PREVENTING SEXUAL VIOLENCE ON CAMPUS

Amid the ongoing national conversation regarding campus sexual assault, this book thoughtfully explores existing programmatic interventions while wrestling with fundamental questions regarding the cultural shifts in our nation's higher education institutions. Stressing the critical importance of student inclusion in policy decisions and procedures, scholars and experts provide complex and nuanced analyses of institutional practices, while exploring themes of race, sexuality, and sexual freedom. This volume addresses many of the unanswered questions in the present dialogue on campus sexual violence, including: What's working and not working? How can outcomes be assessed or measured? What resources are needed to ensure success? This volume provides a truly fresh contribution for higher education and student affairs practitioners seeking to alter, design, or implement effective sexual assault prevention resources at their universities and colleges.

Sara Carrigan Wooten is a Doctoral Candidate in Educational Leadership and Research at Louisiana State University, USA.

Roland W. Mitchell is the Joe Ellen Levy Yates Endowed Professor and Interim Associate Dean for Research Engagement and Graduate Studies in the College of Human Sciences and Education at Louisiana State University, USA.

PREVENTING SEXUAL VIOLENCE ON CAMPUS

Challenging Traditional Approaches through Program Innovation

Edited by
Sara Carrigan Wooten and
Roland W. Mitchell

 Routledge
Taylor & Francis Group

NEW YORK AND LONDON

First published 2017
by Routledge
711 Third Avenue, New York, NY 10017

and by Routledge
2 Park Square, Milton Park, Abingdon, Oxon, OX14 4RN

Routledge is an imprint of the Taylor & Francis Group, an informa business

© 2017 Taylor & Francis

The right of Sara Carrigan Wooten and Roland W. Mitchell to be identified as the authors of the editorial material, and of the authors for their individual chapters, has been asserted in accordance with Sections 77 and 78 of the Copyright, Designs and Patents Act 1988.

Library of Congress Cataloging in Publication Data
Names: Wooten, Sara Carrigan, author. | Mitchell, Roland (Roland W.), author.
Title: Preventing sexual violence on campus : challenging traditional approaches through program innovation / by Sara Carrigan Wooten and Roland W. Mitchell.
Description: New York ; London : Routledge, [2017] | Includes index.
Identifiers: LCCN 2016028788| ISBN 9781138689176 (hbk) | ISBN 9781138689206 (pbk.) | ISBN 9781315537856 (ebk) | ISBN 9781134974849 (Web PDF) | ISBN 9781134974917 (ePub) | ISBN 978113497486 (mobipocket/kindle)
Subjects: LCSH: Rape in universities and colleges--Prevention. | Sex crimes—Prevention.
Classification: LCC LB2345.3.R37 W66 2017 | DDC 371.7/82—dc23
LC record available at https://lccn.loc.gov/2016028788

ISBN: 978-1-138-68917-6 (hbk)
ISBN: 978-1-138-68920-6 (pbk)
ISBN: 978-1-315-53785-6 (ebk)

Typeset in Bembo and Stone Sans
by Florence Production Ltd, Stoodleigh, Devon, UK

CONTENTS

FOREWORD

Rachel Alicia Griffin

ASSISTANT PROFESSOR OF RACE AND COMMUNICATION,
UNIVERSITY OF UTAH

Succeeding *The Crisis of Campus Sexual Violence: Critical Perspectives on Prevention and Response* (Wooten & Mitchell, 2016), *Preventing Sexual Violence on Campus: Challenging Traditional Approaches through Program Innovation* charts progressive trajectories for academic institutions to proactively name, confront, challenge, and transform the cultural norms that sustain the ubiquity of sexual violence in the everyday lives of campus stakeholders such as students, staff, faculty, and administrators. This collection is incredibly timely amid our institutionalized awakening that sexual violence on campuses is undeniably customary[1] alongside the amalgamation of the Dear Colleague Letter (2011) with past and present policy initiatives in the United States[2] that convey to campus leadership that a continuance of neglectfully ignoring sexual violence will indeed be costlier than addressing, preventing, and responding to sexual violence. At a time when U.S. American campuses from coast to coast are scrambling for information, direction, and resources, *Preventing Sexual Violence on Campus* offers an astute entry point in response to rudimentary yet essential institutional inquiries such as: Where do we begin? What is working well elsewhere? What should we do and how will we do it? Against this cultural backdrop laced with urgent concerns of legality and compliance, as a national and international antisexual violence speaker, I experience the necessity of this collection and its predecessor as paradoxically dis/heartening.

As a scholar-activist and survivor of childhood domestic violence and teenage rape, I am sincerely heartened by the brilliant contributions of the collection. Each chapter offers innovative and practical insight into how campuses can actively work against dominant cultural prescriptions of whose bodily integrity is worthy of protection, whose voices and experiences shape the status quo, and who should be involved in and implicated by antisexual violence programming. Jointly, the editors and authors insist that campuses proactively and reactively address sexual violence *differently*, which is monumentally important given how short most institutions fall with regard to compliance, compassion, and humanization. Likewise, this volume unapologetically holds a firm line that mirrors a stance that survivors—myself included—often commonsensically take: Campuses that *are not* actively creating an antisexual violence and pro-reporting climate *are* actively condoning sexual violence. There is no "ish" or "in between" when it comes to the violation of human rights, and acts of sexual violence—ranging from sexual harassment to relational abuse to rape to street harassment to cyberstalking—violate bodily integrity and human rights.

While immensely grateful for the time, energy, and labor invested into both *The Crisis of Campus Sexual Violence* and now *Preventing Sexual Violence on Campus*, I am disheartened by their sheer necessity. My sentiment is captured by Allison (1995), as one voice within a chorus of voices, which unashamedly narrates the injurious presence of systemic, cyclic, and generational sexual violence. Offering a simple and yet damning assertion, she says, "Nothing's different and everything's changed" (1995, p. 89). Since earning my Bachelor's, Master's, and Doctoral degrees, alongside earning tenure, I have delivered well over 100 antisexual violence keynotes and workshops across the United States and Canada. Rhizomatically imagining the travels of antisexual violence speakers as a collective—who perhaps like me have a hovering sense of "home" amid my suitcase's never-fully-unpacked-or-put-away omnipresence—I picture the imagery airlines use to represent their daily flight patterns with overlapping, color-coded lines and dashes that connect cities, states, countries, and continents. Like travel, sexual violence spans our globe, which necessitates that survivors, activists, scholar-activists, crisis workers, and everyday people alike relentlessly advocate against our global culture in which survivors and victims of sexual violence are often ignored, dismissed, shunned, heckled, and accused of lying. This has been happening to us—survivors and victims—globally for centuries. Again, amid the passage of time, improvement of law, and evolution of global society, "nothing's different and everything's changed" (Allison, 1995, p. 89).

Charting sexual violence against women in particular as both global and reprehensibly routine, Stewart (2014) says:

> Global violence against women is ordinary, mundane, everyday, and unremarkable. Whether we are talking about rape in the Congo or in Bosnia or rape in some backwater town in the United States, whether we are talking about the trafficking of girls and women across borders from the Philippines or Thailand to Germany, Japan, or the United States, whether we are talking about the multibillion-dollar porn industry . . . we are talking about the ordinary. (p. ix)

Extending her valuable insight beyond the realm of femininity, sexual violence is tragically ordinary in the everyday lives of people at the intersections of multiple identities including but not limited to gender, race, ethnicity, nationality, class, religion, ability, and age. While cisgender, transgender, and gender-queer women endure sexual violence more commonly than their male counterparts amid globalized patriarchal domination (Meyer, 2015; Stewart, 2014; True, 2012), this reality does not disavow the painful presence of sexual violence in the intersectional lives of cisgender, transgender, and gender-queer men. Advocating for greater inclusivity in the spectrum of antisexual violence advocacy, Patterson (2016) calls for "*queering sexual violence*" to affirm "all of the bodies that experience violence and all the forms that violence takes" (emphasis in the original, p. 5). In contemporary U.S. American society, most campuses purposely reach out to cisgender U.S. American White female survivors, which (intentionally and unintentionally) excludes, for example, queer survivors, survivors of color, male survivors, and international survivors. This is not to even remotely imply that we need to reach out to cisgender U.S. American White female survivors less. Rather, we need to reach out to those at the diverse intersections of multiple identities more purposefully and more often.

Joining in the labor to do so, this volume narrates the obligations that campuses have to *all* of their stakeholders to create and maintain campus environments that actively denounce sexual violence and simultaneously establish accountability measures. Offering guidance on both fronts, the authors communally advocate for: traditional approaches to risk reduction, prevention, and adjudication to be examined as potential sources of victim-blaming; a marked shift toward perpetrator and institutional culpability; the role of bystanders and focus on consent education to be deconstructed and recalibrated in relation to power, privilege, and empowerment; and sustainable programming initiatives that are consciously designed with the knowledge that antisexual violence educators cannot fully rely upon the social institutions of government and/or education to forefront the needs and interests of survivors and victims. This last stance is quite key, because these very institutions have historically functioned to oppress, silence, and punish survivors and victims.

Prompted by Stewart (2014) to illuminate the continued ordinariness of sexual violence in my own everyday life, earlier this week I was driving down the center lane of a three-lane highway in Carbondale, a rural college town in Southern Illinois. Visible in my rearview mirror, an SUV honked from directly behind me and I immediately glanced to check my dashboard lights thinking that perhaps I had an open door or a flattening tire. Then, the SUV hopped into the right lane, sped up next to me, and the male driver lowered his window. Concerned that something was wrong with my car, I did the same with the caution women are often socialized to enact in a world that has proven dangerous for us (i.e., I took my foot off the accelerator, confirmed that my doors were locked, and lowered my window only halfway). Once our cars were aligned, he hollered over the wind and automotive rumble, "You're lookin' good, can I get your number?" Exemplifying sexual intrusion (Jensen, 2009) and street harassment (Bowman,

1993) as manifestations of sexual violence, his behavior was invasive, offensive, and literally unsafe. Yet having had countless, similar experiences, my interpretation, given the coy smile on his face, is that he (and others in the past) felt his behavior was not only "acceptable" but also "flattering." I shook my head "no" in response to his request with pursed lips, rolled up my window, and literally exhaled when the SUV passed me—accompanied by a middle finger jolted into the air and a Southern Illinois University (SIU) Saluki paw sticker on its rear window. I also immediately found myself annoyed at my own relief because I was "grateful" as a cisgender U.S. American woman of color that one "no" had been enough.

Surely I, like many survivors and victims, live with the memories of when one "no," a million "no's," or an absence of an explicit "yes" were not enough to dissuade uninvited hands, mouths without permission, and criminal sexual conduct. Turning back toward the significance of *Preventing Sexual Violence on Campus*, I am less interested in the incident itself and more interested in the cultural and campus ideologies that render the driver's behavior permissible. Presuming that he is connected to SIU given the Saluki sticker on display, I wonder: What is it in our world/culture/community/campus that has taught him to treat women the way he treated me in traffic? And, how can he be taught to unlearn his patriarchal and sexist entitlement? Occurrences reminiscent of my histories with domestic and sexual violence alongside the experience I describe above are exactly why this collection has rigorous intellectual and pragmatic value. My hope is that you are as compelled as I was to engage with each chapter and ponder: What can we learn from *Preventing Sexual Violence on Campus* to change our campus culture as if lives depend on us doing so, because of course they do.

Notes

1 Of importance to note is that survivors, victims, and their loved ones alongside feminists and activists have known this for decades. As such, the advocacy for institutional awakenings on campuses has been long-standing despite the recent, public recognition by the U.S. American government and academic institutions of sexual violence as an enduring and epidemic problem on campuses.

2 For example, the 1972 Title IX Amendment, 1990 Jeanne Clery Act, 1994 Violence against Women's Act and its 2013 reauthorization, 2013 SaVE Act, and 2013 University of Montana "blueprint" resolution (Bhargara & Jackson, 2013, p. 1) are all exemplars of past and present policy initiatives in the U.S. that have been consequential for how campuses address sexual violence.

References

Allison, D. (1995). *Two or three things I know for sure*. New York: A Plume Book.
Bhargara, A., & Jackson, G. (2013). Re: DOJ Case No. DJ 169–44–9, OCR Case No. 10126001. U.S. Department of Justice/U.S. Department of Education. Retrieved from www.justice.gov/sites/default/files/opa/legacy/2013/05/09/um-ltr-findings.pdf.

Bowman, C.G. (1993). Street harassment and the informal ghettoization of women. *Harvard Law Review, 106*(3), 517–580.

Jensen, R. (2009, June). *Beyond multiculturalism: Taking power and privilege seriously in teaching diversity.* Denver, CO: Keynote delivered at The Pedagogy of Privilege: Teaching, Learning, and Praxis Conference.

Meyer, D. (2015). *Violence against queer people: Race, class, gender, and the persistence of anti-LGBT discrimination.* Brunswick, NJ: Rutgers University Press.

Patterson, J. (2016). *Queering sexual violence: Radical voices from within the anti-violence movement.* Riverdale, NY: Riverdale Avenue Books.

Stewart, M.W. (2014). *Ordinary violence: Everyday assaults against women worldwide* (2nd ed.). Santa Barbara, CA: Praeger.

True, J. (2012). *The political economy of violence against women.* New York: Oxford University Press.

U.S. Department of Education, OCR (2011). *Dear Colleague Letter.* Retrieved from www2.ed.gov/about/offices/list/ocr/letters/colleague-201104.pdf.

Wooten, S.C., & Mitchell, R.W. (2016). *The crisis of campus sexual violence: Critical perspectives on prevention and response.* New York: Routledge.

PREFACE

Sara Carrigan Wooten and Roland W. Mitchell

You know that survivors are not statistics. They're our sisters; they're our classmates; they're our friends. They're at every university, every college, in every community—large and small. For all of them, everywhere, we can and we must end sexual and dating violence on campus.

—Vice President Joe Biden, It's On Us to Stop Campus Sexual Assault, 2015

Campus sexual violence remains a seemingly intractable reality for thousands of students every year in the United States. Underreporting, transparent adjudication of complaints, adequate punishment for those found responsible for having committed rape and sexual assault, and the inclusion of students in policy development conversations remain some of the most vexing challenges facing our higher education institutions. However, the movement to eradicate campus sexual violence has spurred a groundswell of promising policy initiatives, largely due to the courageous efforts of student survivors who have refused to be silent about their trauma, their rights, and their demands for change.

Preventing Sexual Violence on Campus: Challenging Traditional Approaches through Program Innovation documents some of the programming initiatives that have been developed as a result of this activist movement. It represents a challenge to traditional ways of thinking about who is at risk of experiencing rape or sexual assault, what their needs may be, and how best to incite fundamental cultural shifts in our nation's higher education institutions as regards attitudes about sexual violence. This volume should not be taken as a comprehensive guidebook for administrators, but rather understood as a constellation of real-time campus advocacy that is taking place and may serve as inspiration for other actors engaging in similar work in higher education. It is our hope as the editors that the lessons gleaned from the authors in this volume might help others to negotiate the institutional challenges posed by their own campuses. The ultimate goal of this volume is that of creating an intricate network of knowledge sharing and diverse prevention programming initiatives that meaningfully and materially help all students in higher education.

This volume reflects the expanding national understanding of who "counts" as a survivor of sexual violence. Where traditional approaches to prevention programming have focused on the assault and rape of heterosexual, gender normative women, particularly White women, we have endeavored to develop a volume that asks how historically underserved student communities are impacted by such violence and how their existence necessitates a significant shift in what prevention programming design looks like and to whom it is targeted. Additionally, this volume is written from the standpoint of the critical importance of student inclusion in the policy decisions and procedures that directly impact their lives. A top-down approach has failed to meaningfully alter the landscape of campus sexual violence. Instead, the gains made over the past five years are directly attributable to survivor-led advocacy. We start this volume from a place of deep faith and profound respect for the knowledge of students regarding how best to achieve substantial advancements on their campuses.

We have organized this volume thematically, with headnotes preceding each selection. A broad range of prevention programming and key issues in the struggle to prevent sexual violence are discussed. Some authors are fierce in their arguments for more inclusive prevention curricula and student participation in the adjudication of assault cases on their campuses. Others are reflective of the specific challenges they have experienced in enacting prevention efforts. However, all of the authors here share a distinct optimism about the future possibilities posed by knowledge sharing among institutions and the development of programming that makes a meaningful difference in the lives of students across the country.

Overview of This Volume

Chapter 1 focuses on how colleges and universities can develop a comprehensive training curriculum for peer advocacy and education around sexual violence, including sexual assault, relationship violence, harassment, stalking, prevention, and intervention. The chapter specifically addresses the critical nature of student involvement in the movement to prevent sexual violence on college campuses. Authors Traci Thomas-Card and Katie Eichele draw on their own experiences to highlight both the successes and challenges in the development, facilitation, and evaluation of an annual 40-hour sexual assault crisis counseling training for undergraduate and graduate students on a college campus. The authors conclude with a discussion on the adaptability of this module to other institutions, and address the ways in which the training may be customized to fit the needs of a specific campus by considering size, student populations, resources, and staffing.

Chapter 2 addresses the adjudication of sexual violence cases in higher education. Author Chris Loschiavo specifically identifies the need for students to be included on hearing panels. Using a training program for student hearing panel members pioneered at the University of Florida, this chapter explores the essential role that students can play in sexual assault adjudication on their campuses. The author ultimately provides valuable insights into the applicability of the UF training program for other universities, including potential challenges as well as benefits for institutional, as well as cultural, change.

Chapter 3 describes the implementation of "A Question of Consent," a prevention program specifically targeted to fraternity men at the University of Houston. Author Beverly McPhail developed the program after growing unsatisfied with the two predominant prevention models used in higher education: risk reduction targeted at women and bystander intervention. This chapter explores some of the successes of the program as well as its challenges, including administrative roadblocks to successful program implementation, the personal commitments required of such programming, and the larger implications of such programs in terms of presenter effectiveness and training.

Chapter 4 interrogates the broad push for bystander intervention programs, where such programs often fail to account for a diversity of identities and experiences held by historically underserved student communities in higher education. Authors Adriane Bang, Annie N. Kerrick, and Christian K. Wuthrich argue that campuses must consider how power and privilege impact the options available to potential bystanders, particularly in the context of the #BlackLivesMatter and #TransLivesMatter movements in the United States. The chapter concludes with a call for intersectional feminist research examining the diversity of needs of campus sexual assault victims and bystanders who are not well represented in the academic literature. Such research would further inform programmatic efforts and help better engage a greater diversity of students in increasingly successful bystander behaviors.

Chapter 5 critically analyzes one of the most popular sexual violence awareness programs in higher education—Walk a Mile in Their Shoes (WaM).[1] Authors Kristina Kamis and Susan Iverson reveal how understandings of sexual violence are dominated by an over-reliance on one dimensional analyses of the problem of sexual violence, and how sexual violence prevention, particularly those efforts targeted at men, would benefit from a challenge to the primacy of gender as the organizing and explanatory factor for sexual violence. To this end, the authors provide a review of literature on sexual violence prevention efforts; describe and discuss findings from a case study of one campus's WaM event, including insight regarding students' (and event organizers') motivations for participating, the impact of the event, and the extent to which this event can alter attitudes; and engage a critical discussion of the possibilities, and limitations, of WaM and similar events, for changing attitudes and mobilizing men to become activists in ending sexual violence.

Chapter 6 uses Shippensburg University as a case study to examine efforts to maintain compliance with Title IX and other legislative mandates with regard to sexual violence and, most importantly, establish a proactive call to action as well as what it takes to ensure its success. Authors Matthew R. Shupp, Stephanie Erdice, and Cecil Howard focus on the strategy of taking the Title IX responsibilities out of the sole employment responsibility of one person or office, and adopting a holistic approach to eradicating sexual misconduct through collaborative efforts throughout the campus. Conclusions are made regarding best practices, recommendations, and ultimately moving beyond strict compliance to proactive engagement. The authors challenge campus staff, faculty, and administrators to build an oversight team dedicated to shifting their campus culture through educating and empowering their community to end sexual misconduct.

Chapter 7 identifies the challenges and opportunities faced by professionals working in interpersonal violence prevention and advocacy programs on college campuses. Authors Lauren "LB" Klein, Jill Dunlap, and Andrew "Drew" Rizzo present findings from the first national study of these programs, utilizing a sample of over 250 schools in addition to interviews with campus-based advocacy and prevention professionals. The authors hope to not only elucidate the trends and gaps in training and services nationwide, but also amplify the voices of these subject matter experts. Key themes include institutional inertia, institutional support and leadership buy-in (or lack thereof), and tensions between pressure for short-term results and the desire to achieve measurable and meaningful cultural change over time. The authors conclude by providing recommendations on how diverse institutions can leverage the knowledge and expertise of campus-based prevention and advocacy professionals about what is and is not working to achieve true campus cultural change.

Chapter 8 explores sexual assault as a community public health issue within a socio-ecological framework at two Catholic institutions. While the national conversation about sexual assault has begun to use the public health approach as a backdrop for making recommendations to colleges and universities, institutions of higher education have traditionally approached sexual assault as a women's center/sexual assault center issue. Further, health education/promotion efforts have addressed sexual practices from a "safer sex" disease prevention perspective, ranging from campaigns to promote condom use to campaigns focused on making consent "sexy." Such approaches, however, are untenable for Catholic institutions of higher education. The goals discussed by authors Mary Geller and Lori Klapperich in this chapter include increasing accountability for perpetrators and enablers, creating a safe atmosphere for reporting sexual assaults, enhancing support for survivors to heal and grow and fostering an empowered community where individuals understand that sexual assault and intimidation are real, and that each community member can and should play a role in prevention and intervention. Using the College of Saint Benedict and Saint John's University as case studies, the authors examine the approaches undertaken by each university with regard to sexual misconduct policy, programmatic interventions, and assessment standards designed to not only capture the scope of sexual assault at these universities, but that also move the campus on the whole toward meaningful cultural change.

Chapter 9 addresses the development and implementation of Project BRAVE, a comprehensive violence prevention program, at Georgia College. Authors Jennifer Graham, Carrie Cook, and Melissa Gerrior describe their process of incorporating evidence-based approaches and utilizing established educational curricula while continuing to monitor their particular effectiveness at Georgia College. This chapter will address the success of Project BRAVE by examining the lessons the authors believe are crucial for the success of a comprehensive violence prevention and response program. By providing a "30,000-foot view" of both the challenges and successes in the implementation of Project BRAVE, the authors hope that other practitioners will be able to take the lessons that they have learned and apply them to their own campuses.

Finally, the afterword briefly addresses the history and legacy of Title IX and other legislation that have made the efforts of the administrators and corresponding programs highlighted in this volume possible. As a concluding commentary, author Laura Dunn offers an insider's perspective into the survivor-led advocacy that has spurred a wave of national support and enhanced policy mandates for higher education institutions when responding to incidents of sexual violence.

While no book on higher education prevention programming could ever hope to be complete, this volume nevertheless offers important insights and considerations in a new age of interest in and solutions for campus sexual violence. It contributes to the innovation and creativity available to administrators and activists in higher education when designing and developing their own programming initiatives. Perhaps most importantly, it raises essential questions about how best to include all students in the decisions and outcomes that will come to bear on their lives. It is our wish that different interest groups involved in the movement to end campus sexual violence will be able to use this volume as a meaningful tool in that struggle.

Note

1   At Kent State, the title for this program is "Walk a Mile in Their Shoes." Although this differs from the national organization, the university changed the title to be more inclusive.

ACKNOWLEDGMENTS

I, Sara, want to express my deepest gratitude to Dr. Caroline Turner, Immediate Past President of the Association for the Study of Higher Education (ASHE). For the 2015 meeting of ASHE, Dr. Turner selected a symposium put together by Roland, myself, and several colleagues to discuss our work examining campus sexual violence for a Presidential Session. This volume is a direct result from that symposium, which drew a phenomenal audience of scholars and practitioners concerned with adequately preventing and responding to incidents of sexual violence on their campuses. During our conversations with audience members, we were actively encouraged to put together an edited collection focused on current approaches to prevention programming taking place in a post-2011 Dear Colleague Letter context. This volume stands as a testament to the very best that our academic communities have to offer when knowledge sharing and collaboration take priority. I also want to sincerely thank our editorial team at Routledge, and specifically Heather Jarrow, for what has truly been a wonderful and generative partnership in producing this volume.

I, Roland, deeply believe no meaningful and sustained challenge to oppression is developed in isolation. Consequently, the dialogue between our contributors, publication team at Routledge, and most notably my coeditor Sara and I—which is found in *Preventing Sexual Violence on Campus*—has provided the perfect context to mount a significant challenge to sexual violence on college campuses. I personally lived this approach to challenging oppression through collective efforts during my affiliation with a close-knit group of colleagues at the University of Alabama from 2000 through 2005. We referred to ourselves as the Post-Qualitative or "PQ" Research Group. We were doctoral students and faculty from academic departments that ranged from Education, Communication Studies, and African American Studies to Kinesiology, History, and Women and Gender

Studies. We studied together, attended conferences, and conducted interdisciplinary scholarly inquiry. The tide that bound this diverse group of individuals was simply a desire to make our academic commitments meaningful and sustained challenges to oppression. Therefore, I dedicate this work to PQ. It is interdisciplinary, intended to build a community around change, and completely focused on addressing arguably the greatest injustice to higher education today.

PART I

Students as Partners and Stakeholders

1

BLENDING VICTIM ADVOCACY AND VIOLENCE PREVENTION WHEN TRAINING STUDENT VOLUNTEERS ON COLLEGE CAMPUSES

Traci Thomas-Card and Katie Eichele

If you build it, they will come. For nearly 30 years, our campus peer advocacy and prevention education program has activated students from diverse academic, gender, and racial/ethnic backgrounds to contribute their time and energy to fight sexual assault, intimate partner violence, and stalking on campus. Each year, our program, based at a large, Midwest, Research Institution, receives inquiries from colleges and universities of all sizes, both private and public, from states and countries all over the world, wanting to learn more about the work our student volunteers do and how our program is set up to train them. We have witnessed through trial and triumph that peer programs allow students to connect with each other effectively while providing campus-based victim advocacy services and prevention education.

As more campuses try to meet the growing needs of their students, a number of institutions are utilizing peer education programs on a variety of topics such as high risk drinking, mental health issues, academics, and leadership. Campuses that have sexual violence prevention programs have been successful at improving awareness and decreasing attitudes that support victim-blaming and rape culture, and increasing bystander intervention efforts on college campuses (Casey & Lindhorst, 2009; Palm Reed, Hines, Armstrong, & Cameron, 2015). However, comprehensive programs that provide both prevention education *and* peer sexual assault crisis counseling and advocacy services are not as common on campuses.

With 1 in 5 college women experiencing rape or attempted rape while in college and 1 in 71 men and 1 in 2 transgender individuals experiencing rape in their lifetime (Kenagy, 2005; Krebs, Lindquist, Warner, Fisher, & Martin, 2007; Black et al., 2011), campuses have had to increase their prevention efforts while simultaneously improving their response strategies. Why is it so helpful to have a comprehensive program that provides both victim advocacy services and prevention education on campuses? Aside from navigating the many protocols and systems that exist within colleges and universities, victim/survivors of sexual and intimate partner violence say their decision-making actually improved when they utilized victim services (Bennet, Riger, Schewe, Howard, & Wasco, 2004). A comprehensive program may ultimately help students access more services and increase the number of reports to authorities. Bennet et al. (2004) found that victim/survivor self-efficacy and coping skills increased through victim advocacy programs, which can help retention and graduation rates of student victims/ survivors. Additionally, peer sexual violence prevention education programs have been found to increase bystander intervention behavior to stop or prevent sexual assaults (Coker et al., 2011; McMahon, Banyard, & McMahon, 2015). Therefore, campuses benefit from having peer advocacy and prevention education programs that train students to teach their peers about violence prevention as well as to be sexual assault advocates who provide crisis counseling, campus-specific information, resources, and referrals.

Before volunteers ever answer a 24-hour hotline call or stand in front of peers to talk about consent or bystander intervention, we ask that they complete a comprehensive 40-hour sexual assault crisis counseling training curriculum. We do this so they can familiarize themselves with the knowledge and skills required to inform and support others around these complex issues. According to the U.S. Department of Justice (2015), nearly every state has domestic violence or sexual assault advocates and subsequent training for those positions. The peer advocacy and prevention education training model we discuss in this chapter mirrors many standard sexual assault crisis counseling trainings already established for community victim advocacy agencies. With the extensive experience we have implementing a campus-based student-focused sexual assault counselor and prevention education training, unique challenges and campus-specific nuances have been discovered that can provide guidance to facilitators hoping to implement a 40-hour campus-based advocacy training at their own institutions.

Our previous work identifies the key components to consider when creating a campus-based sexual violence program: policy development, peer leadership/ advocacy, direct services, education programs, and the importance of creating on-campus and off-campus collaborations to address sexual violence (Thomas-Card & Eichele, 2014). This chapter outlines factors for higher education institutions to consider when creating a comprehensive 40-hour advocacy training for student volunteers who will serve as direct service advocates and violence prevention educators. We begin by addressing the critical nature of student involvement in the movement to prevent sexual violence on college campuses, and assert the need for college campuses to craft a training that is compliant with institutional policy as well as state and federal laws. Next, we outline four pillars to execute such a training: (1) training development, (2) training design, (3) training implementation, and (4) training assessment. We discuss the challenges in developing a 40-hour campus-based training and offer potential solutions that may be used in resolving these issues. We conclude with suggestions to consider in adapting this training model to meet the needs of a wide variety of institutions.

Student Involvement

Most campuses are aware that responding to and preventing sexual and intimate partner violence is a multidisciplinary team effort, requiring strategic planning and assessment, staff to execute those plans, and input from administrators, faculty, staff, and most importantly students to influence the processes. Students *must* be involved in planning and implementing prevention and response strategies to effectively change student behavior. Berkowitz (2010) suggests students often underestimate their peers' discomfort with problem behavior or may feel certain problematic behavior is the norm, and thus hesitate to take appropriate and healthy action. However, through effective peer education and by utilizing a social norms approach where students become the face of social change for each other by encouraging and validating individuals to engage in healthy behaviors (Berkowitz, 2010).

Student Motivations to Volunteer

We know that students are more likely to listen and respond to their peers (Fabiano, Perkins, Berkowitz, Linkenbach, & Stark, 2003). Therefore, we need students teaching students about sexual assault prevention. But how do we get volunteers to show up to begin teaching on such complex issues? Cnaan et al. (2010) indicate students participate in service learning or volunteer opportunities for several important reasons: (1) to help someone in their community, (2) to learn new work-related skills, and (3) to gain experience to benefit their future. Soria and Thomas-Card (2014) revealed similar findings in their study on students' motivations to continue service postgraduation, which revealed that "many college students may pursue community service experiences because of an inherent interest, their belief that they can become better citizens and effect positive change in communities, and perceiving service affording opportunities to learn in different contexts" (p. 61). Our own peer advocacy and education training model is designed to address and promote interests and beliefs that encourage civic behavior among college students.

Public activism efforts clearly demonstrate that students care about sexual assault and intimate partner violence. Not only do they care, but they also want to make a difference. Becoming advocates, educators, or activists are a few ways students attempt to make change. Sometimes, students get involved after experiencing institutional betrayal or "wrongdoings perpetrated by an institution against individuals who trust, or are dependent on that institution" (Smith, Gomez, & Freyd, 2014, p. 459). The desire to do advocacy or activism often comes from experiencing or witnessing marginalization and wanting to create safe spaces (Linder, 2015). Other times, students get involved in advocacy, peer education, and activism efforts for motivations such as the ones described earlier in this section. Linder (2015) believes being an activist includes being informed and raising awareness about oppression and trying to create welcoming and inclusive environments. Our 40-hour advocacy training is designed with this idea in mind, so student-volunteers learn the knowledge and skills needed to create these kinds of open spaces. Students' motivations to become involved in the campus antisexual violence movement as advocates or prevention educators are important for training coordinators to consider in recruiting volunteers, developing curriculum, and assessing their training models.

Compliance

In this section, we examine federal or state compliance needs that facilitators should consider when developing victim advocacy and education trainings and programs. In order to ensure the advocacy and education training is in compliance and meets any and all state criteria, we recommend contacting the state sexual assault coalition, if available. The U.S. Department of Justice Office on Violence Against Women's local resources website (2015) provides access to state coalitions where facilitators can learn if any curriculum standards exist for training sexual assault advocates as well as learn of any state statutes that exist for maintaining the "sexual assault counselor" title (U.S. DOJ, 2015).

Staff at the state sexual assault coalition may be able to provide campus-based centers with technical assistance, guidance, training resources, train the trainer opportunities, or contacts of other agencies that can help set up a volunteer training. Some states do not have compliance standards for sexual assault counselors or the state coalition is inactive; in this situation, the United States Office for Victims of Crime (OVC) provides numerous grants and has worked with many colleges and universities to start advocacy and prevention education programs on campuses.

OVC also provides excellent resources through the Training and Technical Assistance Center's Sexual Assault Advocate/Counselor Training website on what to train advocates on and how to provide competent, effective crisis intervention services. Completing the training through OVC's resources however does not certify trainees as advocates or counselors. That certification is often given at the state level or a recognized victim advocacy agency. Certification is important for providing advocates or educators confidentiality privilege regarding sexual assault, intimate partner violence, stalking, or sexual harassment disclosures, so as not to interfere with federal laws and campus policies outlining "responsible employees" or campus employees or positions that are obligated to report incidents of sexual assault, intimate partner violence, stalking, or sexual harassment to the institution.

Campus advocacy and prevention services funded through a Department of Justice or state grant often provide training requirements for staff and volunteers that can assist facilitators in determining the criteria needed to establish a 40-hour advocacy training. An example of a federal grant that helped our campus program successfully implement volunteer training is the STOP (Services, Training, Officers, Prosecutors) Violence Against Women Formula Grants Program. Specifically, STOP grants help programs shape court advocacy skills, safety planning, crisis counseling services, answering hotline calls, medical advocacy, legal advocacy, and assisting victim/survivors with other mental health issues. Students who have completed our 40-hour advocacy training may accompany victim/survivors to a court hearing, to provide information regarding how to obtain harassment restraining orders or orders for protection, to support a victim/survivor at the hospital during a sexual assault examination, and to provide crisis counseling. Advocates in our program regularly offer these support services to victim/survivors who contact our helpline or come to our office. It is important for colleges and universities to determine early in their planning the scope of responsibilities for student-advocates, as doing so will assist training coordinators in determining the curriculum for the 40-hour training.

In addition to the services listed above, campus programs also have to be prepared to provide student-specific advocacy around academics, financial needs, housing options, and university conduct and Title IX systems advocacy. A prominent state coalition that the OVC has partnered with is the California Coalition Against Sexual Assault (CALCASA). CALCASA has operated as a technical assistance program for campus sexual assault grants and has an excellent resource manual called "Support for Survivors: Training for Sexual Assault Counselors Mini-Book" and a facilitator's guide that outlines standard compliance topics to cover with their trainees who are participating at a general victim advocacy agency (CALCASA, 2008).

Training Development

Planning a 40-hour peer advocacy and prevention education training takes considerable effort on the part of staff and facilitators, resources, and time. We recommend having at least one staff member who is a part of the advocacy and prevention program to serve as the training coordinator and oversee the initiative. The training coordinator then works with other staff members from within and outside of the advocacy and prevention program to design the training, execute recruitment, and facilitate the presentations. A list of collaborating partners is outlined later in the chapter under *Network of Support*. It is helpful if the training coordinator has already attended a 40-hour sexual assault counseling training and if available, a "Train the Trainer" workshop that often times is sponsored by state sexual assault coalitions or other sexual assault advocacy programs. Next, we outline planning questions to consider when developing a campus-based training for direct service advocates and peer educators. We also examine different training design options campus programs may use as well as budgetary needs.

Planning Questions

Once compliance issues are determined, facilitators can craft an outline for their training. Many ideas can get proposed and it is easy to get distracted; therefore, it is helpful to have a plan to operate from and to organize all important and relevant training components. The following list of questions can help focus the direction of a 40-hour advocacy training:

1. What are the mission, goals, and objectives of this program/training/event?
2. What institutional and student behaviors need to change or shift on campus?
3. How large is the population of the institution?
4. Who is the target population served by the direct service advocates and peer educators?
5. What are the ideal characteristics of the peer educators/advocates, given the target population?
6. How many peer educators/advocates will be necessary to reach or serve the population?
7. Does the program have the capacity to train this number of peer educators/advocates?
8. What responsibilities will the peer educators/advocates have?
9. What do the peer educators/advocates need in order to reach these objectives? (Training, materials, supervision, technology, marketing material, etc.)
10. Does the program budget include supervision expenses?
11. How can we make sure young adults can participate and express their opinions about the program as volunteers or clients?
12. What programs/services/organizations are currently in place to support the work we want to accomplish?
13. How much time is needed and what funding is allocated in order to provide the training?

Answering the above questions will help facilitators develop a work plan that outlines the overall goal, specific objectives, and activities for the program. The work plan will identify the resources needed, including staff, equipment, and facilities, and assist with delegating tasks and responsibilities. The work plan should be thought of as a road map that may diverge, so facilitators will need to be flexible so they can respond to the changing needs of the campus populations with whom they work. Changing behaviors is a long process, but that is ultimately what a sexual and intimate partner violence prevention program and training is trying to establish on campuses.

Learning Objectives

Once the training purpose, target audience, and campus needs are identified, facilitators should begin to think about the learning objectives for the training. Our program embraces student development theories; therefore, we keep our learning objectives simple and tangible—we want all volunteers to (1) obtain knowledge, (2) develop skills, and (3) create community (see Appendix II for learning objectives).

Volunteers need to obtain foundational *knowledge* on relevant topics such as social justice, which is the root of sexual and intimate partner violence. They should also learn about the continuum of sexual violence, definitions, policies, bystander behavior, resources and referrals available, etc. However, knowledge alone does not create change.

This is why the second learning objective is to have volunteers *develop skills* they will need for their roles (i.e., active listening skills, good presentation skills, or answering difficult questions and managing conflict). Each year, though we plan scenarios and practice time into every day of training, students tell us in their training evaluations that they want more scenarios, more time to practice the skills, and more opportunities to articulate the knowledge they've learned.

The last learning objective our training focuses on is *creating community*. We observed that when our students did not get a chance to know each other or find a friend to connect with, they became less engaged with the program, more overwhelmed by the content, and in the end were more likely to leave the volunteer position. It is important to realize we are working with students who are still developing their identities, learning their work ethic, and trying to discover what they are capable of. Once our program incorporated community building into our training, we saw a huge increase in both our application numbers and volunteer retention rates.

Training Design

Our campus program has experienced several ways to design and implement a 40-hour training. Training can be delivered on an annual or biannual basis, depending on the number of volunteers needed on campus and the resources available to implement it. One way is to design the training within a two-week time frame, so volunteers get trained and begin working as soon as possible without experiencing too much time in between sessions. We found utilizing two extended weekends on Thursday, Friday, Saturday, and Sunday worked best. Students also told us that their energy and attentiveness did not last longer than five to six hours per day because they were trying to balance training, classes, work, and other commitments. This two-week model also allowed guest speakers to come in on weekdays to present rather than train on the weekend.

Another design option is to host the training over a series of weekends or weeknights. Remember that students have classes and jobs and our program provides academic absence requests to professors if our volunteers have to miss a class or two, but we try not to interfere with class schedules as much as possible. Another challenge to doing this is if students work on weekends and need the income. Additionally, depending on guest speaker schedules, some important trainers may not be able to come in on weekends to work with students.

The last way we have coordinated training is to offer the training as a class for credit over a semester or academic period. Some of the benefits of this model are that topics can be covered in greater detail, facilitators can assign readings and reflective homework, and in-depth discussions tend to take place with more frequency. Some of the challenges to this model may be getting an academic department to sponsor the class, finding someone to teach it, and making sure that the students who take the class understand the volunteer expectations that come with it versus just taking the class for credit.

Budgets

After the training design, timing, and number of students participating are determined, the facilitators can then create a budget. Developing a budget entails estimating the costs of all the stages of the training, including evaluation. The costs of training implementation will vary depending on its structure and size. Some of the expenses to consider include:

1. staff salaries (wages and benefits);
2. advertising/recruitment;
3. room rentals;
4. guest speaker honorarium or recognition;
5. food/snacks;
6. training material (training videos, stress balls, Play-Doh, etc.);
7. training manuals;
8. incentives for peer advocates and educators (Certificates, t-shirts, bags, caps, water bottles, etc.);
9. other supplies (name tags, markers, pens, paper);
10. monitoring and evaluation activities.

Volunteer Job Description and Recruitment

Before the training begins, peer advocates and educators must know what their roles and responsibilities are. That information can be made clear in the volunteer job descriptions. What we found most successful about our training model is that it is designed to prepare two types of volunteers: Direct Service Advocate (DSA) and Violence Prevention Educator (VPE) (see Appendix I for job descriptions). DSAs answer hotline calls, meet with victim/survivors, and provide information and referrals to victim/survivors or their support people. VPEs are trained to be peer educators, presenting signature presentations around issues of sexual assault, intimate partner violence, stalking, consent, bystander intervention, and masculinity. The purpose of training these two roles together is to ensure that no matter what kinds of services they end up providing, they are always prepared to take disclosures from victim/survivors and extend confidentiality to those who do disclose.

In the past, our program only required DSAs to complete the 40-hour training and VPEs complete 20 hours of training. However, as we got more and more requests to present to groups of students, our VPEs encountered more and more disclosures from audience members. In order to protect the confidentiality of those who disclosed to our VPEs which some states provide in their testimony witness laws, our program made the decision to require both volunteer positions to complete the 40-hour advocacy training to guarantee confidentiality under state statutes and give VPEs the skills to handle disclosures. As an added benefit, we found that many of our student volunteers opted to serve in dual roles as a DSA and VPE.

We typically recruit and accept a few more students than necessary to attend training, which is dependent on the capacity of the staff to provide supervision and ongoing training. We know that about two or three students will cancel their commitment at the last minute. In our program, we typically accept 40 student applicants to train. Once the number of volunteers to be trained is determined, facilitators should keep in mind that when working with students, schedules and minds can change. Additionally, during the pre-training interviews, not all applicants who apply will be interested or a good fit for the program due to maturity or their intentions for fulfilling the roles. Other volunteers may leave the program because they graduate, study abroad, have too many other commitments, lose interest, or experience significant changes in their lives.

We have found the most successful peer advocates and educators are not necessarily model students, but rather those students who commit to the program's mission and who really want to participate. Additionally, we have found that recruiting and retaining a diverse group of volunteers—including students who may historically have been underrepresented in the campus antisexual violence movement, for instance, students of color, LGBTQIA+ students, and male identified students—is critical. We have learned that in-person presentations with student organizations to actively recruit these populations of students are more effective than sending only a flyer or e-mail invitation. For this reason, our program does not practice a "first come, first serve" volunteer application confirmation.

Once the volunteer job description and application are available and applications arrive, our program found it helpful to conduct pre-training interviews. These interviews help ensure the applicant understands the role they are applying for, help our program understand why that individual is interested in the position, and help our program determine if they are in a developmental place to take on the responsibility. For example, some applicants are victim/survivors. As we screen applicants, we ask in the application if they have had any personal experiences with sexual or intimate partner violence. During the pre-training interview, we ask them about their disclosure and their healing journey. One of the reasons we ask this important and personal question is because our program does not want to retraumatize a victim/survivor who has not started their healing journey and thus may unintentionally do more harm to clients who are in need of our services. As facilitators review applications and conduct preinterviews, they should assess a volunteer's interest, experiences, and perspective on sexual and intimate partner violence. Peer advocates and educators need to feel comfortable with the information provided in the training so that they communicate it clearly to peers.

Network of Support

Inviting members of the campus and community to participate in training students can aid facilitators in covering a variety of topics important to campus-based peer advocacy and prevention education training. Potential speakers include, but are not limited to, campus security or law enforcement and staff from offices such as: disability services, LGBTQIA+ programs, health services, the international student office, student housing, counseling, and Title IX officers as well as community services such as Sexual Assault Nurse Examiners and local prosecutors. One way to initiate this process is to invite each stakeholder to a kickoff meeting, during which the facilitators present data on the needs the training seeks to address, explain the learning objectives, and ask for a collaborative partnership. Using this process also helps all those different systems connect and learn from each other regarding how they serve victim/survivors.

   One of the most important components of a comprehensive program is that peer advocates and educators are able to refer victim/survivors to existing services. Volunteers must be familiar with the services and staff from those referral organizations, and the service providers must be knowledgeable about the campus peer advocacy and education program. This network of support also helps volunteers increase their commitment as well as increases the program's sustainability to serving victim/survivors. Establishing relationships with campus and community partners aids in creating an environment that demonstrates ending sexual violence on college campuses is a goal that many people work on together, which can alleviate the overwhelming feeling that direct service and violence prevention volunteers may experience when peers challenge their work in this field.

   It is common for peer advocacy and education programs to invest a lot of time and resources in the training of volunteers, and this is certainly important. But when establishing objectives and activities for peer training programs, keep in mind that the final beneficiaries of the program are the other students who *receive* the direct-service advocacy or prevention education, not the peer advocates or educators themselves. The overall objectives of the training should be geared toward helping student volunteers reach the target population as a whole and teaching them best practices to use in both their advocacy and prevention efforts.

Training Implementation

The previous section outlined elements to consider when designing a 40-hour campus-based peer advocacy and prevention education training, including goals and objectives, budget, volunteer roles and responsibilities, as well as the importance of establishing a network of campus and community partners to assist with the training. The next section of this chapter will focus on criteria to consider when facilitators are implementing the training. We discuss content knowledge, learning styles, and formative assessment. We conclude this section by discussing challenges we've encountered in creating this training, and offering potential solutions to institutions who also encounter these issues.

Content

As college and university personnel prepare the topics for their training curriculum, it is imperative to first assess which information must be covered under the state's advocacy training requirements. Sexual assault and domestic violence coalitions will be able to provide guidance on the statutory guidelines for such a training. In addition to state requirements, it is also important to consider what topics are needed and relevant to meet the needs of a particular campus. Students who undergo our 40-hour advocacy training, for instance, receive training on campus policy definitions as well as state law. They also receive additional training on working with LGBTQIA+ students, students with disabilities, and students who are international. Though training on these populations is not required to meet the state statutory guidelines, it is necessary for our campus because our peer advocates and prevention educators provide advocacy and education to students who identify as part of these populations.

We recommend that a 40-hour advocacy training curriculum always include core topics such as an overview of the sexual violence movement as well as definitions and types of sexual violence (for instance, not only should sexual assault, intimate partner violence, and stalking be defined for new advocates, but also forms of violence such as incest, voyeurism, exploitation, etc.). Volunteers will often be confronted with myths and misinformation about these issues; the training should address the most common myths relevant to the issues around sexual assault, intimate partner violence and stalking, and give volunteers detailed information to counter these myths. Additional core topics might include mandated reporting, systems advocacy, victim responses, the public health impact of sexual violence, and perpetrator behavior.

On a college campus, it is also necessary for campus advocacy programs to provide an overview of federal mandates that affect college campuses in terms of victim/survivor response, reporting obligations, and prevention education. Student-advocates and prevention educators need to have a basic understanding of the Clery Act, the Campus SaVE Act, and Title IX. This will ensure that they are able to effectively explain the mandates not only to victim/survivors, but also to the wider campus community.

Learning Styles

When developing a 40-hour advocacy training, both the facilitators' style and approach to teaching must be considered, as well as the various learning styles that volunteers will be accustomed to and find effective. We developed our 40-hour advocacy training by using an anti-oppression, social justice philosophy. Our volunteers come from a variety of backgrounds and experiences with discrimination, oppression, and activism, so as facilitators, we are conscious of and intentional about setting a foundation for our approach. To do so, we incorporate a number of discussions, lectures, and activities into our training that focus on the intersection of sexual violence with other forms of oppression, such as racism, sexism, homophobia, etc. We find that by incorporating team building, name games, social justice story sharing, and other personal sharing while volunteers practice good listening and reflective communication skills helps them not only connect with each other, but also understand what it may be like to be vulnerable and disclose something very personal. Additionally, such an approach allows volunteers to more effectively listen and provide options and information without judgment.

In our experience, not only do our volunteers come from a variety of backgrounds and experiences, they also approach learning in a variety of ways. Facilitators cannot hope to appeal to all learning styles at once. However, in deciding on methods used to teach the training curriculum, facilitators can use a wide variety of methods such as lecture, activity-based/hands-on learning, multimedia, and other visual and oral materials, to ensure they are meeting the needs of those who learn better orally, visually, via expression/action, or through written work at different times throughout training. When developing the curriculum for the training, it is also crucial to keep in mind that volunteers will be comprised of folks who identify as introverted, extroverted, or somewhere along the spectrum of these personality types. Doing so will allow facilitators to craft lesson plans that appeal to volunteers who may enjoy reflective and expressive learning techniques.

Training Assessment

There are a variety of assessment methods that can be used before, during, and after conducting a 40-hour advocacy training for campus advocates and peer educators. When considering the types of assessment that will be most effective, there are a number of factors to consider: purpose, methods, timing, and response. The purpose of a particular assessment can help to determine the most effective method, timing, and response. For instance, it is useful to assess volunteers' knowledge on sexual violence and advocacy skills both before and after the 40-hour advocacy training. This will allow facilitators to learn whether the overall training was successful in achieving its goals. During the training period, we recommend that both formal and informal assessments be used to assess content knowledge, skills, and emotional well-being. Fun quizzes and activities can be implemented at the beginning of each session to determine gaps in knowledge. Informal assessments can be used during the training itself in the form of question and answer sessions and group discussions led by the facilitators. To assess volunteers' proficiency in advocacy skills and peer education, role-plays, case studies, and presentation practices can be conducted under the guidance of the facilitators, whose role would be to provide immediate feedback based on their assessment of the volunteers' skills.

We believe it is also important to assess the participant's emotional well-being throughout the training. The information provided and survivor stories shared often weigh heavily on participants, particularly those who come into the training with little to no knowledge of or experience with sexual violence. The training can be triggering at times for those participants who *do* identify as victim/survivors or concerned people. Vicarious trauma can happen at any point in training, and one way to assess whether this is occurring is to allow time for the volunteers to reflect on what they have learned and how it impacts them. Often, these reflections become a space for volunteers to let facilitators know if something is troubling them.

Facilitators can choose to use both anonymous assessments as well as assessments that ask participants to identify themselves. This decision will be dependent on a number of factors, including, but not limited to: comfort and established trust between facilitators and volunteers, whether the objective of the assessment is to ensure a particular volunteer's readiness to assume the role of advocate or peer educator, or to assess an individual volunteer's well-being. Facilitators can choose to do anonymous assessment but provide volunteers who would like to debrief the option to identify themselves. We used this particular practice in the last 40-hour advocacy training we conducted, and found it to be highly effective. At the end of each session, we asked volunteers to write down any questions or thoughts they had about the day, and invited them to identify themselves should they need to debrief. In each session, we had individuals who chose to do just that, which allowed us to follow up with those volunteers to ensure their needs were met.

In thinking about the evaluation of and response to the various assessments that can be used during a 40-hour advocacy training, it is critical that facilitators review these assessments and strategize plans for moving forward prior to each new training session. Doing so will allow facilitators to be responsive to the needs of the volunteers and to content that needs additional clarification. Additional criteria to consider in designing assessment for the training includes thinking about the method of evaluation, and whether evaluations should be conducted online, via text/phone apps, handwritten, or orally to assess a particular topic or goal of training. In addition, campus-based centers may want to assess volunteers on an ongoing basis. Our volunteers attend monthly meetings during the academic year to provide them with further professional development and advanced training; at each of these meetings, volunteers are asked to complete a handwritten form that allows the staff to assess the effectiveness of each session. In addition to the formative assessments we conduct with student-advocates and prevention educators in our program, we also provide evaluations to the victim/survivors receiving advocacy services as well as the audience members to whom our prevention educators deliver presentations. These external assessments are beneficial for several reasons. Not only do external assessments help guide the professional development and ongoing training we offer to volunteers in our program, but they also provide our agency with information about the advocacy services needed by victim/survivors on a college campus. Additionally, external assessments help to inform our prevention education curriculum by identifying gaps in knowledge and assessing the student body's willingness to intervene in and prevent situations of sexual violence from occurring. Finally, these assessments also contribute to institutional information on campus climate.

Challenges

Over the years, our staff has faced challenges in developing, facilitating, and assessing our training. This is not unusual; as staff gain experience in these areas, training is improved. Staff new to developing such training should expect to encounter a variety of challenges, but should also remain positive that they will learn and grow from these challenges. Such challenges might include, but are not limited to: the recruitment of volunteers, finding facilitators with content expertise who are able to engage a college student audience effectively, space and budget, establishing boundaries and reducing burnout among volunteers.

Each year, our center looks at the needs of the institution as well as the population of volunteers we will have for the next year to determine how our recruitment efforts will be structured. For instance, last year, we began initiatives to increase the number of students of color, international students, and male-identified students. Doing so meant that we recruited volunteers using intentional approaches such as reaching out to staff who may work closely with these students. Yet, this has been a slow process. Historically, the antisexual violence movement has not always been inclusive of people other than White women. While this has changed, there is still stigma to overcome. In our prevention work, we continue to encounter the belief that our center is only for straight, cisgender women, or that sexual violence does not happen in certain communities. It is important when thinking about volunteer recruitment to consider the way that peers influence one another, and to utilize the connections and comfort they have in disclosing to and learning from their peers about sexual violence.

Finding facilitators who are able to effectively engage college students can also be challenging at times. There is a need to balance content knowledge around sexual violence as well as content knowledge about college student development, the unique needs of victim/survivors on college campuses, and state and federal law as well as institutional policy. Our center brings in both campus and community partners to facilitate sections of our training, and achieving this balance has been challenging at times. For instance, we have had external facilitators who may have great knowledge about working with specific populations in the community, but did not necessarily understand the college student experience. We have also hosted speakers who had great knowledge of the campus community, but little understanding of sexual violence and how to connect their expertise to the objectives of the training. As a result, we have worked each year to assess who is invited to training and what their purpose is. Our training coordinator reaches out to these guest facilitators ahead of time to explain our objectives and to assist with training materials as needed. As staff, we work to frame the rationale and connections to what these speakers do with what our volunteers will need to know.

Space and budget can also be challenging depending on the resources available to a particular institution. For example, as our need to increase the capacity of our volunteers has grown, so too has the need for larger space and a bigger training budget. On college and university campuses, space is often challenging. We recommend, if possible, finding one space large enough and equipped with the appropriate technology to meet all training needs. Doing so will avoid confusion around training location, and will allow the volunteers to establish a sense of comfort in the space as they proceed through training. A larger training budget may be an added challenge, particularly when many institutions are cutting funds rather than increasing them. Depending on the needs of an individual institution, we recommend exploring a few potential solutions to reduce costs. First, facilitators might accept fewer volunteers to train at one time. If this is not possible, facilitators might limit the amount of printed materials or snacks provided, or explore whether local restaurants and businesses will provide donations. Of course, this solution may become challenging in and of itself, considering the time and resources needed for staff members to secure the donations.

The topics covered in training and the program in general impact personal beliefs and cultural values. Therefore, it is important for peer advocates and educators to exercise sensitivity to these issues when interacting with others. Volunteers need to recognize that the function of their role is to provide information and referrals, not judgment or trying to impose their own personal values. Exploring issues related to sexuality, religion, gender roles, drug and alcohol use, self-harm, suicide, sexual orientation, decision-making, and risk taking can help volunteers develop respect for different values, lifestyles, and beliefs that are essential to their work. As these can be sensitive issues, it is important to establish upfront that everything discussed in the context of the program will be kept confidential.

As campus-based advocacy and prevention programs grow, outreach needs expand and there may be an increase in the demand for victim-survivor services. This may mean that there is more of a demand placed on the volunteers' time and efforts with the program, so it is important to reduce the burnout peer advocates and educators feel if they perceive they are not achieving their objectives. Our training involves significant discussion around self-care practices as well as presentations on the success of our programs using data from our annual reports and campus surveys. We also invite our volunteers to contribute to the creation of their own goals in their roles as direct service advocates and prevention educators, which allows them to feel a sense of ownership in their work and a feeling of personal impact in the antisexual violence movement.

Adaptability

Thus far, this chapter has covered training development, facilitation, and assessment. We have drawn on our own experiences crafting a 40-hour campus-based sexual assault training for peer advocates and educators, and have highlighted challenges that facilitators can encounter in developing this training. Yet, we recognize that each institution is different. There will be unique factors to consider in adapting this model to craft a 40-hour advocacy training that meets the needs of an individual campus. When thinking about adaptability, it is important to consider several factors: staffing and resources, capacity, content knowledge, and compliance.

Staffing and resources will aid in determining the number of volunteers, or capacity, to whom facilitators can effectively deliver the training and provide ongoing supervision. Our center recruits an average of 40 volunteers for each annual training we offer, a number that has continued to grow as our needs for increased direct service advocacy and peer education have increased. As the number of volunteers continues to grow, so too does the number of full-time staff needed to facilitate the training and provide supervision for students. Our center currently has seven full-time staff members: a Director, an Assistant Director, a Volunteer Coordinator, two staff members focused on Prevention, and two staff members focused on Direct Services. Each of these staff members plays a role in facilitating training topics based on their areas of expertise, and in providing supervision and ongoing professional development for the 80–90 volunteers who serve in direct service and prevention education roles. Smaller campuses may not be able to recruit, train, and sustain that large of a volunteer base. The key is to start small, and to slowly build the program as the needs of the campus grow and funding and other resources increase.

We previously mentioned that reaching out to state coalitions can be a good basis to find out the content and compliance requirements for sexual assault and domestic violence advocacy training. It is also important to be aware of institutional policy. For instance, in our state, sexual assault advocates are considered confidential under state statute (MN 595.02 subdivision K) if they have completed the 40-hour advocacy training and remain working under the direct supervision of an agency such as ours. However, other centers and staff at our institution are not considered confidential, though they may advocate on behalf of students who disclose to them. Educating students, staff, and faculty on which parties are confidential can be a challenge in and of itself. Each state and each institution will have differing laws and policies; thus, it is critical that volunteers undergoing training to become sexual violence advocates and peer educators understand these concepts and are able to fully explain them to peers. It is critical for training coordinators to consult state confidentiality laws as well as state mandatory reporting laws, which involve abuse of children and vulnerable adults. These laws can vary widely from state to state. In addition, training coordinators should consult institutional policies on confidentiality and mandated reporting, as these expectations may differ slightly from the state laws.

In addition to compliance, facilitators must consider the needs of the institutions and the roles and responsibilities potential volunteers will take on after completing a 40-hour advocacy training. For some campuses, student volunteers may provide only triage in terms of direct advocacy services, and professional staff might provide ongoing direct service advocacy. Prevention educators may take on the role of educating not only students, but also staff and faculty. A needs-assessment and campus climate surveys can help facilitators to determine how their training should be crafted to assist volunteers in gaining the knowledge and skills necessary to perform these roles.

In summary, implementing a 40-hour advocacy training for sexual violence advocates and peer educators should be thought of as a cyclical process. Once training has been completed for the year, facilitators should begin to plan for the next training, critically reflecting on both successes and challenges. These simple questions can be used to implement a strategic plan for each subsequent training:

1. What worked well?
2. What areas can be improved on?
3. What was missing?
4. What should be changed?

Conclusion

As national attention grows around the issue of campus sexual violence, more state and federal laws as well as institutional policies require that higher education institutions provide victim/survivor advocacy services as well as prevention education. The impact of this national attention is evident through student activism movements and films such as *The Hunting Ground*. Yet the impact of implementing 40-hour advocacy training on college campuses nationwide remains to be seen. A recent study about campus-based sexual assault advocates identified the following as needs that would improve their abilities to advocate and educate the campus community about sexual violence: "strategies to better serve international students, funding, increased education/awareness, [and] statewide coordination of sexual assault services" (Carmody, Ekhomu, & Payne, 2009, p. 509). Many of these topics have been addressed in this chapter. It is clear that there is a great potential for colleges and universities to foster student leadership and service opportunities, and for these institutions to become leaders in the antisexual violence movement. Doing so, however, will take time, effort, and resources. This chapter has outlined four pillars that higher education institutions can use to craft their own 40-hour advocacy trainings for direct service advocates and peer educators.

Appendix I

Job Description for Direct Service Advocate (DSA)

Requirements

- Successful completion of 40 hours of training;
- commitment to volunteer for at least one year (seniors cannot apply);
- commitment to uphold the volunteer agreement made with the campus sexual assault program;
- mandatory attendance at monthly in-service training meetings;
- interest in working in the antisexual assault and anti-relationship violence movements with victims/survivors and/or with significant people in their lives;
- ability to conduct oneself in a professional and ethical manner, including respect and maintaining healthy boundaries;
- adherence to strict policy of confidentiality;
- understanding of sexual violence as a social justice model and one form of oppression with awareness of the connections between sexism, racism, classism, homophobia, heterosexism, and ableism to violence;
- closure on any issues/victimization with sexual assault, relationship violence, or stalking;
- cannot date or have an intimate relationship with clients that you advocate for at the campus sexual assault program.

Duties

- Provide a minimum of three to five nights per month of on-call coverage for the helpline during the hours that the office is closed.

- Table for the campus sexual assault program at events a minimum of three times a semester.
- Hold in confidence all agency and advocate-client related business.
- Receive regular supervision individually and/or in a group setting.
- Provide advocacy when necessary at any of the three University hospitals.
- Work closely as a team with the other advocate and the staff back-up who are on-call during the same period of time.
- Provide thorough and professional helpline advocacy, information and referrals, and appropriate follow-through.
- Provide appropriate outreach services to legal, medical, law enforcement, and academic agencies.
- Provide follow-up advocacy to clients if appropriate and in consultation with staff.
- Complete paperwork in client folders and for the office in a comprehensive and timely manner.

Other Opportunities

- Become a leader and gain career-building experience.
- Get an opportunity to apply for student staff positions.

Report to: Staff of the campus sexual assault program

Job Description for Violence Prevention Educator (VPE)

Requirements

- Successful completion of 40 hours of training provided by the campus sexual assault program;
- commitment to volunteer for at least one year (seniors cannot apply);
- commitment to honor the volunteer agreement made with the campus sexual assault program;
- mandatory once a month meetings/in-service trainings;
- interest in working in the antisexual assault and anti-relationship violence movements through educational initiatives and public speaking;
- ability to conduct oneself in a professional and ethical manner, including respect and maintaining healthy boundaries;
- adherence to strict policy of confidentiality;
- commitment to practicing upcoming presentations on your own;
- understanding of sexual violence as one form of oppression and awareness of connections between sexism, racism, classism, homophobia, heterosexism, and ableism to violence;

- closure on any issues/victimization related to sexual assault, relationship violence, or stalking;
- cannot date or have an intimate relationship with clients that you advocate for at the campus sexual assault program.

Duties

- Complete at least five presentations each semester.
- Table for the campus sexual assault program at events a minimum of three times a semester.
- Respond promptly after an email has been sent to all VPEs requesting presenters for an upcoming educational presentation.
- Come prepared and attend two mandatory one-hour practices prior to each presentation.
- Present the VPE curriculum or materials with the intended audience at the time and date requested.
- Increase campus awareness of the campus sexual assault program, its service, and the Prevention Education program, encouraging groups and classes to invite VPEs to make a presentation.
- If you are unable to fulfil the responsibilities of a presentation, you must find another VPE to replace you.

Opportunities

- Become a leader and gain career-building experience.
- Apply for student staff positions.
- Build your public speaking skills.

Report to: Staff of the campus sexual assault program

Appendix II: Volunteer Training: Learning Objectives

Knowledge Comprehension

After completing the annual 40-hour training with The Aurora Center, volunteers will be able to:

1. State the responsibilities of a volunteer with The Aurora Center.

    a. Expectations

        i.   Accountability
        ii. Impact

b. Mandated Reporting

c. Direct Service Advocacy

d. Violence Prevention Education

2. Summarize The Aurora Center's philosophical approach to providing services on the University of Minnesota and Augsburg College campuses.

a. Mission, Vision, Values

b. Philosophy

    i. Victim-centered

    ii. Trauma-informed

    iii. Positive prevention

    iv. Vulnerability

c. Free & Confidential Services

3. Recognize the impact of oppression and activism in relation to equity on campus.

a. Intersectionality

b. Privilege & Oppression

c. Activism

d. Mental Health

4. Illustrate the systemic effect sexual violence has on the campus community.

a. Sexuality

b. Concepts

    i. Sexual Assault

    ii. Relationship Violence

    iii. Stalking

    iv. Consent & Affirmative Consent

c. Perpetration Research

d. Power & Control

Knowledge Application

After completing the annual 40-hour training with The Aurora Center, volunteers will be able to:

1. Discover best practices to use during crisis intervention.

a. Affirmation

b. Believing

c. Creating options

2. Interpret how to navigate complex and varying situations requiring critical thinking skills.

    a.   Triage response

3. Show the ability to communicate with clients and empower survivors.

    a.   Listening
    b.   Disclosures
    c.   Education

        i.   Presentations

    d.   Helpline

        i.   On call
        ii. Responding to the hospital

    e.   Empowerment

4. Apply learned techniques to exercise self-care.

    a.   Wellness
    b.   De-briefing
    c.   Confidentiality

References

Aurora Center for Advocacy & Education. (2015a). Volunteer information & application packet. Retrieved from www.umn.edu/aurora.

Aurora Center for Advocacy & Education. (2015b). Volunteer training learning objectives. Retrieved from www.umn.edu/aurora.

Banyard, V., Plante, E., & Moynihan, M. (2004). Bystander education: Bringing a broader community perspective to sexual violence prevention. *Journal of Community Psychology*, *32*(1), 61–79.

Bennet, L., Riger, S., Schewe, P., Howard, A., & Wasco, S. (2004). Effectiveness of hotline, advocacy, counseling, and shelter services for victims of domestic violence: A statewide evaluation. *Journal of Interpersonal Violence*, *19*(7), 815–829.

Berkowitz, A. (2010). Fostering healthy norms to prevent violence and abuse: The social norms approach. In K. Kaufman (Ed.), *The prevention of sexual violence: A practitioner's sourcebook* (pp. 147–172). Holyoke, MA: NEARI Press.

Black, M., Basile, K., Breiding, M., Smith, S., Walters, M., Merrick, M., Chen, J., & Stevens, M. (2011). *The national intimate partner and sexual violence survey (NISVS): 2010 summary report.* Atlanta, GA: Centers for Disease Control and Prevention, National Center for Injury Prevention and Control.

California Coalition Against Sexual Assault (CALCASA). (2008). *Support for survivors: Training for sexual assault counselors: Mini-book.* Retrieved from www.calcasa.org/resources/publications/.

Carmody, D., Ekhomu, J., & Payne, B.K. (2009). Needs of sexual assault advocates in campus based sexual assault centers. *College Student Journal*, *43*(2), 507–513.

Casey, E., & Lindhorst, T. (2009). Toward a multi-level, ecological approach to the primary prevention of sexual assault: Prevention in peer and community contexts. *Trauma, Violence, & Abuse, 10*(2), 91–114.

Cnaan, R., Smith, K., Holmes, K., Haski-Leventhal, D., Handy, F., & Brudney, J. (2010). *Motivations and benefits of student volunteering: Comparing regular, occasional, and non-volunteers in five countries.* Retrieved from http://repository.upenn.edu/spp_papers/153.

Coker, A., Cook-Craig, P., Williams, C., Fisher, B., Clear, E., Garcia, L., & Hegge, L. (2011). Evaluation of Green Dot: An active bystander intervention to reduce sexual violence on college campuses. *Violence Against Women, 17*(6), 777–796.

Fabiano, P., Perkins, H., Berkowitz, A., Linkenbach, J., & Stark, C. (2003). Engaging men as social justice allies in ending violence against women: Evidence for a social norms approach. *Journal of American College Health, 52*(3), 105–112.

Kenagy, G. (2005). The health and social service needs of transgender people in Philadelphia. *International Journal of Transgenderism, 8*(2/3), 49–56.

Krebs, C., Lindquist, C., Warner, T., Fisher, B., & Martin, S. (2007). *The campus sexual assault study (CSA): Final report.* Washington, DC: National Institute of Justice.

Linder, C. (2015). *Strategies of campus sexual assault activists. Roosevelt scholars conference.* Retrieved from: https://drchrislinder.files.wordpress.com/2014/03/roosevelt-scholars-3-28-151.pdf.

McMahon, S., Banyard, V.L., & McMahon, S.M. (2015). Incoming college students' bystander behaviors to prevent sexual violence. *Journal of College Student Development, 56*(5), 488–493.

Palm Reed, K.M., Hines, D.A., Armstrong, J.L., & Cameron, A.Y. (2015). Experimental evaluation of a bystander prevention program for sexual assault and dating violence. *Psychology of Violence, 5*(1), 95–102.

Smith, C., Gómez, J., & Freyd, J. (2014). The psychology of judicial betrayal. *Roger Williams University Law Review, 19*, 451–475.

Soria, K., & Thomas-Card, T. (2014). Relationships between motivations for community service participation and desire to continue service following college. *Michigan Journal of Community Service Learning, 20*(2), 53–64.

Thomas-Card, T., & Eichele, K. (2015) Comprehensive college- or university-based sexual violence prevention & direct services program: A framework. In S.C. Wooten & R.W. Mitchell (Eds.), *The crisis of campus sexual violence: Critical perspectives on prevention and response* (pp. 149–168). New York: Routledge.

U.S. Department of Justice. (2015). *Office on Violence Against Women local resources.* Retrieved from www.justice.gov/ovw/local-resources.

2

AN ACADEMIC CREDIT MODEL FOR TRAINING HEARING PANELS

Chris Loschiavo

Since at least 1986, when a group of professionals met at the Stetson Law and Higher Education Conference to discuss the formation of a professional organization for student conduct professionals, student conduct administrators have advocated for the position that student conduct practices are at their core educational processes. According to founding member of the Association for Student Conduct Administration (ASCA), Don Gehring (2013, p. 1), "It was my dream that an organization be created to assist conduct administrators in staying abreast of the laws and to apply the law in a context of aiding students in their personal development."

In carrying out these educational activities, student conduct professionals believe that students need to play a key role in this process. As indicated in the Preamble to the Constitution and bylaws of ASCA (Kibler, 2013):

> The development and enforcement of standards of conduct and resolution of conflict for students is an educational endeavor that fosters students' personal and social development. Students must assume a significant role in developing and enforcing such regulations in order that they might be better prepared for the responsibilities of citizenship. (p. 8)

This is why many campuses use student hearing panels that are made up of faculty, staff, and (often) students. From 1986 until 2011, this idea of the conduct administrator and the role of hearing panels went largely unchanged.

However, in April 2011, the Department of Education's Office for Civil Rights issued its Dear Colleague Letter (Department of Education Office for Civil Rights, 2011). This letter has arguably had more impact on student conduct practices than anything since the *Dixon v Alabama* court decision, which essentially created the field of student conduct administration. Additionally, the current focus on how campuses handle sexual assault allegations has threatened the very existence of hearing panels. In this chapter, I hope to demonstrate a potential solution that both meets the standards of compliance with federal mandates while also holding true to our belief in student development as student affairs professionals.

Student conduct administration is among the areas most impacted by the federal government's recent focus on sexual violence on the college campus. Documentaries like *The Hunting Ground* (Dick & Ziering, 2015) and *It Happened Here* (Jackson & Nielson, 2015) have shed new light on the various aspects of universities' responses to sexual violence. This increased attention has caused a lot of questioning and debate about the role of campuses in responding to these issues. Regardless of what one believes about the university's role in responding to sexual violence, there is quite a bit of misinformation about the role of the student conduct system in handling these types of complaints.

Within the debate of how to adjudicate campus sexual assault cases is another debate, which has been to a certain extent fueled by the Office of Civil Rights (OCR), about the role of students on hearing panels. The April 2014 Question and Answer Guidance Document produced by OCR states: "Although Title IX does not dictate the membership of a hearing board, OCR discourages schools from allowing students to serve on hearing boards in cases involving allegations of sexual violence" (Department of Education Office for Civil Rights, 2014, p. 30). While OCR has not provided any formal rationale for this position, it has been suggested that student victims will be less likely to report if they know they will have to face a panel of their peers in a hearing. It has also been suggested that students are less able to understand the nuances involved in deciding whether a situation meets the definition of incapacitation and thus cannot be adequately trained to understand this and make a factual determination when presented with a case.

College students are adults who are able to serve on juries of capital murder cases without training. These same students play a critical role in the overall response to sexual violence on campus and that role should not be limited to just that of a passive receptacle of information. Rather, students should have an active role in the management of cases when they arise. This can be done as long as they are provided with adequate training.

This conflict of whether or not students should be able to serve on disciplinary hearing panels provides the backdrop for this chapter. One of the primary reasons OCR has believed that students were inappropriate on these hearing panels is the belief that students cannot be adequately trained to hear this level of cases. At the University of Florida, we were fortunate enough in August 2011 to have the support to make a radical change in the way we trained our student hearing panel members, in particular, our undergraduate student members. In order to train students to hear these kinds of cases so that they understand trauma and its impact on memory, to understand rape myths and rape culture, to learn how to appropriately question victims in a non-victim blaming manner, among other skills, professionals need adequate time to help them learn about these issues. An eight- or 16-hour training is not enough to cover this information adequately. We believed and have since found that by giving students academic credit for their training, we are able to provide a much more detailed level of training to these students so that they truly become experts in many ways. We are now able to spend close to 50 hours of class time with students as they learn how to handle these and other very difficult cases through a three-credit course.

This chapter will take the reader through the steps necessary to implement the Student Conduct Committee training class developed at the University of Florida. My discussion will include how the training was designed for academic credit, curriculum development for the class, as well as some challenges we have experienced with the class and graduate students, professional students, faculty, and staff who cannot take a three-credit course. While this chapter is written from my own perspective in designing this training from start to finish, it should provide readers helpful insight for shaping a similar training in their own institutional context.

Creating the Class

Based largely on our own experiences with some recent (at the time) sexual assault cases, as well as the recently released Dear Colleague Letter, in 2011 the University of Florida was looking for a new way to supplement the hearing panel training offered to our committee members to help make them more effective. For years, we had relied on four hours of general hearing board training with an additional two to four hours of training on sexual violence for those members who wanted the ability to hear those cases. The general training would allow members to hear cases involving academic cheating and plagiarism, as well as theft, damage to property, and alcohol and other drug offenses, among other types of violations. The sexual violence training allowed members to also hear dating violence, domestic violence, sexual assault/misconduct, and stalking cases. The general training was required upon selection and then various topical in-service trainings were offered over the course of each year. The sexual violence training was an annual training requirement. These minimal requirements felt inadequate and we had issues of committee members really struggling with sexual violence cases. The staff members in Student Conduct and Conflict Resolution (a department in the Dean of Students Office at UF) all felt that we were rushed going through many of the training topics, which felt resultantly superficial as opposed to the deep dive that we really needed on some topics. Additionally, we often found that we never had much time to practice the skills involved in hearing these types of cases.

In thinking through alternative training models, it occurred to me that we required resident assistants, peer leaders, and orientation leaders to complete a three-credit training class before they could assume these important leadership roles. Why then, could we not have a similar class for these students who essentially have the authority to remove another student from the campus permanently? The course syllabus for our student orientation staffers served as my inspiration for designing a more rigorous, comprehensive hearing panel training. Based on this and our training outline at the time, I created a draft course syllabus that I shared with my staff. We modified it and came up with more activities and homework assignments until we settled on something we really felt good about. During the 2016 spring semester, we will welcome our fifth cohort of students to the Conduct Committee Training Class. While we have modified the class from its original iteration, it is largely unchanged in terms of major topics covered and overall outline. Once we had a draft syllabus, we discussed potential options for departments that could host the class, as the Dean of Students Office does not have this authority on campus.

We approached a faculty member on our committee from the Department of Sociology, Criminology, and Law. After I explained what we were trying to do, who would teach the class, and what we needed from the Department, we essentially had a class sponsor. The class would be called CCJ 4934, which is an upper division criminal justice designation and counts as an elective course. It was established essentially as a test course, which meant it did not need to go through curriculum committee and could be implemented for the following spring semester.

Class Structure

The shift in training model meant a shift in how we recruited for the Student Conduct Committee. Instead of recruiting members, we were recruiting students to attend the class. We had to make sure in our advertising materials that students knew they needed to hold the class meeting time on their schedule so that they were available at the time the course was offered. We conducted interviews and selected 30 students for our first class. We limited the class to 30 students initially, as this was our pilot and we wanted to be sure we had enough time for grading and evaluation while still managing our caseload in a timely manner. We have since expanded the class to around 40 students per semester.

We conducted group interviews, as it is most important to see how students will work together as that is how deliberations are conducted. In conducting interviews, we were looking for students who understood the educational philosophy of the conduct program as well as those that came in open-minded and could listen and work with a variety of people. We were essentially screening out students on the two ends of the spectrum—those that did not ever see a policy violation and those that felt like anyone who violates policy should be suspended or expelled. The group interviews consisted of two parts. The first part was a ranking exercise, in which the group was given 10 different policy violations that they were supposed to rank individually from most to least serious.

Afterwards, the group had to work together and reach consensus on their rankings. Part two involved a case study. The group discussed what evidence exists of a policy violation, and agreed on appropriate consequences. We were also looking for diverse representation in terms of gender identity, race and ethnicity, age, area of study, etc. Twenty-seven ended up enrolling in our first class. The goal of the class was to more fully explore all of our training topics. The course met three hours per week.

The course was designed to have five quizzes, a diversity project, three in-class presentations, journal entries, hearing panel observations, and a final oral exam. The diversity project involved students having to attend an event that involved a population different from themselves and then writing a reflection paper on the experience. The quizzes were on various subdivisions of the class to ensure students had learned the material from that subtopic. For a complete description of class activities, see the attached syllabus. There were also extra credit opportunities. Reading materials included the University of Florida Student Conduct Code, Division of Student Affairs, Dean of Students Office and SCCR websites as well as *Navigating Past the Spirit of Insubordination: A Model Conduct Code for the 21st Century* (Stoner & Lowery, 2004). We also included several chapters from student affairs books that included information about student conduct, such as *Student Conduct Practice: The Complete Guide for Student Affairs Professionals* (Lancaster & Waryold, 2008).

We had a very strict attendance and tardiness policy. This was done for several reasons. The first reason is that reliability is an important trait in a committee member. We needed to be able to rely on students to be at hearings when assigned. Failure to show for a hearing or showing up late for a hearing looks unprofessional and may cause those participating in the hearing to have less confidence in the process, regardless of which side they are on and what the outcome is. Additionally, the information provided during class was necessary for students to learn to be effective committee members. The class was focused on experiential learning, which requires their physical presence.

Course Content

The course was divided into four primary topic areas: foundations, the conduct process, conduct violations, and sanctioning.

Foundations

After spending the first class session going over expectations, doing introductions, and having the students take a pretest to gauge their knowledge of the conduct process, we jumped into a discussion on the structure of the conduct program and where it fits into the organizational chart of the University of Florida. We also had all students complete a self-assessment because we believed it was important for students to know themselves, their strengths, and weaknesses if they are going to hear cases and ultimately sit in judgment of their peers. From there, we discussed the foundation of student conduct from *in loco parentis* to the *Dixon* case to modern conduct philosophy. During this block of classes, we brought in a guest speaker to focus on diversity and social justice within the context of student conduct. A primary goal we had was to help our students understand the difference between treating the parties equally and equitably, and why our goal is to be equitable as that is the fairest option from a social justice perspective. The last lesson in the foundations subtopic was a discussion of Student Conduct Committee members as leaders and role models.

Conduct Process

Beginning with class five, the course shifted to a discussion of the conduct process. During class sessions, we spent time talking about where the code gives the university jurisdiction over student behavior as well as the role of hearing board members, the role of Student Conduct and Conflict Resolution Staff as hearing panel advisor, and the role of advisors to the respective students. We also talked about accused student and alleged victim rights.

A focus on evidence and interpreting evidence was crucial for the conduct process portion of the course. Our university was a useful resource in locating experts that could teach our students about a number of aspects relevant to the experience of serving on a hearing panel. We brought in a faculty member whose primary area of research was on eyewitness testimony and a study on bias in questioning. This faculty member helped the students in the class learn that how they phrase a question can make a difference in the answers that are shared during the hearing. She also explained how lie detection is much less understood than people think. For example, many people believe they are much better at detecting deception than they actually are, including law enforcement. Finally, the faculty member spent time helping committee members understand how memory actually works. We also spent a great deal of time discussing standard of proof, types of evidence, and weighing of evidence. A key component of this part of the curriculum was communication skills. Committee members were trained in active listening and questioning skills. We even delved into mediation skills such as reframing and restating, and discussed why they were effective for panelists to use in hearings. The conduct process portion of the course ended with a class session focused on determining credibility.

During the conduct process portion of the course, we also provided a session on StrengthsQuest (2010). One of the goals for involvement on the conduct committee is that students also learn more about themselves. StrengthsQuest is a program that helps individuals identify their top five strengths. The philosophy of StrengthsQuest is to focus on working on your strengths rather than emphasizing your weaknesses. It is based on interviews from Fortune 500 CEOs.

One of the philosophies of our class was that we wanted it to be a good professional development experience, and we believed using StrengthsQuest was an effective way of ensuring this.

Violations

After completing a quiz on the student conduct process, we shifted our focus toward learning the various conduct code and honor code violations. We broke these sessions down by asking each student to take a violation of the code, research what it means to analyze key points, and then present their findings to the entire class. In particular, we asked them to focus on the elements of the offense they were assigned. Once the class presentations were completed, a combination of our staff and guest speakers covered our more common or complex violations in more detail. For example, for the session on alcohol, drugs, and hazing, we brought in speakers from fraternity and sorority affairs, our health promotion services office, and our substance abuse specialist from our counseling and wellness center. They discussed things like our medical amnesty policy, how alcohol affects each individual, how BAC is determined, signs of problem drinking, and when a student should be referred for treatment. Our session on driving under the influence involved having a police officer from the University of Florida Police Department or Gainesville Police Department describe what they looked for in field sobriety exercises and where the key decision points were in making a driving under the influence arrest.

We spent a few class sessions discussing sexual assault, dating violence, domestic violence, stalking, and sexual harassment, and brought in several guest speakers to help with the training on these topics. After a discussion of the language used to define these behaviors in our conduct code, and the elements of each offense, we invited a Sexual Assault Nurse Examiner to talk about a sexual assault exam and rape kit. She described how the process worked and what signs and evidence the nurse examiner typically looked for when conducting a rape exam. She also helped committee members understand what things to look for on a rape kit report as an evaluator for the hearings as well as what a rape kit cannot be used to determine. Finally, she helped committee members understand why there may be no signs of trauma in situations where the issue was whether or not the victim was incapacitated and no force was used. Students in the class were given a case study of an acquaintance rape scenario involving incapacitation and were asked to come up with questions they would have of both parties as well as an analysis of how they would handle it as a committee member.

Having a guest speaker from our victim advocates office was an important component of the course. The primary focus of this presentation was on rape myths, victim blaming, trauma-informed questioning, and the role of the victim advocate. The speaker also discussed the neurobiology of trauma and its impact on memory. Victim advocates explained why there is often a delay in reporting these types of offenses to authorities. Finally, they discussed that victims can look and act very differently from what one might expect and that everyone experiences trauma differently.

This victim advocate session was vital to create a balanced hearing panel. If your campus has a hearing panel in place and does not train panelists on these issues, then the panel is in effect evaluating a sexual assault case with most students' preconceived biases in place such as the false belief that rape is often falsely reported or that rape is only committed by strangers jumping out of bushes as opposed to by someone they know. While this session was very important, it is really vital to highlight that just because between 2% and 8% of rape cases are false reports (Lisak, Gardinier, Nicksa, & Cote, 2010), it does not mean the committee members should assume that the case they are reviewing is true. They must make a determination based on the evidence presented; after all, this could be that case that falls in the 2%. It was nuances like this that we felt we could not adequately address in our old training model. It was also important to spend some time talking about what it was like to be accused of sexual assault, so spending time on accused student psychology is also essential.

We then brought in a speaker from our local domestic violence shelter to discuss dating and domestic violence. This speaker placed particular emphasis on the cycle of violence as well as talking more about the psychology of victimization. Additionally, they explained why a victim might stay in an abusive relationship. The speaker also addressed the issue of escalation and how controlling, jealous behavior was part of the dating/domestic violence continuum that could lead to more violent behavior such as hitting, pushing, choking, and sexual assault. In particular, the committee learned about lethality assessments to help determine how dangerous a particular situation might be. Finally, we ended our subtopic on violations by discussing the community impact of various violations. We wanted student members to understand that every case involves at least three parties: the accused student, the victim or most directly impacted party, and the community-at-large. The role of the committee, besides weighing the evidence, was to consider the outcome from the perspective of all three sides.

Sanctions

Our final subtopic was sanctioning. We spent time discussing the University of Florida's sanctioning philosophy, such as which violations were more appropriate for suspension or expulsion from the university. Additionally, the University's philosophy on educational and restorative sanctioning was explained. Some of this was covered through group presentations on campus resources. We had students partner up with one or two other students in the class and research a particular campus resource that might serve as a sanction. Their task was to present the resource and in what circumstances it might be used as a sanction.

The last two class sessions were focused on conflict resolution options and self-care. A primary tenet of UF's conduct philosophy is conflict resolution. Where appropriate, rather than going to a formal hearing, we will divert a case to mediation, a facilitated dialogue, a conflict coaching session, or restorative justice practices. While we have used restorative justice in a number of Title IX cases, we have not used it in a sexual assault case yet. However, if we had the right case, we would consider using it. We also emphasized a restorative justice philosophy to our formal hearings and spent a class session talking about what this meant and why. We ended class with a session on self-care presented by our Counseling and Wellness Center. Some of the issues and hearings our members participated in could be emotional and very stressful; therefore, we wanted to provide them with tools to cope with these issues.

Assignments

Throughout the course, lectures and in-class presentations were supplemented with various assignments. Each of these assignments had a specific purpose that related to either content that directly impacted the student as a committee member or professional development. Eight journal entries on various topics were required. The journal entries were usually reflective pieces, although from time to time we gave a specific topic we asked the class to write about.

To supplement our guest speaker on diversity, we required a diversity project. The project entailed two parts: an observation and information seeking. The observation could consist of attending a lecture or other event that focused on students immersing themselves with a group that was different from themselves. The idea was to learn from a distance. The second component was to interview someone that was different from the student. As committee members, these students are going to come in contact with many individuals different from themselves, so it is important for them to have an opportunity to practice learning from these individuals and understanding different perspectives. After completing these two components, students wrote a three-page paper on what they learned from these experiences.

As mentioned above, we also required a campus resource presentation that was done as a group project. The goal was for the class to present a potential sanction resource, for example, the alcohol, drugs and the law seminar put on by the University of Florida Police Department, to their peers. Students were assigned a particular resource from a preselected list, and course instructors prepared staff members in these areas prior to the students contacting them for interviews about what the resource provided.

Another assignment had students take a particular violation of the conduct code or honor code and present what they learned to their classmates. This assignment typically involved breaking the violation down into its component parts and analyzing what the key aspects were for determining whether a particular behavior violated that section of the code. Within these presentations, students had to provide examples of behaviors that would violate that section of the code. To engage some critical thinking among our committee members, we also asked them to identify a section of the conduct code and/or honor code and propose a revision to it. We asked them to redraft that section with an explanation of why they made the changes they did and how their version was better than what we currently had in place. Part of this activity also involved research into the codes of three other universities to see how those universities addressed similar behavior.

One of the key assignments in the course was a hearing observation requirement. We required every student in the class to observe two hearings during the semester. Their role as observer was to arrive at the same time the committee arrives to hear a case, listen to the hearing preparation, hearing, deliberation, and debriefing, and observe critically. We wanted them to analyze and capture good questions asked by the committee members, as well as those questions that were not effective. Students were required to write a brief paper summarizing their experience with the hearing. In addition, they were to highlight effective and ineffective questions, any information that was missing, any questions they would have asked, assess how the chairperson did in facilitating deliberation, as well as analyze the committee's decision, and finally, identify any questions the observation raised for them about the process, the violation, or the sanctions.

Finally, we had a comprehensive final oral exam. We divided the class into two groups and had the exam take place over two days. Each student had the opportunity to observe half of the class hearing a mock case and provided feedback to those students participating in that hearing board as the first part of their exam. For the second part of the exam, those students then participated in a mock hearing as the panel members themselves and received feedback from their classmates. Conduct staff attended class to observe the hearings and determine grades. Students were graded on their questioning, their evaluation of the evidence, level of participation in deliberation, and overall decision-making. Promptness, preparation, and dress are also evaluated as part of this process.

Challenges

While we are quite happy with the training model we have, it does have some limitations. First, we have only been able to apply it to undergraduate students. We have not yet found a way to get faculty members and graduate or professional students to commit to so many hours of training. Fortunately, our faculty, staff, and graduate and professional student members are aware of the training difference, and often defer to the undergraduate students. In many ways, this may be the strongest argument for why OCR's position on student panelists is flawed. The undergraduate students are the most able to commit to attend this kind of training, so they are arguably the most prepared and well-trained panelists.

In addition to the challenge of limiting this kind of training to undergraduate students, another challenge is the amount of staff time and resources spent in the training class. In addition to preparing the training presentations, staff are also responsible for grading quizzes, papers, and other assignments. A significant amount of time is spent on preparing materials and evaluating them for each assignment and class period. Additionally, due to the amount of work spent grading papers and other assignments, we had to adjust the number of papers and assignments included in the syllabus, as there was less time available to grade these assignments. Because we use full-time conduct staff to handle the teaching and evaluation of these classes, they are subject to the whims of the nature of conduct work, which can mean a significant amount of time hearing cases, preparing for hearings, and ultimately consulting on conduct issues. This makes finding time to grade 30–40 papers very challenging, while also maintaining some work-life balance and keeping up with the demands of investigating and hearing cases.

Another challenge that is foreseeable for other campuses is the idea that there may not be as much student buy-in for the student hearing panel process. This could make it difficult to recruit students to participate on this committee and in switching to a training class format; you may have fewer students willing to spend five or more hours a week on this kind of training. Fortunately, we have not found that to be the case at the University of Florida thus far, as our students are very committed to their role in shared governance.

A final challenge is that the size of the class is limited, because the instructors can only grade so many assignments with their other responsibilities. This has finally caught up to us this year, so we are looking at offering another section of the course during a different semester to help us keep up with the demand for committee members.

Conclusion

Based on each of the four years this class has been provided, the University of Florida has seen a marked improvement in the preparedness of undergraduate hearing panel committee members. Committee members report more confidence in the preparation for their role in hearing cases and staff advisors report better questioning and deliberation by committee members. This training model has also resulted in increased confidence in the conduct system from senior administration and appellate officers. Prior to implementing the training class module, appellate officers sustained 67% of cases; since implementing the class, the rate of sustained cases by appellate officers has risen to 75%. Recruitment has become easier overall, as the class seems to have raised the prestige of this leadership role among undergraduate students on campus. Additionally, due to the initial commitment students make to the training, we have improved retention of student committee members.

One of the primary criticisms of student panelists is that just knowing that students sit on the panel could cause a silencing of victims being willing to participate in the conduct process. Our experience at UF seems to run counter to this theory, as approximately 50% of complainants request a panel hearing on our campus. It is worth noting that students can choose between the faculty, staff, and student panel or an Administrative Hearing. During our intake meetings with alleged victims, we explain the various hearing options and discuss the training undergone by all of those involved in the adjudication process.

In addition to the wonderful feedback from our participants and committee members and the increased confidence in the hearing process, we have some general feedback from some of the federal decision makers who are making policy decisions and recommendations about campuses' response to sexual violence. As a conduct professional since 1999, I have seen as well as adjudicated my share of sexual violence cases. I have also trained student hearing panel members every year of my career. How and on what topics I train my hearing members has evolved over time. Additionally, as past president of ASCA, an association that is the voice of 3300 professionals at over 1800 institutions across the country, I have a good idea of what is happening nationally. Finally, I have had the opportunity to meet face-to-face with White House staffers involved in the *Not Alone* (2014) report, the OCR, and staff members from the Offices of Senator McCaskill, Gillibrand, Blumenthal, Rubio, and others. I have had the opportunity to share the Student Conduct Committee training model that we utilize at the University of Florida with each of these constituents. At each of these meetings, the stakeholders were clearly surprised such a training model exists. They were also impressed with its thoroughness and actually asked the question "Why doesn't everyone do this?" While this training may not work for every campus and we are not suggesting every campus has this capability or student desire to be involved, for many campuses this presents a viable option for training student panelists.

Campuses have a long history of using students on their disciplinary hearing panels, and this training model could be adapted so that campuses that have adequate student investment and interest can continue to use these hearing panels, which are so important to student accountability and institutional governance. Additionally, students have a unique understanding of student culture and the dynamics involved in student relationships. When we remove students from the decision-making process, we lose this added information. Finally, an added benefit is the university has another 40 or so students with a high level of sexual violence training each year that go out and interact with their peers.

While this training model has proven very effective for the University of Florida, part of the reason for its effectiveness is our campus culture. We have a large student body of approximately 53,000 students, most of whom are very actively engaged on campus. Our students seek out leadership positions, and the more prestigious, the better. Our campus also has a strong tradition of student governance, which lends itself well to committing to something like this training. As indicated in the ASCA Gold Standard Report of 2014 (pp. 18–19), understanding your campus culture is one of the key components of deciding what type of resolution model for Title IX will work for your campus. Before deciding whether or not to attempt this kind of training, you must be sure you have a campus culture that supports it, the resources to provide it, and student buy-in to your process (Bennett, Gregory, Loschiavo, & Waller, 2014, pp. 18–19).

References

Bennett, L., Gregory, M., Loschiavo, C., & Waller, J. (2014). Student conduct administration and Title IX: Gold standard practices for resolution of allegations of sexual misconduct on college campuses. Retrieved from www.theasca.org/files/Publications/ ASCA%202014%20Gold%20Standard.pdf.

Dick, K. (Writer, Director), & Ziering, A. (Producer) (2015). *The hunting ground* [DVD]. United States: Chain Camera Pictures.

Dixon v. Alabama State Board of Education, 294 F. 2d 150 (5th Cir. 1961).

Gehring, D. (2013). The history and founding of the association. In D. Waryold & J. Lancaster (Eds.), *The state of student conduct: Current forces and future challenges: Revisited.* (pp. 1–6). Texas, TX: Association for Student Conduct Administration.

Jackson, L. (Director), & Nielsen, M.S. (Producer) (2015). *It happened here* [DVD]. United States: Cinedigm.

Kibler, W. (2013). Preamble to the constitution of the Association for Student Conduct Administration: Reflections upon the crafting of the preamble and the relevance it has today. In D. Waryold & J. Lancaster (Eds.), *The state of student conduct: Current forces and future challenges: Revisited* (pp. 7–9). Texas, TX: Association for Student Conduct Administration.

Lancaster, J.M., & Waryold, D.M. (2008). The professional philosophy of student conduct administration. In J.M. Lancaster & D.M. Waryold (Eds.), *Student conduct practice: The complete guide for student affairs professionals* (p. 6). Sterling, VA: Stylus.

Lisak, D., Gardinier, L., Nicksa, S.C., & Cote, A.M. (2010). False allegations of sexual assault: An analysis of ten years of reported cases. *Violence Against Women, 16*(12), 1318–1334.

StrengthsQuest. (2010). Retrieved from www.strengthsquest.com/home.aspx.

Stoner II, E.N., & Lowery, J.W. (2004). Navigating past the "spirit of insubordination": A twenty-first century model student code of conduct with a model hearing script. *Journal of College and University Law, 31*(1), 1–78.

U.S. Department of Education Office for Civil Rights. (2011). Dear Colleague Letter. Retrieved from www2.ed.gov/about/offices/list/ocr/letters/colleague-201104.html.

U.S. Department of Education Office for Civil Rights. (2014). Questions and answers about Title IX and sexual violence. Retrieved from www2.ed.gov/about/offices/list/ocr/ frontpage/faq/rr/policyguidance/sex.html.

3

A QUESTION OF CONSENT

Engaging Men in Making Responsible Sexual Decisions

Beverly A. McPhail

Although sexual assault and sexual assault prevention programs have a long history on college campuses, the problem has only recently received national attention, primarily due to student activism, federal intervention, and media attention. A recent study of 27 institutions of higher education (IHE) found that 16.5% of college seniors across all surveyed universities experienced sexual contact involving penetration or sexual touching as a result of physical force or incapacitation since entering IHE (The Association of American Universities, 2015). The study revealed that nonconsensual sexual contact by force or incapacitation varied across college campuses and by demographics with rates higher for undergraduates than graduate or professional students; higher for cisgender women and transgender, gender queer, or nonconforming (TGQN) individuals than for cisgender men; and higher for freshmen than for seniors (AAU, 2015).

In 2010, as the director of the Women's Resource Center at the University of Houston (UH), I decided to deliver a sexual assault primary prevention program tailored to men on campus. There was no current campus programming directed toward men and, due to my feminist[1] worldview, I found "rape prevention" programs that targeted a female audience problematic. I had some difficulty finding a program that I liked or could afford with our department's limited resources. Since necessity is the mother of invention, I developed my own program called "A Question of Consent," based on my experience as a feminist scholar and social work practitioner in the antiviolence against women field.

This chapter will outline a brief history of sexual assault prevention on college campuses while making the case for developing programs that target men. I will provide a full description of A Question of Consent, including its content as well as some of the limitations I have found with its implementation. The program is similar to other prevention programs that define and detail gaining sexual consent, but is unique in its explicit inclusion of sexuality as a component of sexual assault prevention.

Primary Prevention on College Campuses

Traditional Programs

Primary prevention efforts are "approaches that take place *before* sexual violence has occurred to prevent initial perpetration or victimization" (Centers for Disease Control and Prevention, 2004, emphasis in original, p. 3). In earlier prevention efforts, "primary prevention" was often misdirected at women, as they were the most frequent victims of sexual violence. However, attempting to teach women how to prevent their own sexual assaults often had the unintended consequence of victim blaming, as women were held responsible for preventing their own rapes and blamed if they could not. Today, such programs are more appropriately termed "risk reduction" programs, which are interventions designed to reduce women's risk for sexual victimization, often by identifying potential high-risk situations and learning to act in response (Orchowski, Gidycz, & Raffle, 2008). Risk reduction programs are conducted by many sexual assault advocates as well as law enforcement, and provide strategies for rape avoidance, such as being careful about posting one's geographic location on social media, asking a friend to walk with you across campus, using only headphones in one ear to stay aware of surroundings, and not leaving your drink unattended while at a party or bar (Rape, Abuse & Incest National Network, 2016).

Another popular prevention program directed at women and often offered through the campus police department is the Rape Aggression Defense (RAD) program. RAD involves learning to fight off a physical attack by a stranger. However, most rapes on college campuses do not involve a physical attack and are perpetrated by someone the victim knows. For example, one study of college women found that, in almost 80% of rape and sexual assault victimizations, the victims knew their offender (Sinozich & Langton, 2014). Also, the RAD program offers no empirical evidence of its effectiveness.[2]

Another popular primary prevention program is the bystander intervention program, which engages with students as potential allies rather than perpetrators or victims, increases awareness of the problem of campus sexual assault, and instills a sense of responsibility for the problem, while also teaching effective intervention skills (Carr, 2008). DeGue et al. (2014) report that bystander programs have some empirical evidence that they work, but call for further research. Henriksen, Mattick, and Fisher (2016) also cite empirical support for bystander intervention training, but they also ask: (1) Are the positive effects long-term? (2) Does the fact that in most campus rapes the perpetrator and victim know each other create more complex dynamics than when a bystander is deciding whether or not to intervene with a stranger? (3) If most sexual assaults occur in private, how often can bystander interventions occur? My own criticism of bystander intervention programs is that they address students as bystanders in the lives of others rather than actors in their own lives. Most people will be involved in situations of consent and nonconsent in their own lives as well as in the lives of others.

Targeting Groups at High Risk for Sexual Assault Perpetration

Although all men do not rape, they are nevertheless the primary perpetrators of campus sexual assault. In their study of campus sexual assault, Sinozich and Langston (2014) found that 97% of perpetrators were men. Factors associated with male sexual aggression include rape myth acceptance (false beliefs about rape that tend to legitimize rape), lack of empathy for rape victims, use of alcohol, and hostility toward women (Stephens & George, 2009). Although media reports on campus sexual assaults frequently focus on athletic teams and fraternities as high-risk groups, the research has been mixed.

In a meta-analysis of 29 studies, Murnen and Kohlman (2007) found that participation in men's college athletics or fraternities was associated with attitudes related to sexual aggression, hypermasculinity, and rape myth acceptance. In a review of 305 sexual assault insurance claims, 15% of male perpetrators were athletes and 10% were members of a fraternity (United Educators, 2015). Humphrey (2000) was able to differentiate between high- and low-risk men's athletic teams and fraternities based on upper-level student's perceptions of the likelihood in which the group's parties created an atmosphere conducive to sexual assault. The study found that perceived high-risk sports teams and fraternities were more likely to report committing more sexually aggressive acts, scored higher on hostility toward women, higher on a measure of male peer support for sexual assault, and higher on alcohol drinking frequency and intensity. The author concluded that not all men's athletic teams and fraternities are equal in their propensity to engage in sexually aggressive behaviors, suggesting the need for more targeted interventions (Humphrey, 2000).

A Focus on Sexuality

History of the Etiology of Sexual Assault Motivations

When trying to prevent a phenomenon, it is helpful to understand what causes it in the first place. The causal factors can then be used to inform and target prevention and educational programming. However, our understanding of what causes sexual violence has changed over time. The history of sexual assault etiology includes rape being considered a property crime against the father of the raped woman, the belief that rape was a perversion and that rapists were mentally ill, and that rape was a sex crime committed by an offender unable to control his sexual impulses (Donat & D'Emilio, 1992). However, with the advent of the second wave of the women's movement, feminists reconceptualized rape as being motivated by power and control, rather than sexual desire, in order to maintain a gendered hierarchy (Brownmiller, 1975; Connell & Wilson, 1974). Davis (1981) expanded the feminist understanding of rape by constructing an intersectional and historical analysis that examined rape through the lens of capitalism as well as gender and race. Since the 1970s, this paradigm has been the prevailing explanation of perpetrators' motives for committing sexual assault in prevention and educational programs, which are largely informed by the feminist perspective.

However, McPhail (2016) knits multiple feminist theories together to better account for the complexities of rape and to acknowledge that rape is a sexual act committed due to multiple motivations in which male sexual entitlement plays a major role. From a public health perspective, Tharp et al. (2013) identify a constellation of risk factors for sexual violence perpetration, such as unhealthy sexual behaviors, experiences, or attitudes, including multiple sexual partners, impersonal sex, early initiation of sex, exposure to sexually aggressive peers, and peer pressure to have sex. Traditionally, campus sexual assault prevention programs have not focused on the social constructions of male sexuality or risk factors for male sexual aggression. Vivolo, Holland, Teten, Holt, and the Sexual Violence Review Team (2010) suggest that adopting a public health model for sexual violence prevention could include addressing sexual risk factors.

Sexual Scripts

Sexual assault prevention programs do not often explicitly attempt to address the sexual scripts of college students. Sexual socialization occurs through the influence of intrapersonal, interpersonal, and environmental or sociocultural sources (Gagnon & Simon, 1973). Frith and Kitzinger (2001) note that sexual scripts are blueprints that guide sexual behavior and decision-making, including widely shared understandings about the sequence and pattern of sexual encounters, although they are gender and culture specific. Feminists are often attracted to sexual script theory, as it identifies sexuality as a learned behavior, rather than purely biological or individualistic; therefore, what is learned can be unlearned.

Two major findings of sexual script theory are that heterosexual activities occur in a certain sequence and males and females learn different sexual scripts. For instance, traditional male sexual scripts can include the message that men are to actively seek out sexual partners and have an uncontrollable sexuality once aroused, in contrast to the sexual scripts of heterosexual women that include the message to passively wait to be chosen for sex and to desire love rather than sex. In a sexual assault prevention program with a focus on sexuality, there is an attempt to confront old sexual scripts, including those influenced by pornography, while introducing new ones.

Sexual Education

One major difficulty in sexual assault prevention and education programming is that the majority of women and men arrive on campus with little sexual education. In 2006, 87% of U.S. public and private high schools taught abstinence as the most effective method for pregnancy, HIV, and STD prevention (Guttmacher Institute, 2012). Additionally, 37 states require that sex education include abstinence, even though abstinence-only programs have not been shown to delay sexual activity and may instead deter contraceptive use among sexually active teens (Guttmacher, 2012). Abstinence-only sexual education teaches abstinence from sexual activity outside of heterosexual marriage as the expected standard for all, while warning of the psychological and physical dangers of all other choices (Guttmacher, 2009). In contrast, comprehensive sexual education teaches young people the skills to make responsible decisions about sexuality and how to develop healthy relationships, including the prevention of dating violence and sexual violence. Kay and Jackson (2008) posit that not addressing issues of rape, sexual assault, or coercion while simultaneously teaching that girls have the responsibility for controlling male sexual urges provides excuses for sexual violence while promoting victim-blaming attitudes.

Pornography

In addition to noting what sexual education young college men do not receive, it is important to look at the informal "sexual education" that they do. Carroll et al. (2008) found that 86% of young men in their study reported using pornography within the past year, almost half (48.4%) reported weekly use or more, and about 20% used it daily or every other day. Another study found the average age of first viewing pornography for males was age 10 and that early viewing was related to later suppression of sexual intimacy, although this varied depending on the genre of pornography (Stulhofer, Busko, & Landripet, 2010). Bleecker and Murnen (2005) found that fraternity members had a higher number of degrading sexual images of women in their dorm rooms than non-fraternity members and that the images were correlated with greater rape myth acceptance. An early study (Li & Davey, 1996) found that fraternity members ranked pornography as their second source of sexual information (behind peers and before parents), while sorority members ranked pornography as their least important source of sexual knowledge (sixth out of six). These findings led the researchers to suggest that sex education programs should incorporate media literacy lessons to enable young people to critically assess pornography. Pornography or viewing sexually explicit materials (SEM) can also impact sexual scripts and sexual decision-making, although the specific impacts are debated.

Today's concerns about the consequences of men viewing pornography is not primarily based on morality, but other concerns:

The fear, of course, is that adolescent boys are no longer learning what it takes to evolve healthy partnerships, that they are using online porn as their model for real-world sexual relationships. And this well may be a legitimate concern since online porn typically has no storyline, no emotional connection, no build up to the sexual performance, and no concern for physical or emotional safety. There is no talking, no negotiating, no seducing, no romancing, and no tenderness. Usually kissing and foreplay are totally absent. All that's there is an endless stream of idealized body parts and sexual acts. (Weiss, 2014, para 3)

This leads to concerns by Zimbardo and Duncan (2012) that boys' brains may be rewired by pornography consumption, resulting in unrealistic demands for sexual novelty, simulation, and excitement. Additional unintended consequences of pornography consumption can include difficulty achieving erection and orgasm with an in-person partner, compulsive use of pornography, greater criticisms of their partner's body, and a decrease in self-esteem of partners (Weiss, 2014).

Development of A Question of Consent

In developing my own sexual assault prevention program that targeted men, I took the previously outlined research into account. In addition to addressing traditional notions of sexual consent, I also addressed male sexuality, sexual scripts, and sexual pleasure. The following is a program overview.

The Campus Environment

The UH was founded in 1927 and recently became a Carnegie-designated Tier 1 research university (University of Houston, 2014). UH is an urban institution located in the fourth largest city in the United States with a student population of over 40,000. UH is the second most ethnically diverse major university in the nation with racial minorities (this includes the categories of African American, Latino, Asian American, and American Indian) comprising 57% of undergraduates (Forbes, 2010).

Program Overview

A Question of Consent is an interactive sexual assault prevention program targeted to fraternity men that addresses safer sex, consensual sex, and pleasurable sex. Table 3.1 provides an outline of program content. In sum, the program includes statistics on sexual assault (prevalence and reporting rates), how to gain sexual consent, a review of the affirmative sexual consent standard, a discussion of the role alcohol plays in consent, and ends with how to make sex mutually pleasurable. The consent topics are pretty standard: sexual permission must be given, verbal consent is better than nonverbal, consent must be gained for each sexual act, silence is not consent, and an unconscious, incapacitated, or underage partner cannot provide consent. Content also included the common psychological responses to danger and trauma: fight, flight, and freeze, with women most likely to use the latter. I also taught that enthusiastic consent is preferable. The program was enhanced by the use of real-life incidents, analogies, and sexual double standards (see Table 3.2).

What makes A Question of Consent different from other sexual assault prevention programs is its focus on sexuality and having pleasurable, as well as consensual, sex. The focus on mutual sexual pleasure was a deliberate strategy to move away from viewing sex as "scoring," or a sexual conquest, to one of mutual sexual satisfaction. Most men seemed interested since they frequently expressed a desire to be good lovers, and it changed the focus from viewing all fraternity members as potential rapists to responsible sexual partners.

The primary goals of the sexuality component of the program utilized social norms theory (Lee, Guy, & Perry, 2008) to educate the attendees about pornography, discuss female sexual pleasure,[3] and suggest that there are good reasons for delaying sex utilizing social norms theory. Social norms theory recognizes that although students are greatly impacted by their peer's attitudes and behaviors, they often hold mistaken beliefs about those attitudes and behaviors, that is, often overestimating their peer's unhealthy choices while underestimating their peers' healthy choices (National Social Norms Institute, 2016). Therefore, health marketing and educational efforts often focus on correcting the misperceptions in an attempt to encourage more healthy attitudes and behaviors. First, I addressed their use of pornography by stating that although it might make good masturbatory material, pornography does not provide an accurate sexual education about female sexual desire or response. I noted that pornography is most often made for and by men. I suggested they look at feminist or lesbian porn to see more authentic female sexual response. I would say that although I could not speak for all women, most college women I had talked with did not want ejaculate on their face or to be doubly penetrated.

I used the book *Porn for Women* (Cambridge Women's Pornography Collective, 2007) to illustrate what women find arousing. The book is a tongue-in-cheek look at what excites heterosexual women, including a boyfriend who helps with chores, who asks her about her day, or just likes to snuggle. My intention here was to show that instead of focusing on being sexual acrobats as often portrayed in the male role in pornography, pleasing their partners could often be accomplished by just being a nice and thoughtful person. I would also mention some potential problems that could develop through extensive porn use, detailed earlier, such as difficulty with sexual intimacy, erections, and orgasm.

I also educated heterosexual men on the role and function of the clitoris, with its over 7,000 nerve endings, in female sexual pleasure since most women do not orgasm from vaginal stimulation alone (Rankin, 2010). I recommended the book *She Comes First* (Kerner, 2004), termed "the thinking man's guide to pleasuring women." I would end the sexuality component with the suggestion that there were good reasons to delay sexual activity for a multitude of reasons including religious or cultural beliefs, avoiding impregnation or getting a sexually transmitted infection, and learning to know their partner without the complications of sex, as well as the advantages of gaining sexual maturity and confidence with age. I also informed them of the tendency of most young men to artificially inflate the numbers of their sexual partners due to their greater belief in the prestige of sexual success (Johnson & Fisher, 2009). Therefore, if they were trying to achieve the high number of sexual partners claimed by fellow fraternity members, those most likely were not realistic goals.

TABLE 3.1 A Question of Consent Program Outline

A Introduction

1. Introducing the presenter (inclusion of two jokes in order to use humor to reduce defensiveness)
2. Explaining the benefits of program content for women, fraternity members, and fraternity organizations
3. Introducing the acceptance of diverse sexualities
4. Detailing the importance of safer sex practices
5. Providing sexual assault statistics, prevalence, and reporting

B Consent Dynamics

1. Defining of consent and the affirmative consent standard
2. Reviewing consent characteristics (better verbal, freely given, conscious, enthusiastic; silence not consent; consent can be withdrawn at any time; sometimes yes means no with an underage partner; an unconscious person cannot provide consent)
3. Using a range of consent analogies and real-life stories while eliciting their opinions of each scenario (See Table 3.2)
4. Discussing different ways of asking for consent

C Alcohol Use and Consent

1. Exploring range of alcohol intake from influence, impairment, intoxication, inebriation, and incapacitation
2. Describing gender differences in alcohol absorption
3. Listing signs of alcohol incapacitation
4. Discussing the difficulty of determining partner's level of impairment
5. Reviewing behavior that may not be criminal, but is "dickish" (lying about your feelings for someone, playing with partner's emotions, agreeing to commitments you know you will break) (adapted from Moss, 2011)

D Sexuality

1. Moving from discussing safer and consensual sex to pleasurable sex
2. Addressing pornography use
3. Addressing female pleasure

TABLE 3.2 Use of Analogies, Real-Life Incidents, and Double Standards

Concept or Situation	Training Example
Sexual double standard	The more sexual partners a man has, the more likely he is to be called a player; the more sexual partners a woman has, the more likely she is to be called a slut or ho.
Sexual double standard	The more alcohol a woman drinks, the *more* responsible she is held for her behavior; the more a man drinks, the *less* responsible he is held for his behavior.
Sexual double standard	A woman will generally say she cares so much about her male partner that she *will not* request he wear a condom, while a man will generally say that he cares so much about his female partner that he *will* wear a condom.
Sexual double standard	When asked about their number of sexual partners, both women and men tend to lie. Women artificially deflate their numbers while men artificially inflate theirs.
Showing acceptance for multiple sexual identities	I would ask an attendee if he was right or left-handed. I would then ask how he chose to be right or left-handed. Most acknowledged that they were born that way and did not make a conscious choice. I furthered that analogy to talk about sexual minorities, that fewer folks are left-handed, it can make their lives more difficult, sometimes people try to make them right-handed, but they really can't change the orientation.
When attendees complain that asking for consent is hard	I ask them what happens if their large group goes for coffee later and they need to add more chairs to their table to accommodate everyone. I ask if they see a woman reading alone at a table with four chairs would they go up and just take one of the chairs while assuming she is not waiting for others to join her? The group agrees they would ask if they could take the chair. So I say, "If you would ask for permission for such an inconsequential act as to remove a chair at a coffee shop, wouldn't you ask for permission to put your body parts in another person's orifices and vice versa?"
Consent case	I tell them of the real-life case of WikiLeaks founder Julian Assange, who after speaking at an event in Sweden went home with a woman (Davies, 2010). She agreed to have sex if he would wear a condom. He said he didn't like to wear them so she said there would be no sex. He relented, wore a condom, and they had sex. They fell asleep and she later awakes to find him inside her once again. She asks if he is wearing a condom and he is not. She charges him with rape. I ask the young men what they think of the situation. For the most part, they agree that she negotiated condom use as a condition of sex and he violated that condition, so the second act was without

Continued . . .

TABLE 3.2 Continued

Concept or Situation	Training Example
	her consent, and therefore, it was rape. We also talk about how she was also sleeping and could not give consent. Sometimes the young men want to discuss her sexual proclivities since it was casual sex, but we talk about how that information is inconsequential. I also use this case to teach that they must have consent for each sexual act, even if it is with the same person who agreed to a prior act.
Consent situations	I tell them about a case of rape that occurred in Austin, Texas, where a woman was raped at knifepoint by a stranger in the middle of the night in her apartment. She asked him to wear a condom to protect herself from pregnancy and STIs and he did. After he left she called the police who found and arrested him. However, a grand jury later refused to indict him, saying she gave consent when she asked him to wear a condom and he agreed. The national reaction was strong and negative. A second grand jury indicted him and he was found guilty at trial (NYT, 1993). I explain that when there is force or threat of force, consent is a moot point.
Rape double standard	I propose this hypothetical: I ask if they walk to their cars after the presentation and they get car-jacked, how many would immediately call the campus police? All say they would. Then I ask, would you expect the police to ask if you said "no," and ask how you said "no," and how hard you fought for the car, and why did you drive such a nice car to campus anyway? They agree those questions would not be asked. I compare that to how women who are raped often do not report the rape, and if they do, they get asked all of those questions and more.
Attendees suggest if the man is drunk then he is not responsible and the woman may be responsible if she was drinking	I use an analogy created by Harry Brod (Jhally, 2010). Brod asks a college audience whose fault it is if a student is driving a vehicle and hits a young woman who is walking across the street in a crosswalk. All agree it is the driver's fault. What if it is subsequently revealed that the woman in the crosswalk was drunk? All agree, it is still the driver's fault. What happens when the police come and the driver attempts to deny responsibility by saying he was also drunk? All agree that makes his responsibility greater, not less.
If disgust is expressed about the mechanics of gay sex	Sometimes when I ask about the climate for gay or bisexual men in the fraternity, a young man will express disgust about what he thinks gay men do sexually. I then ask them all to imagine the sex that two people most

Continued . . .

TABLE 3.2 Continued

Concept or Situation	Training Example
	likely had to produce them. They do and all are pretty disgusted at the images in their heads. So I try to normalize their distaste for what other people do sexually.
When they ask how drunk is too drunk for them and their partner to have consensual sex	I say that there is a defined alcohol level (0.08) for drunk driving in Texas, but not one that distinguishes between having buzzed consensual sex and rape. I say they might calculate their potential partner's state of intoxication by knowing her genetic propensity to black out, how much she drank, her food intake, her weight, body fat, type of drugs/alcohol, vomiting, and alcohol tolerance. Realizing the futility of making such an assessment, I advise them to avoid sex with new partners who have been drinking.
When attendees ask for examples of how to ask for consent	I usually read from a list of consent questions I was given, some that are funny, others suggestive, and others corny.[4,5] I end by saying, "These might not get you laid, but they will get you consent."
If guys say they cannot trust women to have consensual sex one night without reporting it as rape in the morning if they come to regret the sexual encounter	I say overcoming such fears means trusting their partner and if they do not know a particular partner well enough to know that they would never do such a thing, maybe they should get to know the other person better over time in order to build trust. I also say that when I am talking to young women on campus about sexual matters, I make it a point to distinguish between sex without their consent and sex they regret.
Asking for consent will sound stilted and ruin the sexual mood	In a robotic voice I say they fear consent will sound like, "Thank you for letting me touch your left breast, may I please now touch your right breast?" I say that asking for consent can be fun, sexy and playful. I add that sex can be more pleasurable if they are not thinking they could get charged with rape the next day.
Bystander behavior	Although this program is not a bystander intervention program, I do mention bystander behavior as a tool to interrupt a potential sexual assault. I make two specific points: (1) Often courage in men is depicted as being a soldier in battle or a fire fighter running into a burning building. However, I try to expand the notion of courage to include attempting to stop a potential sexual assault. (2) I say that their fear of the consequences of intervening, that is, making a fraternity brother angry at him, must also be balanced with the cost for *not* intervening, which they often do not calculate. I refer to several anecdotal stories I have heard over the years of men who did not step in and then felt badly afterwards, especially if they later saw the young woman struggling emotionally and academically.

Continued . . .

TABLE 3.2 Continued

Concept or Situation	Training Example
Objections to suggestions to limit alcohol use before sex because it acts a social lubricant and confidence builder	I would note that extended foreplay is also a social lubricant and confidence booster.
Don't really want to talk about sex, would rather "just do it"	I acknowledge that it is more intimate to actually talk about sex than to "just do it." But I remind them that it is in the talking that condom use and consent is negotiated. I mention that in BDSM relationships there is often a written contract of do's and don'ts. I say that could be a model for all sexual relationships. I add if they are too uncomfortable talking about sex, maybe they are not yet ready for a sexual relationship.

Program Characteristics

Target Audience

Since the research indicates that members of fraternities and sports teams may have a higher propensity to rape, I focused my efforts on these two high-risk groups. In a review of the literature, Vladutiu, Martin, and Macy (2011) found in general that sexual assault prevention programs that were most effective targeted single-gender audiences, so I decided to present to all-male attendees (although sometimes they invited female guests and that was fine with me). Although I attempted to reach out to the athletics department at my university multiple times using both personal connections and cold-calling, I could never get in the door to present A Question of Consent to male athletes. Everyone was very polite by phone or email, but there was never any follow-through on their part. The "stiff- or straight-arm" technique used in football, that is, when a ball carrier wards off a would-be tackler by pushing them away with a straight arm, was successfully employed off the field by the athletic staff. This stiff-arm technique is accentuated by the fact that athletes are often physically segregated from other students, residing in their own dorms, and athletic administrators often operate more independently than in other university departments. Crosset (2016) notes that resistance by athletic programs can be due to staff feeling that male athletes are being unfairly stigmatized.

I was more successful with the Greek community as the Student Affairs staff that oversaw the Center for Fraternity and Sorority Life on campus allowed me to pitch my program to the Interfraternity Council (IFC) during their weekly meeting. There were 24 fraternities on campus and the majority did not have a fraternity house. Eleven of those fraternities were designated traditionally African American, Latin, Asian, or South Asian. I presented to approximately 10 different fraternities, several of them repeatedly reaching over 500 young men, with 2 of the fraternities being ethnically or racially specific.

Learning Objectives

The overall goal of the presentation was to educate fraternity men on how to make sex safer, consensual, and pleasurable in order to create more ethical sexual citizens. Thus, the focus was on their sexual desires and sexual decision-making, with some skill-building components in how to ask for consent. Specific learning objectives included: (1) distinguish between situations of consent and nonconsent; (2) identify ways to ask for consent; (3) explain the relationship between consent and alcohol use; (4) explain some unintended effects of viewing pornography; and (5) recognize ways to make sex more pleasurable for their partners and themselves.

Values

The values embedded within the program reveal a feminist framework with respect for all genders as sexual beings (although increasingly some students are identifying as asexual); belief in the importance of equalitarian (sexual) relationships; mutual sexual respect; valuing consent with enthusiastic consent a goal; respecting the sexual boundaries of all; acknowledgment and acceptance of a range of sexual identities; valuing the right of all people to say "yes" and "no" to sexual activity; and valuing consensual, safer, and pleasurable sex.

Risk Factors Targeted

Risk factors have been empirically and theoretically derived that are associated with a greater likelihood to perpetrate sexual violence (Tharp et al., 2013). The risk factors targeted through this intervention were those at the individual level: gender, alcohol and drug use, and exposure to sexually explicit media and societal factors including social norms that support sexual violence, male superiority, and sexual entitlement while maintaining women's inferiority and sexual submissiveness. Relationship risk factors included association with sexually aggressive, hypermasculine, and delinquent peers, although clearly those are not characteristics of all fraternities.

Location

Often sexual assault prevention programs are conducted in large auditoriums with hundreds of people, for instance, during orientation. However, I would go to the men's fraternity house or alternately a classroom with just their fraternity members, and occasionally some of their guests. The setting was more intimate and they seemed to feel more comfortable being on their home turf. I usually went during their regularly scheduled weekly meeting time, which was helpful as the fraternity mandated their attendance.

In Their Best Interest

Often men are engaged in sexual assault prevention programs as allies and friends or as rescuers of women. While both of those motivations can be helpful (although the notion of riding in on a white horse to "rescue" women is problematic), it can also be helpful to identify male self-interest. Although I introduced myself as the director of the campus Women's Resource Center and an advocate for women, I also said I was there to assist them. Sometimes I would mention that I was the mother of grown sons to establish my bona fides; however, what I most often said was, "I am here so you graduate with your name on a diploma and not a sexual offender registry." I also reminded them that their poor choices could not only land them in trouble as individuals, but could also result in their fraternity's suspension or expulsion from the university.

Even though my goal was rape prevention, I also addressed the fears of the men in the room. They were not concerned about being raped, but rather being falsely accused of rape. This topic usually organically surfaced and I would address it with two points. First, I would let them know that peer-reviewed research (important at our newly designated Research I university) found that only between 2% and 10% of rape allegations were found to be false (Lisak, Gardinier, Nicksa, & Cote, 2010). I also reminded them that the vast majority of women on college campuses do not report rape to the police, therefore, refuting the myth that women vindictively "cry rape" for other motivations. For instance, Sinozich and Langton (2014) found that only 20% of college students reported their rapes to police, while women in the same age group who were not students reported their rapes to police in higher numbers (33%).

However, I also found it important to acknowledge their fears. I reassured them that when I spoke to young women I was always clear that rape is an unwanted sexual experience, not a regretted one. I would also say that if men had these fears, one remedy would be to get to know their sexual partner better and establish a sense of trust before engaging in sexual activity.

UH adopted the affirmative consent standard in its newly revised sexual misconduct policy in 2012 (University of Houston, 2012). Frequently called the "yes means yes" standard, the policy shifts responsibility for establishing consent from the sexual assault victim to the sexual initiator. That is, instead of asking the victim, "Did you resist, say no, or fight?" the alleged perpetrator is asked, "How did you ask for consent and how did you know you had it?" Although it is said that "ignorance of the law is no excuse," I felt that it was important to inform and educate young men on the new standard to which they would be held accountable.

Materials

A frequent trope of painful presentations is the notion of "death by PowerPoint." PowerPoints can also disengage and disconnect the attendees from the speaker and seem too much like their academic classes. Relying on technology to work in a fraternity house can also be problematic. Instead, I created PowerPoint slides and had them blown up to poster board size (24" by 36") and adhered them to foam board.[6] So my only materials were an easel and the poster boards. I used them as an outline for my talk.

Time

After I had created A Question of Consent, I looked for a fraternity to pilot it. I had worked with a fraternity president on a committee for Greek affairs and on the basis of that relationship he agreed to have me present the program to his fraternity. His one stipulation was that I only speak for 15 minutes. I was flabbergasted at how he could think that such a sensitive and important topic could be covered in 15 minutes. In an attempt to meet his request, I did my first presentation in a fast-paced and somewhat jumbled 30-minute time frame. I learned that even 30 minutes was not enough time and in the future I said my presentation would take an hour and tried to keep it closer to 45 minutes.

The fraternity president's request for a 15-minute sexual assault prevention program was not a slight to the topic or me, but rather due to real time constraints faced by the fraternity. In giving this talk repeatedly to fraternities and getting to know many young men, I came to admire many of these young men who lead quite busy lives. They had mandated events from their national organizations, their local chapters, and often the Student Affairs department. They participated in service projects, study halls, fundraisers, homecoming, carnivals, and talent shows. Fraternity officers had even greater responsibilities than general members. I always respected their limited time and kept my presentations to no more than an hour. One way I shortened my program is that many of the young men were turned off by my first attempts at explaining trigger warnings and confidentiality. They grew restless and I learned to drop those preliminaries and get right to program content.

Use of Humor

Two words not associated very often are "rape" and "humor." Although rape is absolutely no laughing matter, it is helpful to engage men with the use of humor. Often when they attend sexual assault prevention programs, men are expecting a grim, finger-pointing lecturer, which can result in a defensive stance. However, to break through that defensiveness, humor is a helpful tool.

Our culture today is one of "edutainment" and even college professors try to make their lectures more entertaining to engage their multi-tasking, attention-deficient students. For example, I would usually say, "I know you are wondering what this older gray-haired woman can tell you about sex, but if my generation didn't know something about sex, your generation wouldn't be here" (a line I borrowed from a late night comedian). I would also say that I was the perfect person to give the talk because I was "a cougar." Immediately that would get a laugh, as "cougar" is a slang term for a woman who seeks sexual relations with much younger men. So while they were relating that term to me, I would hold up our school's hand sign and say, "Go Coogs!" since our school mascot is a cougar. They would laugh at the discrepancy from what they first thought I meant by identifying as a cougar and the reality of what I meant in terms of school spirit.

Addressing Male Culture

Social norms are rules and standards that guide one's behavior, while gender norms are the rules and norms that guide and constrain masculine and feminine behavior (Mahalik et al., 2003). Mahlik and his fellow researchers developed a scale, the Conformity to Masculine Norms Inventory (CMNI), in order to identify the predominate masculine norms of the United States. They found 11 distinct factors, including winning, emotional control, power over women, risk-taking, violence, primacy of work, dominance, playboy, self-reliance, disdain for homosexuals, and pursuit of status. They write:

> In a way that is similar to how social norms influence people to engage in specific social behavior, gender role norms also operate when people observe what most men or women do in social situations, are told what is acceptable or unacceptable behavior for men or women, or observe how popular men and women act. As a result, males and females come to learn what is expected of them when living their gendered lives. (p. 3)

Prevention programs that focus on social norms rely on the fact that peer pressure is a primary influence on shaping college students' behavior and some campus behaviors are influenced by incorrect perceptions of how their peers think and behave (Lee et al., 2008). For example, some prevention programs inform college students that their fellow students are not drinking alcohol as much as they might assume, in an attempt to get them to drink less. Therefore, prevention efforts seek to teach college students what the current social norms are and how to *conform* to social norms when they lead to healthier behaviors.

In contrast, sexual assault prevention programs attempt to teach young men to distance themselves from gender norms that they have often been taught to strive toward. The latter is a more difficult task. Many young men have been sexually unsuccessful in high school and are determined to fulfill the male gender role norms of being a playboy, being dominant or violent, and having power over women.

Another part of addressing male/fraternity culture is acknowledging the existence of the social norms "cock-blocking" and the "bro code." Cock-blocking is a male prohibition between interfering with another man's sexual conquests, and the bro code acknowledges the importance of homo-social relationships over heterosexual ones, summed in the phrase "bros before hos." During the presentation, these phrases were acknowledged and addressed.

Use of Analogies, Real-life Incidents, and Sexual Double Standards

To better engage the men, I used real-life incidents for them to consider whether the sexual activity was consensual or nonconsensual. I also used analogies to help them better understand obtaining consent. I also related sexual double standards, which elucidated the unfairness inherent in some gendered expectations and judgments. Although some men have difficulty understanding a broader feminist agenda, they understood the concept of unfairness. (A list of the most common ones used during the presentation is located in Table 2.)

Use of Incentives

Incentives are difficult on a small budget, but I was able to offer three incentives that were generally appreciated. Sometimes their national fraternal organizations required sexual assault prevention training and frequently those involved bringing in a paid speaker. I could fulfill that requirement at no cost and with great convenience, as I came to their residence at their regular meeting time. Second, I would provide money for pizza at the end of the presentation. (I quickly learned that ordering pizza when I first arrived was an attention killer when the pizza was delivered mid-presentation). Last, each attendee who filled out an evaluation got a stadium cup in our school colors of red and white, imprinted with "Got Consent?" and the website, phone number, and physical address of the Women's Resource Center. These cups became a desired item with other fraternities calling to obtain the cups and then learning what it took to earn them.

Presenter

Although peer sexual assault prevention programs have their place, DeGue et al. (2014) reviewed the literature for successful prevention programs and found that effective programs have presenters who are "stable, committed, competent, and can connect effectively with participants" (p. 357). During one semester, I was able to team present with a psychology intern who was also a former fraternity member. We were well-received on several fronts: (1) having a presenter with a Greek background seemed to open doors and lower resistance, (2) having a male and female on the team seemed helpful and comfortable, and (3) having an older and younger presenter also provided a good balance.

Program Evaluation

The UH and the Department of Student Affairs and Enrollment Services (DSAES) are very data-driven, and assessments were a routine part of all programming. Over my 8 years at UH, program assessments grew more sophisticated with a shift from only recording the number of program attendees to gauging student satisfaction to attempting to measure student learning and skill building. My evaluations changed over time in response. I handed out paper and pen surveys after each evaluation, which asked how they liked the program and what they learned using Likert scales. Later renditions of the evaluation included this fill-in-the-blank question: "As a result of this training I am more likely to _____" and then rate that answer on a scale of 1–10 ranging from not likely to very likely.

Students were surprisingly willing to fill out the forms and response rates were high, although not measured (Remember, to get the stadium cup they had to fill out the evaluation). One time I attempted to use a survey monkey tool to collect evaluation data at a later time by giving the fraternity president the link to share with fraternity members. I did not receive a single response.

After one presentation, the program evaluation found the modal response to the statement, "I found the sexual consent presentation to be helpful," to be 4 (agree) with a mean of 3.81. However, when it came to the self-report of predicted behavior change, the modal response was 3 (neutral) with a mean of 2.45. These findings clearly point to the difficulty of transforming participant satisfaction and attitude change to subsequent behavior change. One outlier worth mentioning was an attendee who circled all his answers to the questions asking whether the program was helpful, interesting, or would lead to personal behavior change with "strongly disagree." Clearly, a more robust evaluation is called for to evaluate the effectiveness of this program.

Surprisingly to me, my program was most often enthusiastically received by fraternity members. I usually received a big round of applause at the end of the presentation. I found that they had often not been exposed to such concepts and they were hungry for information and frank talk about sexuality. Being addressed as sexual beings instead of potential rapists also engaged the men.

Marketing and Mandating the Program

I marketed the program at the beginning of each semester to fraternities by attending their weekly IFC meeting. I would bring the "Got Consent" cups and a handout describing the program and providing contact information. I would attempt to be engaging and a little funny to increase interest and reduce defensiveness. I would then wait for the fraternities to contact me. Response was uneven at best. Some fraternities invited me each year, while other fraternities never contacted me. Additional recruitment measures included word of mouth, working through sorority women I knew who were connected with fraternities, and also a tactic I call "reverse tabling," that is, when fraternities were at events tabling on their own behalf, I would approach them about my program.

During talks I would conduct with sorority women, I would encourage their members to commit to not partying with a fraternity unless the fraternity had attended my sexual assault prevention training. Upon hearing this suggestion, sorority members would often snap their fingers (a sign of assent and approval), but as far as I know none of them used this power that they possessed to urge their brother fraternity to receive training.

To present to a greater number of fraternities, I met with an assistant vice president of Student Affairs and the director of the Center for Fraternity and Sorority Life to request that the program be made mandatory for all fraternities. My request was met with some resistance and was never granted. The resistance seemed to be the result of multiple reasons, largely unspoken.[7] First, the Wellness Center on campus had previously taken responsibility for sexual assault prevention programming and although the Center was not currently conducting any programming on this topic, it was viewed as their "turf." Also, the Women's Resource Center was viewed by the larger Student Affairs division as having a feminist ideology, which was one of our stated values. However, the Student Affairs' interpretation of our feminist stance was erroneous, falling into the common misperception that feminism means being anti-male. In contrast, the Wellness Center was viewed as ideologically neutral. Additionally, the Student Affairs department had multiple mandatory meetings and trainings for the Greek system and they seemed reluctant to further burden fraternities with another mandatory program. It should be noted that my request for mandatory training was made prior to the federal government's mandates on sexual assault training. After my departure from the position and due to the new federal guidelines, UH, like college campuses across the country, ramped up its sexual assault prevention programming.

Program Limitations

Due to work primarily within the prevention science and public health fields, empirical evidence now exists about what works and what does not work in prevention programs in general and sexual assault prevention programs in particular. Nation et al. (2003) identified nine "principles of prevention" found in effective programs: (1) comprehensive, (2) appropriately timed, (3) utilized various teaching methods, (4) sufficient dosage, (5) administered by a well-trained staff, (6) provide opportunities for positive relationships, (7) socioculturally relevant, (8) theory driven, and (9) include outcome evaluation. Table 3.3 examines how A Question of Consent measures up against these criteria, which reveals some of the strengths and limitations of the program.

TABLE 3.3 Principles of Prevention Applied from A Question of Consent

Principles of Prevention	A Question of Consent
Comprehensive	The program is one-dimensional, focusing on consent with single targeted population, but could be one vital part in a more comprehensive sexual assault prevention program taking place campus-wide.
Appropriately timed	Since college-aged men and women are at higher risk for sexual assault victimization and perpetration, the program is appropriately timed, although an argument can be made that targeting even younger audiences would be more beneficial since violence perpetration often happens before college and shortly after arrival (DeGue et al., 2014).
Varied teaching. methods	Utilizes a single teaching method, a small group lecture with some interaction.
Sufficient dose	Program was presented a single time to fraternities, although a couple of fraternities asked for the program each year; as a stand-alone, it does not provide a sufficient dose.
Fosters positive relationships	The program does foster positive relationships as the fraternity is doing something as a group and engaging with each other and further developing peer support and networks; the audience also developed a relationship with the presenter, as some would come to me on other issues in my office at a later date.
Sociocultural relevance	The program was socioculturally relevant as it was targeted to the cultural beliefs and social norms of male and fraternal cultures, but did not include any specific content for racial/ethnic groups.
Well-trained staff	The presenter developed the program and was a long-time educator in the antiviolence against women movement.
Theory-driven	The program is based upon the theory that rape is motivated by a desire for sex as well as power and control (McPhail, 2016). It also borrows from social norms theory and sexual script theory.
Includes outcome evaluation	A rudimentary evaluation was given after each presentation to assess self-reported satisfaction, learning, and anticipated behavior change. However, the effects were not measured over time and also could not assess behavior change or a decrease in number of sexual assaults.

One limitation of the program and its evaluation is that all of the fraternities that attended a presentation invited the speaker to present. This self-selection process could have resulted in only low-risk fraternities attending the program and filling out the evaluations, thus artificially inflating the positive response to the program. However, in one instance I was invited because the fraternity was on probation and required a sexual assault prevention program as a stipulation for getting off probation status. However, even this mandated audience was open to learning and received the material well. Another limitation was my ignorance about Greek cultures and organizations. I did not know the differences between the various fraternities and could not identify high- and low-risk fraternities. I should have done more homework.

Another limitation of the program is that it is labor and time intensive to present to small groups of men during evenings and requires a skilled presenter with a lot of experience and knowledge about the topic as well as a comfort speaking to men about sexuality. Also, in a perfect world, the program would be longer and involve more interaction between presenter and audience. An additional limitation is that teaching men new sexual scripts while challenging their old ones is difficult, as they have viewed pornography for years and lived in a culture of male sexual entitlement their whole lives, leaving their sexual scripts pretty set and most often out of their conscious awareness. Such education needs to be conducted in age-appropriate ways from elementary school through middle and high school with refresher, rather than introductory, courses in college.

Additionally, the program does not directly address male sexual entitlement that McPhail (2016) notes is a key motivation for rape. The last, and major, limitation is that the program purports to expand the sexual scripts of men while also preventing sexual miscommunication. However, Kitzinger and Frith (1999) dismiss the notion that sexual assault occurs due to miscommunication and instead posit that "male claims to not have 'understood' refusals which conform to culturally normative patterns can only be heard as self-interested justification for coercive behavior" (p. 295).

Conclusion

The continued prevalence of rape on college campuses and the renewed attention to the issue by the federal government, student activists, and the media provide a unique opportunity to reexamine sexual assault prevention programs. An expanded focus on sexuality could be a helpful path to both captivating male attention and understanding. The prevalence rate of campus sexual assault demands continued attention, innovation, and hard questions. Brownmiller (1975) ends her foundational book with the words, "my purpose in this book has been to give rape a history. Now we must deny it a future" (p. 404). I share that goal and hope that my targeted prevention program can serve as a model and inspiration for others doing the important work of sexual assault prevention and education.

Notes

1   There are multiple ways of defining feminism with multiple schools of feminist thought, which results in "feminisms." My definition as used in this article is valuing women while seeking to end sexism, racism, classism, homophobia, and other oppressions.
2   I could not find any information on program evaluations that had been conducted on the Rape Aggression Defense (RAD) class. I contacted the email listed on the website, www.rad-system.com and received no response.
3   Although I acknowledge a range of sexualities and that rape occurs within LGBT relationships, since the majority of fraternity men were heterosexual, I focused on heterosexual relationship dynamics. A course tailored to the LGBT population would be helpful, especially since the AAU survey found such high rates of victimization among this population.
4   An unattributed handout of a list of sample questions to use when asking for sexual consent, which is available by request from the author at bevmcphail@icloud.com.
5   If I would have had additional time, I might have used the following sexual consent exercise that I only saw presented later at the Delaware Coalition Against Domestic Violence conference by Angela Seguin and Joanne Sampson (2014) called "Wanna Smush?" (inspired by the words Snookie of the reality television show *Jersey Shore* used to ask for sex). Exercise description available by request from this author at bevmcphail@icloud.com.
6   PowerPoint slides and notes are available from the author upon request by contacting bevmcphail@icloud.com.
7   To ascertain the reasons my program was not made mandatory for all fraternities, I contacted the two men I had met with. Neither returned my email.

References

Ali, R. (2011). *Dear colleague letter: Sexual violence.* Retrieved from www2.ed.gov/about/offices/list/ocr/letters/colleague-201304.pdf.

Association of American Universities. (2015). *Report on the AAU campus climate survey on sexual assault and sexual misconduct.* Rockville, MD: Westat.

Boonstra, H.D. (2009). Advocates call for a new approach after the era of "abstinence-only" sex education. *Guttmacher Policy Review, 12*(1), 6–11.

Brownmiller, S. (1975). *Against our will: Men, woman, and rape.* New York: Simon and Schuster.

Cambridge Women's Pornography Collective. (2007). *Porn for women.* San Francisco, CA: Chronicle Books.

Carr, J.L. (2008). *Preventing sexual violence through empowering campus bystanders. Shifting the paradigm: Primary prevention of sexual violence. An ACHA Toolkit.* Linthicum, MD: American College Health Association.

Carroll, J.S., Padilla-Walker, L.M., Nelson, L.J., Olson, C.D., Barry, C.M., & Madsen, S.D. (2008). Generation XXX: Pornography acceptance and use among emerging adults. *Journal of Adolescent Research, 23*(1), 6–30.

Centers for Disease Control and Prevention. (2004). *Sexual violence prevention: Beginning the dialogue.* Atlanta, GA: Centers for Disease Control and Prevention.

Connell, N., & Wilson, C. (1974). *Rape: The first sourcebook for women.* New York: New American Library.

Crosset, T.W. (2016). Athletes, sexual assault, and universities' failure to address rape-prone subcultures on campus. In S.C. Wooten & R.W. Mitchell (Eds.), *The crisis of campus sexual violence: Critical perspectives on prevention and response* (74–91). New York: Routledge.

Davis, A.Y. (1981). *Women, race & class*. New York: Vintage Books.

Davies, N. (2010). 10 days in Sweden: The full allegations against Julian Assange. *The Guardian*. Retrieved from www.theguardian.com/media/2010/dec/17/julian-assange-sweden.

DeGue, S., Valle, L.A., Holt, M.K., Massetti, G.M., Matjasko, J.L., & Tharp, A.T. (2014). A systematic review of primary prevention strategies for sexual violence perpetration. *Aggression and Violent Behavior, 19*, 346–362.

Donat, P.L.N., & D'Emilio, J. (1992). A feminist redefinition of rape and sexual assault: Historical foundations and change. *Journal of Social Issues, 48*(1), 9–22.

Forbes Magazine (2010). *Full list: The most diverse colleges*. Retrieved from www.forbes.com/2010/12/10/most-diverse-best-colleges-lifestyle-education-minorities_slide.html.

Frith, H., & Kitzinger, C. (2001). Reformulating sexual script theory: Developing a discursive psychology of sexual negotiation. *Theory & Psychology, 11*(2), 209–232.

Gagnon, J.H., & Simon, W. (1973). *Sexual conduct*. Chicago, IL: Aldine.

Guttmacher Institute. (2012). *Facts on American teens' sources of information about sex*. Retrieved from www.guttmacher.org/sites/default/files/pdfs/pubs/FB-Teen-Sex-Ed.pdf.

Henriksen, C.B., Mattick, K.L., & Fisher, B.S. (2016). Mandatory bystander intervention training. In S.C. Wooten & R.W. Mitchell (Eds.), *The crisis of campus sexual violence: Critical perspectives on prevention and response* (169–183). New York: Routledge.

Humphrey, S.E. (2000). Fraternities, athletic teams, and rape. *Journal of Interpersonal Violence, 15*(12), 1313–1322.

Jhally, S. (Director), Morris, S., & Young, J. (Producers). (2010). *Asking for it: The ethics and erotics of sexual consent, a lecture with Dr. Harry Brod* (DVD). United States: A Media Education Foundation Film.

Johnson, P.K., & Fisher, T.D. (2009). The power of prestige: Why young men report having more sex partners than young women. *Sex Roles, 60*, 151–159.

Kay, J.F., & Jackson, A. (2008). *Sex, lies, and stereotypes: How abstinence-only education harms women and girls*. New York: Legal Momentum.

Kerner, I. (2004). *She comes first: The thinking man's guide to pleasuring a woman*. New York: HarperCollins.

Kitzinger, C., & Frith, H. (1999). Just say no? The use of conversation analysis in developing a feminist perspective on sexual refusal. *Discourse & Society, 10*(3), 293–316.

Lee, D.S., Guy, L., & Perry, B. (2008). *Sexual violence prevention. Shifting the paradigm: Primary prevention of sexual violence. An ACHA Toolkit*. Linthicum, MD: American College Health Association.

Li, Q., & Davey, M.R. (1996). Pornography as a source of sex information for college students in fraternities and sororities. *Journal of Health Education, 27*(3), 165–169.

Lisak, D., Gardinier L., Nicksa, S.C., & Cote, A.M. (2010). False allegations of sexual assault: An analysis of ten years of reported cases. *Violence Against Women, 16*(12), 1318–1334.

McPhail, B.A. (2016). Feminist framework plus: Knitting feminist theories of rape etiology into a comprehensive model. *Trauma, Violence, & Abuse, 17*(3), 314–329.

Mahalik, J.R., Locke, B.D., Ludlow, L.H., Scott, R.P.J., Gottfried, M., & Freitas, G. (2003). Development of the conformity to masculine norms inventory. *Psychology of Men and Masculinity, 4*(1), 3–25.

Moss, E.H. (2011, September 26). *You can get laid without being a jerk*. The Good Men Project. Retrieved from http://goodmenproject.com/featured-content/you-can-get-laid-without-being-a-jerk.

Murnen, S.K., & Kohlman, M.H. (2007). Athletic participation, fraternity membership, and sexual assault aggression among college men: A meta-analytic review. *Sex Roles, 57*, 145–157.

Nation, M., Crusto, C., Wandersman, A., Kumpefer, K.L., Seybolt, D., Morrissey-Kane, E., & Davino, K. (2003). What works in prevention: Principles of effective prevention programs. *American Psychologist, 58*, 449.

National Social Norms Institute. (2016). *Social norms approach: overview.* Retrieved from http://socialnorms.org.

New York Times (1993, May 14). *Man is convicted of rape in case involving condom.* Retrieved from www.nytimes.com/1993/05/14/us/man-is-convicted-of-rape-in-case-involving-condom.html.

Orchowski, L.M., Gidycz, C.A., & Raffle, H. (2008). Evaluation of a sexual assault risk reduction and self-defense program: A prospective analysis of a revised protocol. *Psychology of Women Quarterly, 32*, 204–218.

Rankin, L. (2010). *What's up down there?: Questions you'd only ask your gynecologist if she was your best friend.* New York: St. Martin's Press.

Rape, Abuse & Incest National Network. (2016). *Staying safe on campus.* Retrieved from https://rainn.org/get-information/sexual-assault-prevention/campus-safety-sexual-assault.

Seguin, A.D., & Sampson, J. (2014). *Wanna smush: How do you ask for consent.* Paper presented at the Powerful partnerships: 20 years of the Violence Against Women Act and the path ahead meeting of the Delaware Coalition Against Domestic Violence, Newark, DE.

Sinozich, S., & Langton, L. (2014). *Rape and sexual assault victimization among college-age females, 1995–2013.* Washington, DC: U.S. Department of Justice, Office of Justice Programs, Bureau of Justice Statistics. NCJ 248471.

Stulhofer, A., Busko, V., & Landripet, I. (2010). Pornography, sexual socialization, and satisfaction among young men. *Archives of Sexual Behavior, 39*, 168–178.

Tharp, A.T., DeGue, S., Valle, L.A., Brookmeyer, K.A., Massetti, G.M., & Matjasko, J.L. (2013). A systematic qualitative review of risk and protective factors for sexual violence perpetration. *Trauma, Violence, & Abuse, 14*(2), 133–167.

United Educators. (2015). *Confronting campus sexual assault: An examination of higher education claims.* Bethesda, MD: United Educators Insurance.

University of Houston (2012). *Sexual misconduct policy.* Number 01.D.08. (Revised August 25, 2015). Retrieved on November 9, 2015 www.uh.edu/af/universityservices/policies/sam/1GenAdmin/1D8.pdf.

Vivolo, A.M., Holland, K.M., Teten, A.L., Holt, M.K., & Sexual Violence Review Team. (2010). Developing sexual violence prevention strategies by bridging spheres of public health. *Journal of Women's Health, 19*(10), 1811–1814.

Vladutiu, C.J., Martin, S.L., & Macy, R.J. (2011). College- or university-based sexual assault prevention programs: A review of program outcomes, characteristics, and recommendations. *Trauma, Violence, & Abuse, 12*(2), 67–86.

Weiss, R. (2014, January 20). *Is male porn use ruining sex? Psychology Today.* Retrieved from https://psychologytoday.com/blog/love-and-sex-in-the-digital-age/201401/is-male-porn-use-ruining-sex.

Zimbardo, P., & Duncan, N.D. (2012). *The demise of guys: Why boys are struggling and what we can do about it.* (Kindle version). Retrieved from www.amazon.com/Demise-Guys-Boys-Struggling-About-ebook/dp/B00850HTHO.

PART II

Challenging Assumptions About Race, Gender, and Sexuality

4

EXAMINING BYSTANDER INTERVENTION IN THE WAKE OF #BLACKLIVESMATTER AND #TRANSLIVESMATTER

Adriane Bang, Annie Kerrick, and Christian K. Wuthrich

> Oppression is the root cause of violence, and we must work from an anti-oppression and social justice framework to prevent it.

> —The Oregon Sexual Assault Task Force, 2015

High profile studies have operationalized campus sexual assault as a hetero-normative, nonconsensual sexual act and revealed the pervasiveness of alcohol-facilitated assaults perpetrated against young women by young men they know (Krebs, Lindquist, Warner, Fisher, & Martin, 2009; Lisak & Miller, 2002). These contributions have increased practitioners' understandings about the prevalence of campus sexual assault, provided insight into the predatory behaviors of assailants, and informed the development of some of the most well-known collegiate bystander programs. While informative, these studies are not, as we might expect, exhaustive; a diversity of identities and experiences are left out of ongoing discussions on the prevalence and reduction of campus sexual assault. To date, intervention programs have yielded promising data and could be bolstered with the integration of research focused on the experiences of college student victims and bystanders of diverse sexual orientations, racial backgrounds, and/or gender identities.

The 2011 Dear Colleague Letter energized advocates, students, lawmakers, and practitioners to seek solutions to reduce sexual violence on the college campus. In best applying guidance provided in the letter, professionals may turn to the fields of social work and health promotion, which have been instructive in examining how to engage positive change, for example, through the theory of risk and protective factors and data on promising prevention practices. Today, colleges and universities rely on a number of federal, state, and local laws that, when combined with best and promising practices in these fields, seek to improve the health and physical safety of students.

In addition to published theoretical approaches, promising practices, and the guidance of current laws, it is of equitable importance to consider grassroots response to current social issues. Ripe, at this time, is the issue of state violence against people who are Black and Trans★,[1] most notably through activism related to #BlackLivesMatter and #TransLivesMatter. These two movements—which come from decades of activism—demand consciousness of institutionalized White supremacy and transphobia as well as a strategy to end state-facilitated violence (Black Lives Matter, n.d.; Office of Justice Programs, Office for Victims of Crime, 2014; Rök Jóns, 2015). Core to these movements is the concept that equity, justice, and safety cannot be realized until we focus on the most marginalized amongst us. Third wave feminism aligns well with these movements, as the philosophy calls for an examination of oppression through an intersectional lens—addressing the complexity of social issues by examining the matrix of social identities, systems, and issues, rather than focusing on how one (typically privileged) identity experiences a social issue (Haslanger, Tuana, & O'Connor, 2012).

This chapter uses a conceptual framework that considers the interdepence of intersectional feminism and ecology of a student's life, known in the prevention field as the social-ecological model. The social-ecological model considers the relationships within and between a variety of interpersonal, environmental, and community factors that must be addressed simultanously to prevent and eliminate violence (Centers for Disease Control and Prevention, 2015). Violence prevention using the social ecological model considers a multitude of personal, environmental, and community factors such as how substance abuse escalates violence, the availablity of safe spaces for students to congregate for social activities, community responses to difference, and as identified in this chapter inclusive educational strategies developed for specific communities.

This chapter begins with a review of relevant literature on violent crime and substance abuse before summarizing legal and policy considerations that have provided the impetus for prevention programming. This chapter concludes with a proposed intervention model designed to elevate protective factors and reduce risks by being more inclusive through partnering with campus diversity offices, gender equity centers, and community groups to further evolve prevention programs.

Campus Violence and Implications

Studies have long documented the social factors that put community members at risk for adverse experiences, such as sexual violence. Those doing antiviolence work confront the fact that college students with marginalized identities are not well represented in the literature; however, these students are often at the highest risk for victimization. Specifically, the Centers for Disease Control and Prevention's (CDC) National Intimate Partner and Sexual Violence Survey found that those with marginalized identities have the highest risk of sexual violence, noting that among all identities, the 12-month prevalence of intimate partner rape, physical violence, or stalking is highest for women who: are multiracial non-Hispanic (53.8%), are bisexual (61.1%), and earn less than $25,000 in annual income (9.7%) (Black et al., 2011; Walters, Chen, & Breiding, 2013). Lesbian, Gay, Bisexual, and Transgender (LGBT) focused organizations, such as The National Gay and Lesbian Task Force, have found rates of sexual violence for Transgender (Trans★) identified individuals are as high as 50% (Grant, Mottet, Tanis, Harrison, Herman, & Keisling, 2011). The National Coalition of Anti-Violence Programs (NCAVP, 2012, 2010) attributes the high rates of violence experienced by these populations to oppressive actions on an individual level, as well as institutional; for example, people being targeted for sexual violence because they have marginalized identities, and further being unable to access providers and systems that are informed, respectful, and safe.

Additional factors predicting Trans★ and marginalized student populations' experiences can be identified among the various meta communities that comprise campus social circles, networks, and cultural attributes of the college campus. Holistically considering the environment in which a student participates, specifically those associated with their educational experience can be used to reduce risk and enhance protective factors (Stone, Becker, Huber, & Catalono, 2012). Because alcohol consumption is such a huge issue on many college campuses, the following illustrates the significance of the strategies offered in this chapter. Research on alcohol consumption concludes excessive use contributes to violence and victimization among the cisgender population (Wechsler, Lee, Nelson, & Kuo, 2002; Hingson, Heeren, Winter, & Wechsler, 2005). It is also clear that psychological and environmental stressors drive some maladaptive behavior such as using alcohol and drugs as a coping mechanism. In one recent study examining heavy episodic alcohol use patterns, Trans★ identified young adults "were significantly more likely to have been in physical fights, physically assaulted, verbally threatened, and sexually assaulted than their nontransgendered-identified (sic) counterparts" (Coulter et al., 2015, p. 253). As illustrated later in this chapter, risk and protective factors include but are not limited to race, gender, socio-economic status, family history of substance abuse and parental mental health, college attendance, and peer groups. In other words, students with fewer challenges and greater support such as participating in communities that value and support them though purposeful and safer activities have more protective and fewer risk factors, which reduce the odds for interpersonal violence. To increase bystander program efficacy, we must acknowledge the intersectionality of oppression as well as the fact that not all student victims/survivors are White, young, female-identified, or heterosexual.

Research and prevention programming over the last several decades have increased practitioner knowledge of promising practices. Despite an enhanced focus on education, learning and behavioral outcomes have lagged. In an effort to improve outcomes and transform campuses, Congress and the U.S. Department of Education have acted independently to challenge campuses to focus on student safety and eliminate discriminatory policies and practices. The court system has provided some clarity of intersecting laws, but the matters of safety continue to evolve. The next section provides an overview of these efforts.

The Problem of Current Bystander Models: Excluded Groups

Since the 1990s, researchers have promoted bystander intervention programs as a potential method of preventing sexual assault and other forms of violence on college campuses (Coker et al., 2011). In recent years, calls to employ bystander intervention programs to reduce sexual violence on college campuses have come from the White House and two of the major public funders of sexual violence response and prevention programming: the CDC and the U.S. Department of Justice Office on Violence Against Women (Centers for Disease Control and Prevention, 2014; United States Department of Justice, Office on Violence Against Women, 2015; White House Task Force to Protect Students from Sexual Assault, 2014). Each of these sources touts bystander intervention programming, specifically "Bringing in the Bystander" and "Green Dot," as promising programs to reduce rates of sexual assault on college campuses around the country.

The goal of all bystander intervention programs is to increase the likelihood that more people in a specific community act in a way that predicts and encourages bystander intervention, that is, to increase community protection factors. However, this is a somewhat circular argument because the predictors of bystander intervention behaviors include people modeling the behaviors, recognizing potentially dangerous situations, taking responsibility to act in any given situation, and identifying intervention techniques that minimize physical and social risk (Coker et al., 2011). A person's community and position of power in society heavily affect all of these predictive behaviors. Without community support for interventions or positions of equal power allowing those from marginalized communities to safely intervene in situations, it's unlikely that those from diverse racial and ethnic groups will have the same response to bystander intervention programs as those involved in program evaluations.

Up to this point, bystander intervention program evaluations are limited and a minority of published studies focuses solely on marginalized student populations. While current research supports the claims that these programs increase bystander intervention behaviors—and in the case of Green Dot, reduces rates of sexual violence—educational interventions must be more focused to include students of color, students who are LGBT, and students of other marginalized, high-risk populations.

Green Dot

Green Dot harnesses the peer and cultural influence of respected and influential peer and social group leaders to create meaningful change across the campus community. The goal of Green Dot is to increase proactive bystander intervention behaviors, ultimately resulting in a reduction of sexual violence within the community (Coker et al., 2011). The program is promoted by the Office on Violence Against Women, is used by many campuses and high schools, and was recently shown effective in reducing sexual violence at the University of Kentucky (Coker et al., 2015). However, it is important to note that one of the creators of Green Dot is a faculty member at the University of Kentucky and that the university itself is 76% White and 7.6% African American (National Center for Education Statistics, 2015). The exact demographics of those who actively participated or otherwise engaged with the program are unclear, although the article summarizing the study provides that 14.2% of the freshman class during program implementation was non-White (Coker et al., 2015). Because the publicly available study data does not assess rates of interpersonal violence (inclusive of sexual violence) within any specific racial group, these findings may not apply equally across the broader higher education community.

Green Dot programming presents three intervention methods: direct, distraction, and delegation. Direct intervention is essentially verbally or physically stepping into a situation as it occurs. Distraction involves stopping a situation by removing attention on one of the parties in the situation through a ploy, for example "accidentally" spilling a drink on someone and then taking them to the bathroom to get cleaned up. Finally, delegation involves calling on someone better prepared to directly intervene in a situation. Delegation usually involves summoning law enforcement or other authority figures and is generally described the safest intervention method in high-risk situations. As with the prior portions of the program, this section is problematic because it does not directly address increased risk factors certain subpopulations experience, distrust of law enforcement, or power imbalances experienced in many communities. For example, the work of Potter, Fountain, and Stapleton (2012) discuss that bystander intervention in the LGBT community may present additional complications because of potential stigma associated with that community, heightened risk of violence for people assisting LGBT identified targets, and the like. Also, the strained relationship between many law enforcement agencies and people from socially disadvantaged neighborhoods or otherwise marginalized communities is well documented (e.g., Schneider, 1999). Therefore, if a student comes from a community that has been historically mistreated by and does not trust law enforcement, or is involved with an otherwise marginalized community in which socially supported power structures hamper a person's ability to safely and effectively intervene in a situation, it seems unlikely that exposure to a 90 minute to four-hour program will counter these effects.

Bringing in the Bystander

Bringing in the Bystander programming encourages the development of a sense of responsibility for other members of the community to prevent violence before it is perpetrated (Banyard, Moynihan, & Plante, 2007). Although Bringing in the Bystander (BIB) has not been empirically shown to be effective in reducing sexual violence, the CDC notes that the program might work to prevent sexual assault perpetration as it has been shown to be "effective in reducing risk factors for sexual violence or related outcomes using a rigorous evaluation design" (Centers for Disease Control and Prevention, 2014, p. 8). BIB, as promoted by The Prevention Innovations Research Center (2015), is customizable, and as such it is not possible to conduct uniform research on efficacy across campuses.

In their description of the program, Banyard et al. (2007) assert that the ". . . bystander model gives all community members a specific role, which they can identify with and adopt in preventing the community problem of sexual violence" (p. 464). "Roles" identified by Banyard et al. are the interrupter, the messenger, and the ally (2007, p. 464). The interrupter feels comfortable interrupting violence as it occurs or situations that may lead to violence. The messenger vocally opposes social norms that support sexual violence, including sexist jokes, catcalling, and the like. Finally, the ally supports victims of violence after the fact, to process what happened and access appropriate resources. Trained program facilitators provide participants specific examples and information that participants may use to fulfill one or all of these roles (Boise State, 2013). One challenge of this model is facilitators' familiarity with diverse communities and the examples they may provide for any one of these given roles, as the scenarios shared and solutions discussed are generally based upon facilitator experiences, community-supported intervention techniques, and level of comfort that they can safely (both physically and emotionally) intervene in the provided examples. Therefore, facilitators' roles are highly subjective and experience-based and may not align with the experiences and needs of the program participants, especially those who fall outside of a White, heterosexual, and middle to upper class demographic.

In addition to examples of roles a person may take on, the program provides participants the opportunity to identify and discuss predictors of bystander intervention. Research on the major predictors of bystander intervention began in the 1960s after the rape and murder of Kitty Genovese in the vicinity of many witnesses (e.g., Darley & Latane, 1968). Since that time, academics have come to generally agree upon four major predictors of bystander intervention: diffusion of responsibility, evaluation apprehension, pluralistic ignorance, and modeling (Coker et al., 2011). Without going into detail regarding these factors, it is important to note that each of them is heavily influenced by cultural beliefs and community climate around interventions because by definition they each involve other people in the community acting in one way or another. This point is important because the typical college student comes to campus with 18 years of experiences and beliefs built around their specific communities. Banyard et al. (2007) evaluated the effectiveness of Bringing in the Bystander using a fairly racially and ethnically homogeneous sample of students. The researchers admit that there are demographic factors that may "hamper or enhance prosocial bystanding related to sexual violence" (p. 478). The gender identity of the treatment students is unknown, but likely does not include enough individuals identifying as Trans* to provide evidence of effectiveness within that community.

After identifying the predictors of bystander intervention, the program provides participants information on options for intervention, both in terms of timing and style (Boise State, 2013). The program identifies opportunities to intervene on a spectrum from things that happen often, and are not usually viewed as harmful, to things that happen less often and are usually recognized as harmful (Boise State, 2013). BIB also provides examples of the types of behaviors that fall at different places along this spectrum ranging from "catcalling" to rape and murder. Of course, where specific behaviors fall on this spectrum is fairly subjective, which becomes obvious when students are asked to place behaviors on the spectrum. Based on our personal experiences facilitating Bringing in the Bystander sessions at Boise State University, we speculate that student beliefs around the harmfulness of behaviors are based on their specific socializations prior to entering college. For example, we posit that men perceive catcalling ("Hey, bring that fine ass over here!") as a much less harmful activity than do women, who are more likely to experience the behavior. Furthermore, greater levels of acceptance of certain behaviors, including catcalling, are deeply rooted in the cultural and societal norms promoted within individual students' home communities and social groups. In other words, this is another cultural factor that is not necessarily directly addressed by the program. Instead, the program assumes that student participants have a generally accepted understanding of where specific behaviors fall on the spectrum. Again, this approach fails to account for the wide range of experiences students have when they come to campuses.

Finally, the program asks participants to develop a plan of action for intervention (Boise State, 2013). The purpose of the plan of action is to make students concretely think about a scenario requiring intervention they may experience at some point in the future and to write a specific plan of intervention for that scenario. While we believe this is a useful component of the program, it again assumes that students accept that there are situations in which it is appropriate and helpful (both to themselves and to their community) to intervene and that there are methods of intervention that are viable options, which is not always the case.

An Intersectional Model

Advocacy in second wave feminism has influenced the development of policy, programmatic funding, and research on victims with privileged identities

(Wooten, 2016). Crenshaw (1989) highlighted that leaving women of color out of important movements has served to further marginalize their experiences. She posited a model that examined the complexity of identity and experiences, called intersectionality. Using an intersectional model as a conceptual framework has several advantages, including considering how diverse identities are impacted by and sometimes left out of primary prevention as well as efforts to boost protective factors.

As noted on their website, Alicia Garza, Patrisse Cullorse, and Opal Tometi created #BlackLivesMatter to be an intersectional movement, following an incident where a 17-year-old boy (Trayvon Martin) was followed and shot to death by George Zimmerman, a man who claimed to be acting in self-defense (Black Lives Matter, n.d.). The incident and the shooter's resulting acquittal fueled the development of grassroots movements such as #BlackLivesMatter. The founders clarified that the movement served to bring awareness of state violence against a number of marginalized groups, noting "Black Lives Matter affirms the lives of Black queer and Trans folks, disabled folks, Black-undocumented folks, folks with records, women and all Black lives along the gender spectrum" (Black Lives Matter, n.d.).

In the midst of the proliferation of this hashtag, people using social media began to use #TransLivesMatter, to bring attention to oppression perpetrated against Trans★ individuals (Rök Jóns, 2015). Variations of the hashtags have also been used, such as #SayHerName, which serves to bring awareness to the high level of violence enacted against Black and Trans★ women (Crenshaw, Ritchie, Anspach, Gilmer, & Harris, 2015). Members of the movements have turned to social media as well as published reports, blogs, staged protests, and even disrupted public events to bring awareness to the anti-Black, transphobic actions in policing and the broader community.

Over the last year, Black Lives Matter activists expanded their efforts to numerous campuses, demanding, ". . . a more diverse faculty, more ethnic-studies classes, improved mental-health services for students of color, and policies for dealing with incidents that the activists find offensive" (Somashekhar, 2015). The challenge of practitioners failing to consider intersectionality of violence is that resulting prevention efforts are strictly focused on White, cisgender, heteronormative perspectives. Dominant educational models driven by a non-inclusive discourse have proliferated on college campuses at the expense of nondominant groups. It is movements like this that help to reiterate the imperative that all campus efforts to end violence be inclusive, and recognize and address the elevated risk of the violence perpetrated against historically marginalized student populations.

Social-Ecological Model

In the collegiate environment, students are part of a system linked to many other communities, and as such the approach suggested in this chapter encompasses a social-ecological systems framework (Bronfenbrenner, 2005). Promising interventions will harness the power of intersectionality by utilizing a pro-social risk and protective factor model. Initially conceptualized to combat adolescent alcohol and drug use under a framework of community health, the risk and protective factor model is now commonplace in social work and counseling (Hawkins, Catalano, & Miller, 1992).

The environment in which students live has an important impact on their wellbeing. For example, scholars studying homophobic bullying in school have identified "individual-level characteristics, such as sex and sexual orientation, have been consistently identified as salient risk and protective factors . . ." (Hong & Garbarino, 2012, p. 273). For students who are LGBT and/or of marginalized racial identities, a social-ecological model incorporates individual characteristics, social relationships between subgroups, and the greater community with which students have interactions (see Figure 4.1). If we are to improve the

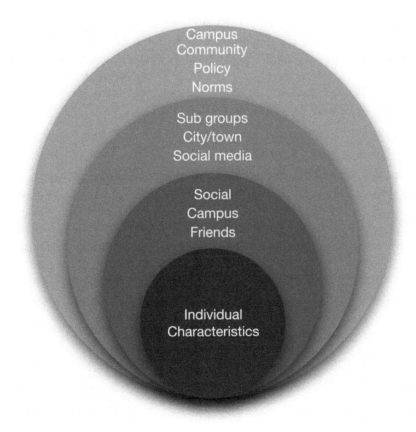

FIGURE 4.1 Socio-Ecological Model

wellbeing of all students—especially with respect to the #TransLivesMatter and #BlackLivesMatter movements—holistic improvements must be made across the social-ecological levels, including in higher education communities and beyond. Improvements should include greater support programs, addressing institutionalized marginalization and micro-aggressions.

While college students who are LGBT and/or of marginalized racial identities face new opportunities in enrollment, they also arrive on campus with their past experiences and connections to communities intact. Certainly LGBT and historically marginalized students who have experienced family and community encouragement, school systems supportive of their identities, and reside in less conflict prone areas may have more "grit," which adds to their resilience or protective factors. However, many students entering college directly from high school indicate pervasive harassment by peers and indifference from school personnel, which has eroded the protective factors made possible by the educational environment (D'Augelli, Grossman, & Starks, 2006; Grossman et al., 2009; Kosciw, Diaz, & Greytak; Sausa, 2005). Practitioners may need to look no further than the communities they serve to acknowledge the harm caused by bullying, harassment, and xenophobic peers, administrators, and society at large. The complexity of individual- and community-level relationships calls for an approach that recognizes risk and protective factors. Implications for practitioners using this model require educational programs and support structures to reduce risks and enhance protective characteristics.

Toward a More Inclusive Model

Additional research and further programmatic development, focused on perpetration of violence against students of nondominant racial and gender identities as well as LGBT students, is paramount. Further, greater sensitivity in responding to culturally sensitive and diverse situations and increased awareness about how students can use bystander intervention skills to interrupt sexual violence is lacking from current programmatic efforts. This section introduces a model for practitioners to develop a customizable curriculum, unique to their campus (see Figure 4.2).

Develop Understanding of Diverse Experiences

Recognize how current research and programs perpetuate invisibility

While robust bodies of research have clearly documented the dynamic of male college students perpetrating sexual assault against females, the literature is sparse regarding experiences as they relate to sexual orientation, gender identity, and/or

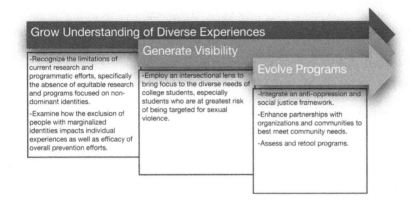

FIGURE 4.2 Intersectional Educational Model

race, particularly as they relate to campus sexual assault. Studies overwhelmingly operationalize gender on a binary and nearly omit mention of sexual orientation and other marginalized identities (Ciarlante & Fountain, 2010; Edwards et al., 2015; Wooten, 2016). For example, the NCAVP notes that the CDC included heterosexual, gay, lesbian, bisexual, and male and female identifiers in the 2010 National Intimate Partner and Sexual Violence Study focused on sexual orientation; however, the organization missed the opportunity to query experiences of Trans* or Queer identified people (2013). Campus specific research is needed to better understand the experiences of various subgroups, as ". . . college campuses may vary in their specific mix and risk of protective factors, as well as the needs and strengths of their student population and the surrounding community" (Centers for Disease Control and Prevention, 2014, p. 11). While this chapter focuses on race, gender identity, and sexual orientation, we acknowledge research on campus sexual violence should expand target populations to include students with disabilities, students in committed relationships, as well as the efficacy of bystanders engaging authority figures when victims belong to a culture that practices honor killings.

Examine the impact of invisibility

Problematizing invisibility yields the lived consequences of marginalized populations and ultimately challenges our ability to understand the experiences of our most-at-risk populations (The National Coalition of Anti-Violence Programs, 2013). Programs like Green Dot and Bringing in the Bystander normalize Lisak's description of campus sexual assault as a party-related, alcohol-facilitated occurrence. While such situations are documented as common, they are not representative of the range of students' experiences. As Crenshaw (1991) cautioned, "Strategies based solely on the experiences of women who do not share the same class or race backgrounds will be of limited utility for those whose lives are shaped by a different set of obstacles." Wooten (2016) also iterated the limitations that narrow understandings of sexual violence have had on both program development and federal level policy (e.g., The Violence Against Women Act).

The limited focus described throughout this chapter informs our efforts to engage college students in bystander intervention. As noted above, participants in various programs are encouraged to involve trained responders or delegate to others, in efforts to increase safety. This method is in contrast to decades of research, and the advocacy of newer movements like #BlackLivesMatter and #TransLivesMatter, which highlight the systemic homophobia, transphobia, and racism apparent in policing systems. To better understand the limitations of such an approach, consider the NCAVP's member survey that examined LGBTQ and HIV-affected intimate partner violence, which found ". . . in nearly one-third of incidents (29.7%) in 2012 the police mis-arrested the survivor as the perpetrator of violence. . ." (2013, p. 48). Further, INCITE!, a radical feminist organization for women of color notes, ". . . the criminal justice system is itself not an alternative. It not only does not provide safety for women as an overall strategy . . . but actually puts women in greater danger of violence, particularly state violence" (2003, p. 2). Concerns shared by INCITE! are also echoed in a report produced by the African American Policy Forum, which details the disproportionate amount of police violence against Black women (Crenshaw et al., 2015). Resultantly, Grant et al. (2011) found that only one-third of Trans★ and gender non-conforming individuals feel safe contacting police, as such efforts are not guaranteed to increase safety, but rather, are likely to yield harassment and physical or sexual violence at the hands of officers, medical professionals, or staff or peers in the jail system.

Calling on law enforcement may also feel like a non-option for victims or bystanders when considering the wellbeing of the person engaged in violence. For example, a victim or bystander may be concerned about reporting when the person who has committed violence is undocumented or Trans★, for fear of how they will be treated in the criminal justice system (The National Coalition of Anti-Violence Programs, 2013). Additionally, if the offender is of a dominant identity and the victim is not, there may be hesitation to accept assistance from bystanders wanting to engage law enforcement. For all these reasons, our most-at-risk students may hesitate to alert law enforcement and campus personnel. We assert that prevention efforts, such as engaging youth in a mentoring program or lobbying for policy change post incident must also be explored as possible alternatives when risk of further injury or death is high or when an individual does not have direct influence over corrupt systems, groups, or individuals.

Generate Visibility

Employ an Intersectional Lens

Gender-based violence does not merely exist on a plane of sexist behaviors. An instructional model that accounts for intersecting oppressions provides a more in-depth, accurate examination of the issue. In her seminal work on intersectionality, Crenshaw declared, "Because the intersectional experience is greater than the sum of racism and sexism, any analysis that does not take intersectionality into account cannot sufficiently address the particular manner in which Black women are subordinated" (1989, p. 58). Private and state-funded antiviolence organizations such as INCITE!, The Idaho Coalition Against Sexual and Domestic Violence, Move to End Violence, Creative Interventions, The Oregon Sexual Assault Task Force, Prevent Connect, The Virginia Sexual and Domestic Violence Action Alliance, The NCAVP Programs, and The Chicago Task Force on Violence Against Girls and Young Women have endorsed Crenshaw's perspective and integrated this framework into their violence prevention efforts (Creative Interventions, 2012, pp. 2–23). Generating visibility of nondominant experiences through practice, assessment, and research will help us better determine if current programs meet the needs of our most-at-risk students, inform how we educate bystanders, and explore viable alternatives for interventions.

Evolve and Offer Programs with Research and Community Input

Integrate Frameworks and Findings

Numerous scholars have identified promising practices in violence prevention and bystander intervention education (Brown, Banyard, & Moynihan, 2014; CDC, 2014; Coker, et al., 2015; Nation, et al., 2003). We echo Brown, Banyard, and Moynihan (2014) who cautioned, ". . . educational programs need to be sensitive to different barriers and facilitators to helping for different groups of students, including students of color" (p. 360). We argue the importance of integrating findings from the above recommended research. Examining these findings will empower practitioners to further develop programs and better instill in participants those skills that are culturally informed, relevant, and inclusive.

Davis, Parks, and Cohen (2006) created The Spectrum of Prevention for sexual violence to outline various behaviors—overlaid on the social-ecological model—in which bystanders could engage in to prevent sexual assault. Casey and Lindorst (2009) echoed the need for this model, noting that it allows practitioners to adequately address risk factors. The intersectional model blends well with this approach, potentially resulting in practitioners who are better able to address risk and protective factors and bystanders who are increasingly empowered to engage

Sexual Violence and the Spectrum of Prevention	
1 Strengthening Individual Knowledge and Skills	Enhancing an individual's capability of preventing violence and promoting safety
2 Promoting Community Education	Reaching groups of people with information and resources to prevent violence and promote safety
3 Educating Providers	Informing providers who will transmit skills and knowledge to others and model positive norms
4 Fostering Coalitions and Networks	Bringing together groups and individuals for broader goals and greater impact
5 Changing Organizational Practices	Adopting regulations and shaping norms to prevent violence and improve safety
6 Influencing Policies and Legislation	Enacting laws and policies that support healthy community norms and a violence-free society

FIGURE 4.3 The Spectrum of Prevention: A Tool for Comprehensive Action and Norms Change

with peers and advocate for changes in language, actions, and policies that impact a diversity of identities.

Combining these factors may modify programmatic content in a number of ways. For example, content may move beyond a mere highlight of the rate of violence experienced by nondominant identity groups to a discussion of the cultural factors that perpetuate sexual violence across identities. Bystanders would broaden their approach from recognizing and responding to expressions of sexism, to also intervening in situations that may also present as transphobic, racist, or otherwise marginalizing. To do this, program participants may reflect on how sexism in mainstream media may also be accompanied by layers of transphobia, biphobia, and/or racism as well as connected to sexual violence. Programs may also encourage bystanders to advocate for healthier representations of consent and relationships that feature people of diverse racial and gender identities. The aforementioned organizations and state coalitions provide leadership in empowering bystanders to organize and respond to policies and programs that perpetuate or make it difficult to address sexual violence across identities.

Enhance Partnerships with Organizations and Communities

Organizations engaged in this multifaceted work note the importance of collaboration with target communities and organizations (Centers for Disease

Control and Prevention, 2014; Ciarlante & Fountain, 2010). With such partnerships, practitioners can critically examine risk and protective factors found in populations on their campuses, as well as how partnerships may best address such concerns. Violence prevention work is maximized when we address the intersections of oppression, as we are more fully addressing the precipitating factors of violence.

When interventions are developed in the community, they may be more accessible, safe, more sensitive to power and privilege, and perhaps more likely to be used. As advocated by Casey and Lindorst (2009), a high level of community involvement ". . . assures the relevance of the prevention program to the needs and realities of the community" (pp. 98–99). We also encourage practitioners to involve community members in meetings, information sharing, program creation and implementation, and leadership positions.

Assess and Retool Programs

Once research is expanded and incorporated into programmatic efforts, we must evaluate the efficacy across populations using the most rigorous research designs possible. Practitioners are encouraged to share this specific need for research with faculty, graduate students, and community organizations, all of which may be better positioned to engage in research. The CDC (2014) offers insight into effective evaluative methods, noting, "Rigorous outcome evaluation research benefits the field as a whole and can provide valuable feedback to individual campuses on the impact of their initiatives" (p. 12). Promotion of findings will continue to evolve programs and generate further awareness of interventions sensitive to our most-at-risk populations.

The Future of Prevention Programs

Because the future of campus-based prevention programming is necessarily informed by our collective histories, a brief synopsis of the evolution of crime prevention on college campuses, specifically sexual assault, is important.

Prevention and the Legal Mandate

Since at least the mid-nineteenth century, courts, and later the federal government, have imposed varying duties on universities to prevent and respond to crimes affecting their student bodies (Fisher, 1995; Lake, 2013). Most recently, the U.S. Department of Education, Office of Civil Rights (OCR) clarified that universities must prevent and remedy sexual harassment under Title IX. Further, OCR's April 2011 Dear Colleague Letter clarified that this obligation extends to sexual violence affecting a campus community. One of the direct consequences of the 2011 Dear Colleague Letter was an enormous and nearly immediate increase in the number of complaints filed by student victims of sexual assault with OCR (Anderson, 2015). These complaints served as an important indicator that sexual assault on college campuses is not just happening, but is happening at epidemic levels—with nearly one in four college women reporting some form of sexual assault during their college careers (Cantor et al., 2015).

To bring awareness to the issue and to reduce the prevalence of sexual assault on our college campuses, President Barack Obama established the White House Task Force Addressing Sexual Assault on College Campuses in January 2014. The Task Force promptly published a report entitled "Not Alone," which provided an overview of the problem of sexual assault on college campuses and suggested programming targeted at reducing rates of such violence, including the implementation of bystander intervention and other primary prevention programming (2014). Coinciding with the release of the taskforce report, the U.S. Department of Education issued a lengthy guidance document further clarifying the application of Title IX to sexual assault (2014). Also in 2014, Section 304 of the Violence Against Women Reauthorization Act of 2013 amended the Clery Act and established broad categories of training programs that institutions must offer students, staff, and faculty on an annual basis (Violence Against Women Reauthorization Act of 2013, 2013; Jeanne Clery Disclosure of Campus Security Policy and Campus Statistics Act, 1990). Required training includes primary prevention programming such as bystander intervention (Higher Education Act of 1965, as amended).

With this federal mandate, nearly every college and university in the country is under an affirmative obligation to provide primary prevention programming within campus communities. While not specifically addressed, by federal law or guidance, certainly institutions of higher education should utilize primary prevention programming that is effective at reducing sexual violence both within the broader community and within traditionally marginalized communities. While bystander intervention programs currently promoted to reduce interpersonal violence on college campuses show promise, their effect within marginalized communities is largely unknown.

Moving Forward

In the course of this chapter, we assert protective factors can be strengthened by offering programs that are informed by an intersectional lens, the social-ecological model, an understanding of privilege and oppression, and the spectrum of the sexual violence prevention model. Also highlighted is the lack of data on how intersecting oppressions influence the behaviors and experiences of bystanders, victims, and perpetrators. Practitioners should be aware of the limitations of current prevention programming, including lack of data demonstrating they are effective in traditionally marginalized communities, including Trans★ and Black communities.

In developing a mass of data through program evaluation, and optimistically partnering with faculty, graduate students, or organizations to engage in researching and publishing literature on these correlates (intersectionality, risk and protective factors, the socioecological model, bystander intervention, and campus sexual assault), practitioners can further refine an understanding of promising and best practices for countering violence perpetrated on individual and systemic levels and begin to evolve programs to better serve students with nondominant identities. Such research would further inform programmatic efforts and help better engage a greater diversity of students in increasingly successful bystander behaviors across the spectrum of prevention. Ultimately, engaging in and partnering with third parties to advocate for research focused on the intersections of identities and campus sexual violence would promote a strengthened understanding about what interventions may be most relevant, accessible, and applicable.

Educators accomplish their best work in a college community when they are inclusive of diverse communities, share the message of prevention, and empower bystanders to be better able to address the complexity of violence experienced in their communities. As practitioners, our goal is to increase protective factors for both individuals and, ultimately, the community. To do so, we must partner with diverse organizations, advocate for greater representation of marginalized identities in research and programs, participate in program evaluation, and examine our findings to counter sexual violence from a more effective, holistic perspective.

Note

1   The term Trans★ is an all-inclusive term, encompassing a diverse array of gender identities, including but not limited to Transgender and Gender Non-Conforming.

References

Anderson, N. (2015, March 4). Schools facing investigations on sexual violence: Now more than 100. *The Washington Post*. Retrieved from www.washingtonpost.com/news/grade-point/wp/2015/03/04/schools-facing-investigations-on-sexual-violence-now-more-than-100.

Banyard, V.L., Moynihan, M.M., & Plante, E.G. (2007). Sexual violence prevention through bystander education: An experimental evaluation. *Journal of Community Psychology, 35*(4), 463–481.

Black Lives Matter. (n.d.). *About the black lives matter movement*. Retrieved from http://blacklivesmatter.com.

Black, M.C., Basile, K.C., Breiding, M.J., Smith, S.G., Walters, M.L., Merrick, M.T., Chen, J., & Stevens, M.R. (2011). *The national intimate partner and sexual violence survey (NISVS): 2010 summary report*. Atlanta, GA: National Center for Injury Prevention and Control, Centers for Disease Control and Prevention.

Boise State University. (2013). *Bringing in the Bystander: Creating community responsibility*. PowerPoint Presentation. On file with author.

Bronfenbrenner, U. (2005). Ecological systems theory. In U. Bronfenbrenner (Ed.), *Making human beings human: Bioecological perspectives on human development* (pp. 106–173). Thousand Oaks, CA: Sage.

Brown, A.L., Banyard, V.L., & Moynihan, M.M. (2014). College students as helpful bystanders against sexual violence: Gender, race, and year in college moderate the impact of perceived peer norms. *Psychology of Women Quarterly, 38*(3), 350–362.

Cantor, D., Fisher, B., Chibnall, S., Townsend, R., Lee, H., Bruce, C., & Thomas, G. (2015). *Report on the AAU campus climate survey on sexual assault and sexual misconduct.* Rockville, MD: Westat.

Casey, E.A., & Lindhorst, T.P. (2009). Toward a multi-level, ecological approach to the primary prevention of sexual assault: Prevention in peer and community contexts. *Trauma, Violence & Abuse, 10*(2), 91–114.

Centers for Disease Control and Prevention (CDC). (2014). *Preventing sexual violence on college campuses: Lessons from research and practice.* Atlanta, GA: Centers for Disease Control and Prevention.

Centers for Disease Control and Prevention (CDC). (2015). *The social-ecological model: A framework for prevention.* Retrieved from www.cdc.gov/violenceprevention/overview/social-ecologicalmodel.html.

Ciarlante, M., & Fountain, K. (2010). *Why it matters: Rethinking victim assistance for lesbian, gay, bisexual, transgender, and queer victims of hate violence and intimate partner violence.* New York: National Center for Victims of Crime and The National Coalition of Anti-Violence Programs.

Coker, A.L., Bush, H.M., Fisher, B.S., Swan, S.C., Williams, C.M., Clear, E.R., & DeGue, S. (2015). Multi-college bystander intervention evaluation for violence prevention. *American Journal of Preventive Medicine, 50*(3), 295–302.

Coker, A.L., Cook-Craig, P.G., Williams, C.M., Fisher, B.S., Clear, E.R., Garcia, L.S., & Hegge, L.M. (2011). Evaluation of Green Dot: An active bystander intervention to reduce sexual violence on college campuses. *Violence Against Women, 17*(6), 777–796.

Coulter, R., Blosnich, J., Bukowski, L., Herrick, A., Siconolfi, D., & Stall, R. (2015). Differences in alcohol use and alcohol-related problems between transgender— And nontransgender-identified young adults. *Drug and Alcohol Dependence, 154,* 251–259.

Creative Interventions. (2012). *Creative interventions toolkit: A practical guide to stop interpersonal violence.* Retrieved from www.creative-interventions.org/wp-content/uploads/2012/06/CI-Toolkit-Complete-Pre-Release-Version-06.2012-.pdf.

Crenshaw, K. (1989). *Demarginalizing the intersection of race and sex: A black feminist critique of antidiscrimination doctrine, feminist theory, and anti-racist politics.* Retrieved from http://allisonbolah.com/site_resources/reading_list/Demarginalizing_Crenshaw.pdf.

Crenshaw, K.W. (1991). *Mapping the margins: Intersectionality, identity politics, and violence against women of color.* Retrieved from http://socialdifference.columbia.edu/files/socialdiff/projects/Article__Mapping_the_Margins_by_Kimblere_Crenshaw.pdf.

Crenshaw, K.W., Ritchie, A.J., Anspach, R., Gilmer, R., & Harris, L. (2015). *Say her name: Resisting police brutality against black women.* African American Policy Forum. New York: Centre for Intersectionality and Social Policy Studies.

D'Augelli, A., Grossman, A., & Starks, M. (2006). Childhood gender atypicality, victimization, and PTSD among lesbian, gay, and bisexual youth. *Journal of Interpersonal Violence, 21*(11), 1462–1482.

Darley, J.M., & Latane, B. (1968). Bystander intervention in emergencies: Diffusion of responsibility. *Journal of Personality and Social Psychology, 8*(4), 377–383.

Davis, R, Parks, L.F., & Cohen, L. (2006). *Sexual violence and the spectrum of prevention: Towards a community solution.* Enola, PA: National Sexual Violence Resource Center.

Durate v. State, 88 Cal. App. 3d 473 (Cal. App. 1979).

Edwards, K.M., Sylaska, K.M., Moynihan, M.M., Banyard, V.L., Cohn, E.S., Walsh, W.A., Ward, S. K., & Barry, J.E. (2015). Physical dating violence, sexual violence, and unwanted pursuit victimization: A comparison of incidence rates among sexual-minority and heterosexual college students. *Journal of Interpersonal Violence, 30*(4), 580–600.

Fisher, B.S. (1995). Crime and fear on campus. *The Annals of the American Academy of Political and Social Science,* 539, 85–101.

Grant, J.M., Mottet, L.A., Tanis, J., Harrison, J., Herman, J.L., & Keisling, M. (2011). *Injustice at every turn: A report of the national transgender discrimination survey.* Washington, DC: National Center for Transgender Equality and National Gay and Lesbian Task Force.

Grossman, A., Haney, A., Edwards, P., Alessi, E., Ardon, M., & Howell, T. (2009). Lesbian, gay, bisexual, and transgender youth talk about experience and coping with school violence: A qualitative study. *Journal of LGBT Youth, 6,* 24–46.

Haslanger, S., Tuana, N., & O'Connor, P. (2012). *Stanford encyclopedia of philosophy: Topics in feminism.* Retreived from http://plato.stanford.edu/entries/feminism-topics/.

Hawkins, J., Catalano, R., & Miller, J. (1992). Risk and protective factors for alcohol and other drug problems in adolescence and early adulthood: Implications for substance-abuse prevention. *Psychological Bulletin, 112,* 64–105.

Higher Education Act of 1965 (as amended by Section 304 of the Violence Against Women Reauthorization Act of 2013). *20 U.S.C. § 1092 (f)(8).*

Hingson, R., Heeren, T., Winter, M., & Wechsler, H. (2005). Magnitude of alcohol-related mortality and morbidity among U.S. college students ages 18–24: Changes from 1998 to 2001. *Annual Review of Public Health, 26*(1), 259–279.

Hong, J.S., & Garbarino, J. (2012). Risk and protective factors for homophobic bullying in schools: An application of the social-ecological framework. *Educational Psychology Review, 24*(2), 271–285.

INCITE! (2003). *Women of color against violence community accountability principles/concerns/strategies/models working document.* Retrieved from www.incite-national.org/page/community-accountability-working-document.

Jeanne Clery Discolsure of Campus Security Policy and Campus Crime Statistics Act. (1990). *20 U.S.C. § 1902(f).*

Kosciw, J., Diaz, E., & Greytak, E. (2008). *The 2007 national school climate survey: The experiences of lesbian, gay, bisexual and transgender youth in our nation's schools.* New York: GLSEN.

Krebs, C.P., Lindquist, C.H., Warner, T.D., Fisher, B.S., & Martin, S.L. (2009). College women's experiences with physically forced, alcohol- or other drug-enabled, and drug-facilitated sexual assault before and since entering college. *Journal of American College Health, 57*(6), 639–647.

Lake, P. (2013). *The rights and responsibilities of the modern university: The rise of the facilitator university* (2nd ed.). Durham, NC: Carolina Academic Press.

Lisak, D., & Miller, P.M. (2002). Repeat rape and multiple offending among undetected rapists. *Violence and Victims, 17*(1), 73–84.

Miller v. State of New York, 62 N.Y.2nd 506, 467 N.E.2nd 493, 478 N.Y.2nd 829 (1984).

Nation, M., Crusto, C., Wandersman, A., Kumpfer, K.L., Seybolt, D., Morrissey-Kane, E., & Davino, K. (2003). What works in prevention: Principles of effective prevention programs. *The American Psychologist, 58* (6–7), 449–456.

National Center for Education Statistics. (2015). College navigator: University of Kentucky. Retrieved from http://nces.ed.gov/collegenavigator/?q=University+of+Kentucky&s=all&id=157085#enrolmt.

The National Coalition of Anti-Violence Programs. (2013). *Lesbian, gay, bisexual, transgender, queer and HIV-affected intimate partner violence in 2012.* Retrieved from www.avp.org/storage/documents/ncavp_2012_ipvreport.final.pdf.

The National Coalition of Anti-Violence Programs. (2009). *Hate violence against the lesbian, gay, bisexual, transgender, and queer communities in the United States in 2009.* Retrieved from www.avp.org/storage/documents/Reports/2009_NCAVP_HV_Report.pdf.

Office of Justice Programs, Office for Victims of Crime. (2014, June). *Responding to transgender victims of sexual assault.* Retrieved from www.ovc.gov/pubs/forge/sexual_numbers.html.

Oregon Sexual Assault Task Force. (2015). *Intersections of oppression and sexual violence.* Retrieved from http://oregonsatf.org/wp-content/uploads/2011/02/Intersections-of-Oppression-and-SV-Paper-Final-9.29.15.pdf.

Potter, S.J., Fountain, K., & Stapleton, J.G. (2012). Addressing sexual and relationship violence in the LGBT community using a bystander framework. *Harvard Review of Psychiatry, 20*(4), 201–208.

Prevention Innovations Research Center. (2015). Bringing in the Bystander® Regional Training. Retrieved from http://cola.unh.edu/prevention-innovations-research-center/regional-training.

Rök Jóns, R. (2015). *On the origins, circulation & deployment of #TransLivesMatter.* Retrieved from www.hastac.org/blogs/ragnarok/2015/03/01/origins-circulation-deployment-translivesmatter-0.

Sausa, L. (2005). Translating research into practice: Trans youth recomendations for improving school systems. *Journal of Gay and Lesbian Issues in Education, 3*(1), 15–28.

Schneider, S.R. (1999). Overcoming barriers to communication between police and socially disadvantaged neighbourhoods: A critical theory of community policing. *Crime, Law & Social Change,* 347–377.

Somashekhar, S. (2015). How black lives matter, born on the streets, is rising to power on campus. *The Washington Post.* Retrieved from www.washingtonpost.com/national/how-black-lives-matter-born-on-the-streets-is-rising-to-power-on-campus/2015/11/17/3c113e96-8959-11e5-be8b-1ae2e4f50f76_story.html.

Stone, A.L., Becker, L.G., Huber, A.M., & Catalano, R.F. (2012). Review of risk and protective factors of substance use and problem use in emerging adulthood. *Addictive Behaviors, 37*(7), 747–775.

United States Department of Education, Office for Civil Rights. (2011, April 4). Dear Collegue Letter.

United States Department of Education, Office for Civil Rights. (2014, April 29). Questions and Answers on Title IX and Sexaul Violence.

United States Department of Education, Office for Civil Rights. (2001, January). Revised Sexual Harassment Guidance: Harssment of Students By School Employees, Other Students, or Third Parties.

United States Department of Justice, Office on Violence Against Women. (2015, May 13). *Responding to campus sexual assault.* Retrieved September 25, 2015, from The United States Department of Justice Website: www.justice.gov/ovw/responding-campus-sexual-assault.

Violence Against Women Reauthorization Act of 2013. (2013, March 7). *PL 113–4, 127 Stat. 54.*

Walters, M.L., Chen, J., & Breiding, M.J. (2013). *The National Intimate Partner and Sexual Violence Survey (NISVS): 2010 findings on victimization by sexual orientation.* Atlanta, GA: National Center for Injury Prevention and Control, Centers for Disease Control and Prevention.

Wechsler, H., Lee, J.E., Nelson, T.F., & Kuo, M. (2002, January 01). Underage college students' drinking behavior, access to alcohol, and the influence of deterrence policies. Findings from the Harvard School of Public Health College Alcohol Study. *Journal of American College Health, 50*(5), 223–236.

White House Task Force to Protect Students from Sexual Assault. (2014). *Not alone: The first report of the White House task force to protect students from sexual assault.* Washington, DC: The White House.

Wooten, S.C. (2016). Heterosexist discourses: How feminist theory helped shape campus sexual violence policy. In S.C. Wooten & R.W. Mitchell (Eds.), *The crisis of campus sexual violence: Critical perspectives on prevention and response* (Chapter 3, pp. 33–50). New York: Routledge. Retrieved from http://boisestate.worldcat.org/title/crisis-of-campus-sexual-violence-critical-perspectives-on-prevention-and-response/oclc/918135237.

5

POWERFUL OR PLAYFUL?

A Case Study of "Walk a Mile in Her Shoes"

Kristina M. Kamis and Susan V. Iverson

Sexual assault continues to occur at an alarming rate on college campuses across the United States (Baum & Klaus, 2005; Karjane, Fisher, & Cullen, 2005; Krebs, Lindquist, Warner, Fisher, & Martin, 2009). For decades, campuses have been mandated through the Clery Act to provide programming to reduce incidents of dating violence, sexual assault, and stalking. Approaches to prevention range from basic awareness programming to educating bystanders, and include events targeted at particular populations such as men (McMahon, Postmus, Warrener, & Koenick, 2014; Moynihan, Banyard, Arnold, Eckstein, & Stapleton, 2010, 2011). Many studies have examined these sexual violence prevention efforts in U.S. higher education (Ahrens, Rich, & Ullman, 2011; Chekwa, Thomas, & Jones, 2013; Coker et al., 2011; Gidycz, Orchowski, & Berkowitz, 2011; Moynihan et al., 2015; Paul & Gray, 2011). While such studies are useful in their description of prevention approaches, limited empirical evidence exists regarding the effectiveness of these efforts, and even less interrogates such approaches from a critical lens.

In an effort to shift prevention efforts from focusing primarily on victim support and awareness, an increasing number of colleges and universities have begun organizing events aimed at mobilizing men to become part of the solution to combat sexual violence against women (Macomber, 2012). Through one such event, "Walk a Mile in Her Shoes" (WaM), men walk one mile in high heels to raise awareness of sexual violence against women. However, whether this event is effective in achieving its intended purpose is under question. Recent research found that by asking men to wear high heels, WaM may be reinscribing existing gender and sexual inequalities and reifying the normative assumption that sexual violence means male violence against women. Resultantly, men perform their prevention of sexual violence as a gender transgression (Barber & Kretschmer,

2013; Bridges, 2010; Masters, 2010). As well, even when men claim to be activists in preventing sexual violence against women, they too often still perpetuate the problem. For instance, men may be vocal advocates for ending interpersonal violence through their participation in an event, but still behave in sexist ways, fail to interrupt sexist and misogynistic behaviors that they observe, and sometimes perpetrate sexual violence themselves (Atherton-Zeman, 2009).

The "'reality' of male sexuality and the 'inevitability' of violence against women" (Gibson-Graham, 1996, p. 81) adheres to a dominant normative script: Sexual violence is a form of gendered violence committed by men against women. Framed in this way, prevention efforts such as WaM reify hetero-normative and heterosexist constructions of sexual violence and fail to identify other dimensions of identity as important (Phipps, 2010; Wooten, 2016).

In this chapter, we (1) provide a review of literature on sexual violence prevention efforts, and specifically those efforts targeted at men; (2) delineate our use of gender theory as a conceptual frame for this critical inquiry; (3) discuss findings from a qualitative case study of one campus's WaM event that sought to understand the goals of the event and the gendered meanings produced at the event; and (4) conclude with a delineation of implications for practice and future research. Our aim is to reveal how sexual violence prevention, particularly those efforts targeted at men, would benefit from a challenge to the primacy of gender as the organizing and explanatory factor for sexual violence.

Review of Literature

Prior to the feminist movement of the 1970s, the problem of sexual violence was widely attributed to women's unregulated bodies. In turn, women were told not to wear suggestive clothing or stay out late (Terry & Doerge, 1979; Workman & Orr, 1996). Feminist activism challenged this problem definition with initiatives to "take back the night" and educate women on how to resist and defend against sexual violence (Searles & Follansbee, 1984). Research on such initiatives (e.g., self-defense) has reported positive outcomes, including a decreased likelihood of being raped (Daigle, Fisher, & Stewart, 2009; Orchowski, Gidycz, & Raffle, 2008) as well as more self-reported assertiveness and a greater perceived ability to resist potential perpetrators (Daigle et al., 2009; Hollander, 2014; Weitlauf, Smith, & Cervone, 2000). Yet, critiques also exist, as it is widely agreed that men's sexual violence perpetration cannot be prevented unless men become active participants in standing up against violence (Bridges, 2010; Flood, 2011).

Men and Sexual Violence

Although men can be victims of sexual violence, they are most often perpetrators (Flood, 2011). According to the Centers for Disease Control and Prevention (2014), approximately 18.3% of women have been raped during their lifetime and 5.6% have experienced other forms of sexual violence, compared to 1.4% and 5.3% of men, respectively. This is especially evident on college campuses. According to Krebs et al. (2009), 19% of females experienced at least one attempted or completed act of sexual violence while in college. As well, 37.4% of female rape victims were first raped between the ages of 18 and 24 (Center for Disease Control and Prevention, 2014).

Moreover, much existing research has found that gendered violence stems from a patriarchal society that supports male dominance over women (Flood, 2011; Fulu et al., 2013). When men internalize this sexual inequality, they recognize rape and sexual violence as a way to exert control over women. In this case, rape serves as a manifestation of dominance guided by power and anger rather than passion (Brownmiller, 2013; Groth & Birnbaum, 2013). This is evidenced in heterosexual families, where there is more likely to be high levels of violence against women when the male holds dominant decision-making power (Flood, 2011). In addition, men who hold traditional or adverse gender-based attitudes toward women are more likely to perpetrate physical or sexual aggression (Carr & VanDeusen, 2004; Rosenbaum & O'Leary, 1981; Schumacher, Feldbau-Kohn, Slep, & Heyman, 2001; Telch & Lindquist, 1984). Thus, men should be the targets of sexual violence prevention in an effort to instill in them a sense of ownership for the problem, and to disrupt attitudes toward female subordination and male dominance (Kaufman, 2001; Sweetman, 1997).

Men and Prevention

Many prevention efforts exist to mobilize men in ending sexual violence against women, including as targets of antiviolence campaigns (e.g., "my strength is not for hurting"), active members in sexual violence education programs, and activists in changing public policies toward rape and sexual violence (Casey & Smith, 2010; Flood, 2011; Krebs et al., 2009; Masters, 2010; Murphy, 2009). Some scholars have suggested that rape myth acceptance interventions (e.g., sexual assault education) are effective at reducing rape myth acceptance among college men both immediately and two months following completion of the program (Foubert, 2000; Foubert & Marriott, 1997; O'Donohue, Yeater, & Fanetti, 2003). Rape myths are widely accepted ideologies that justify sexual violence against women and make them liable for their sexual victimization (Deming, Covan, Swan, & Billings, 2013), and several studies have found that when rape myths are accepted on college campuses, sexual assault is more likely to occur (Abbey, McAuslan, Zawacki, Clinton, & Buck, 2001; Carr & VanDeusen, 2004; Hamilton & Yee, 1990; Muehlenhard & Linton, 1987). Consider, for example, the prominent rape myth that women never really mean "no"—a myth that is perpetuated in films portraying force as sexually arousing or women saying "no" while swooning under a man's sexual advances. Thus, reducing rape myth acceptance among college men is an important focus of many sexual assault interventions on college campuses (Aronowitz, Lambert, & Davidoff, 2012; Hammond, Berry, & Rodriguez, 2011; McMahon, 2010; O'Donohue et al., 2003; Sawyer, Thompson, & Chicorelli, 2002).

"The Men's Program" is one specific intervention program targeted directly at college men. This program is designed to teach men how to help female rape victims, use bystander interventions in high-risk situations, and alter their rape-supportive actions while encouraging others to do the same (Langhinrichsen-Rohling, Foubert, Brasfield, Hill, & Shelley-Tremblay, 2011). To do this, each program starts with a powerful empathy component followed by bystander training, both delivered by highly trained men (Langhinrichsen-Rohling et al., 2011). Much existing research has found that the program effectively increases empathy, sexual violence awareness, and the likelihood to intervene in a questionable situation, and decreases rape-supportive behaviors, rape myth acceptance, and the likelihood to rape among men who participate in the program (Chapleau, 2015; Foubert & Perry, 2007; Langhinrichsen-Rohling et al., 2011).

Some scholars have identified the importance of establishing peer networks for men to develop the attitudes and behaviors to "do something" about sexual violence (Piccigallo, Lilley, & Miller, 2012). Protest marches are one of those spaces in which alliance building can occur. In the 1970s, women organized "Take Back the Night" (TBTN) marches and rallies to reclaim women's rights to move freely in their communities (Lederer, 1980). These events were originally formed by and to exclusively empower women; however, in the subsequent decades, men have begun (and been allowed) to participate, and related events targeted primarily at men have emerged. Men's involvement in TBTN marches and similar events such as "Walk a Mile in Her Shoes" have not only served to create empathy but also to open spaces for male victims, provide male role models, and to disrupt dichotomous constructions of gender by acknowledging the realities of transgender violence (Urback, 2013). However, limited research exists on men's involvement in marches protesting sexual violence, and those studies suggest that men may at best sympathize with the cause but fail to become politically conscious about "cultural definitions of masculinity that valorize competition, aggression, and the sexual conquest of women" (Barber & Kretschmer, p. 44; Bridges, 2010).

Conceptual Framing

This study is conceptually framed by gender theory, what Allan (2004) refers to as "a body of theories that examines how cultural expectations about femininity and masculinity shape understandings of women and men as gendered selves" (p. 278). Gender was too long presumed as "two fixed, static and mutually exclusive role containers" (Kimmel, 1986, p. 521). However, this notion has been effectively disputed and is now (and for our purposes) understood as "a set of socially constructed relationships which are produced and reproduced through people's actions" (Gerson & Peiss, 1985, p. 327). Gender theory contends that dominant expectations of masculinity and femininity are largely learned and performed, rather than rooted in one's biology (Allan, 2004; Lorber, 2004).

Gender is "something that one does, and *does* recurrently, in interaction with others" (West & Zimmerman, 1987, p. 140, italics in original). Gender includes sociocultural identity markers that signal one's maleness or femaleness expressed through clothing, jewelry, and footwear, such as high heels as a marker of femininity. Gender is a performance tied to culture; therefore, gender norms can shift depending on time and place (Kimmel, 1995). Further, gender is not exclusive of other dimensions of identity (such as race/ethnicity, sexuality, class, age), and we align with those scholars who recognize multiple masculinities and femininities that reflect variation when gender intersects with minoritized identity statuses (Crenshaw, 1991; Tevis & Griffen, 2014). However, dominant constructions of gender suggest a hegemony of maleness and femaleness (Lazar, 2005), which is central to this analysis.

Hegemonic masculinity, as Connell (1987) indicates, serves to legitimize and naturalize certain ways of *doing* maleness, and to marginalize alternative forms of masculinity, especially those associated with femininity. Connell adds that hegemonic masculinity represents the "maintenance of practices that institutional-izes men's dominance over women" and is associated with hyper-violent masculinity (p. 185). Further, some have reported that homosociality—"the nonsexual attractions held by men (or women) for members of their own sex" (Bird, 1996, p. 121)—and spaces that enable homosocial male bonding (e.g., fraternities, athletic teams) are "associated with attitudes conducive to sexual harassment of women" (Flood & Pease, 2009, p. 134). Yet others have identified "hybrid masculinity" that occurs when aspects of femininity are incorporated into hegemonic masculinity, and the implications of this hybridization, for disrupting gender norms (Arxer, 2011; Messner, 2007; Yeung, Stombler, & Wharton, 2006). For this chapter, we wondered in what ways might appropriating hybrid masculinity, that is, walking a mile in high heels, or what Bridges (2010) refers to as "performances of drag," disrupt hegemonic masculinity?

Methods

This qualitative case study sought to describe the purpose and objectives of sexual violence prevention programming targeted at men, and specifically one campus's WaM event, in an effort to understand the goals of the event and the meanings produced at the event.

Context: The Event

Case study research, according to Stake (1995), is a choice of what to study rather than a methodology. The context for this case study is the WaM event, from the planning through implementation, on one campus. WaM is an award-winning international program (Awards & Honors, n.d.); founded in 2001, the WaM campaign self-promotes as the "men's march to stop rape, sexual assault & gender violence" and has grown to a "world-wide movement with tens of thousands of men" walking to raise awareness on college campuses (Walk a Mile in Her Shoes, n.d.). Rooted in the saying, "You can't really understand another person's experience until you've walked a mile in their shoes," WaM asks men "to literally walk one mile in women's high-heeled shoes" in an effort to start a conversation "about something that's really difficult to talk about: gender relations and men's sexualized violence against women" (Walk a Mile in Her Shoes, n.d.). At Great Lakes University (GLU, a pseudonym), WaM adheres to the international campaign's event objectives (stated above and on the WaM website), but also sets some of its own. WaM seeks to create an "enriched experience for those who participate, [to] increase faculty and staff participation, better marketing, future funding sources, and [to] increase shoe donations."

Kamis [first author] served as a member of the seven-person WaM planning team, and attended biweekly meetings from January through April. Other members of the planning team included the director of the GLU sexual violence response center (who also serves as WaM event director), a female graduate assistant who works at the GLU women's center, and four individuals (three men, one woman) recruited from on-campus offices. The event, held in April as part of Sexual Violence Awareness Month programming, occurred on a mild spring day. Participants approached one of three registration tables: one for Greek Life, one for preregistered walkers, and one for those registering on-site. Registrants were men and women, but were routed in different directions after checking in: Men went inside to pick out shoes and participate in games, including limbo, hula hoop, and relay races, while women went to an indoor viewing area to observe the spectacle of men attempting to play games in high heels.

The GLU event began with an opening ceremony that included a welcome speech delivered by the event director, followed by speeches from the undergraduate student government president and an athletic coach. Participants were then directed outside to begin the walk. Most of the 300 participants were White males, of traditional age (18–24), and from Greek life or athletics. Several females also walked, but were not required to wear high heels. At the conclusion of the event, prizes were awarded for the Best Shoe, Highest Heel, First to Fall, Laziest Shoe, Best Runway Walk, and Ugliest Shoe.

Data Collection

Stake (1995) delineates three characteristics of case study research: First, the case is a program, event, process, or one or more individuals. For our purposes, WaM serves as the case. Second, Stake indicates that the case must be bound by time and activity. Our study of WaM began during the initial planning meetings in January and continued through the event in April. Finally, Stake states that data should be collected through various methods over a definitive period of time. In this section, we describe the sources of data collected from January through April 2015.

One note regarding our use of the term "participants." In order to distinguish between study participants and WaM event participants, we refer to those who participated in WaM as "walkers" and all those individuals who were part of this study (from staff on the planning team, to walkers) as "participants." Additionally, we secured human subjects' approval through the institutional review board and all participants gave informed consent to participate.

Data were collected from multiple perspectives over various points of time. Questions, for the electronic questionnaire and interviews, were grounded in the literature and served to elicit responses that would address our research purpose. All interview and questionnaire participants were recruited via email; they were informed that their participation was voluntary, their responses would be confidential, they could skip any questions, and could withdraw their participation at any time. In what follows, we elaborate on the multiple data points:

1. The six planning committee members were invited to participate in interviews before and after the event, and four staff (one woman, three men) consented to participate, completing pre-event interviews during the week prior to the event. The pre-event interview included six questions assessing the staff member's goals for the event, strategies for increasing attendance, which groups s/he targets for the event, and why s/he thinks high heels are a part of the event. These four staff also completed post-event interviews in the two weeks following the event. The post-event interview included five questions assessing the staff member's reflections of the event, whether the event achieved his or her goals, what s/he believes men took away from the event, and what s/he thinks can be done to improve the event.

2. Walkers who preregistered were sent a link to a pre-event questionnaire using Qualtrics. The aim was to reach a larger number of respondents than would be possible through interviews. However, only nine respondents completed the pre-event electronic questionnaire, which included eight open-ended questions asking about the walker's motivation for attendance, perception of the event's purpose and use of high heels, beliefs about feminism, and knowledge of bystander training.

3. All walkers (preregistered and on-site registrants) were invited to reflect on the event and their participation, by either completing a post-event electronic questionnaire or participating in an interview.

    a. Twelve walkers completed the post-event questionnaire, consisting of eight open-ended questions asking about the walkers' reflections of the event, ways in which s/he had been impacted by the event, ways in which s/he will apply what s/he learned at the event to everyday life, and what s/he thinks can be done to improve the event. The post-event questionnaire was made available 3 days following the event and stayed available for 1 week.

b. Five walkers participated in post-event interviews, sharing their reflections on the event, ways in which s/he had been impacted by the event, articulating how s/he will apply what s/he learned at the event to everyday life, and identifying what can be done to improve the event.

4. Kamis maintained a research journal throughout the project and completed field notes of my observations during the event. Specifically, she focused on walkers' interactions, the ways in which speakers and event staff communicated the event's purpose and mission, and the overall logistics of the event.

In sum, data were collected from 30 participants.

Data Analysis

Case study research seeks to answer "how" and "why" questions in an effort to understand a phenomenon. To achieve that end, we employed the analytic technique of explanation building, as suggested by Yin (2003). Explanation-building is an iterative process that poses questions of the data, seeks patterns in the "answers" to those questions, and repeats the analytic process until themes emerge. Braun and Clarke (2006) observe that "no hard-and-fast" rules determine what "counts as a theme"; rather "the 'keyness' of a theme is … whether it captures something important in relation to the overall research question" (p. 82). We additionally employed "theoretical thematic analysis," which explicitly acknowledges and utilizes the researcher's "theoretical or analytic interest" in the subject (Braun & Clarke, 2006 p. 84). This case study was theoretically framed by feminist and gender theories, and these informed interpretive judgments during data analysis. A recognized risk in this analytic process is that a researcher could prematurely impose "keyness" of themes in the data. To combat this, we sought "rival explanations" (Yin, 2003) as themes emerged in order to "see how far they fit or fail to fit the expected categories" (Hartley, 2004, p. 329).

Findings and Discussion

A Worthy Cause to Support

When WaM participants were asked why they participated, most expressed a desire to support a good cause or that they were passionate about the message of the event. For instance, one walker stated "I think it [WaM] has a very powerful message behind it and I have always wanted to participate." Similarly, another walker reported being "passionate about supporting awareness of sexual assault and violence." Still another walker, who self-identified as a member of a student group against sexual assault, indicated being "passionate about the message behind the event." Many staff on the planning team similarly attributed their involvement with the event to their passion for the message. For instance, one staff person stated:

> This was an issue that I just felt really strongly about personally; certainly there's events and there's groups (sic) all over campus that you can get involved in. Whatever you're passionate about, whatever it is, whatever societal cultural issue it is that you really feel passionate about. For me, this is pretty much that issue.

Coupled with supporting a cause about which one was passionate, participants identified "fun" as a motivation for attending the event. For instance, one walker stated, "Besides the fact that it's a worthy cause to support, I saw a photo in the [campus news] with several guys in heels and it looked like it would be fun." Similarly, another walker commented, "I had heard about the event before and it sounded like it was for a really good cause. Plus, I already like to walk around campus so I thought it would be fun!" Another walker shared, "It looked like it would be a fun event, plus it is spreading a great message and I wanted to be a part of it."

Increasing Participation

Ensuring the event would be fun is tied to a goal articulated by the event planning team: increase participation. For instance, one staff person's goal was to "get more students involved, make it bigger, and hopefully reach students and try to make a difference . . . but hopefully we can expand our reach." Similarly, another staff person stated:

> I'd like to see increased turn out . . . So again, if we can increase the numbers from last year, I think that would be a step in the right direction. I would say that's my primary goal, just to see more students involved.
> Additionally, another staff person stated "My goals for the event this year include [increased] participation."

One strategy to increase participation of men was to target, and if possible require, certain male-identified campus organizations to participate (e.g., Greek life and athletics). For instance, one staff person stated, "I'd love to see more people take part in it to make it such a bigger event." Another staff person remarked,

> I know that through traditional students selecting to show up, we know that the group tends to be small, so if we could find other groups with some sense of obligation . . . we can have a more diverse set of individuals there.

Hoping to reach beyond these male-identified groups, another staff person stated,

> Even though we are heavy on the athletes and heavy on Greek life, you kind of have like the bread and butter . . . but then seeing how we can get the participation like that from other groups . . . [m]andating that peer tutors or mentors or other people show up.

Still another staff person saw Greek life's involvement as important for public image, stating,

> Greek life has been huge . . . I know that Greek systems in the overall media are fairly poorly portrayed that [GLU] has been working, . . . but also Greek life has been trying to improve that image and by getting these populations involved, helping bring that awareness in from those who might be most in need.

This targeted recruitment was evident at the three check-in tables during registration: one for preregistered walkers, one for those registering on-site, and one for Greek life. The Greek life table was the most crowded and headed by a Greek life administrator who checked in and awarded "Greek points" to participating fraternities and sororities. The preregistered table was visited mostly by athletes who were required to attend by their coaches. The on-site registration table had the least amount of traffic. However, from Kamis's observation of those individuals who registered on-site, they were generally motivated by extrinsic reasons. For instance, as two students approached the on-site registration table, one said to the other "Will you register with me? I just want a shirt." Another student approached me before registering for the event and asked how to receive proof of attendance for a class. After explaining that proof of attendance would be given at the end of the event, the student sighed and walked away (Kamis, field notes).

With too much focus on increasing participation (and perhaps extrinsic rewards like t-shirts), achievement of other objectives may have been missed. One of those objectives is for men to view themselves as allies in the fight against sexual violence. However, ensuring men's participation seemed to eclipse this objective. For instance, on event day, one staff person observed:

> It's so great to see how many men decided to come out. Women are more connected to the issue, so it's almost their obligation to come. But men, they don't have as much a reason to be here and support this women's issue.

Another staff person stated, "I think the goals are to get more people involved so we can engage and impact more students on campus and faculty and staff."

By constructing men's participation as optional support of a worthy cause, the event missed its opportunity to demonstrate how men can be agents of change and support feminist issues. Instead, men were praised for coming out to support an issue in which their involvement was considered atypical.

Disrupting (or Reinforcing?) Gender and Sexual Inequalities

High heels are central to the event. Heels, along with other articles of clothing (i.e., short skirts, low-cut shirts), have long been culturally associated with sexual promiscuity, and used as rationale for why women might be more susceptible to rape (Terry & Doerge, 1979; Workman & Orr, 1996). Thus, high heels are a symbol of gender and sexual inequalities. However, participants at WaM instead associated high heels with femininity and performing a female identity. For instance, one walker asserted that "high heels are associated with women and what better way to 'walk a mile in their shoes' then by wearing their shoes!" Another walker observed that "high heels are a classic symbol of women and using them helps men understand what it's like to wear them," while still another walker said that high heels "represent a powerful woman." When a photographer asked one walker for a picture in his heels, the individual instantly posed in a feminine fashion, leaning to one side with his hand on his hip. Another walker commented "I'm a pretty woman" while putting on his high heels. In both instances, rather than disrupting social constructions of gender and sexuality, they instead reinforced hegemonic masculinity to show that their effeminate behavior was atypical. In addition, during the opening ceremony, a speaker asked for "girls to come to stage to teach these guys to walk in heels." This not only reinforced gender inequalities, but also supported the binary notion that femininity is exclusively female and men cannot be feminine.

Walkers generally seemed to perceive high heels as a superficial experience of a woman's world. This is especially illustrated in one post-interview with a male walker. While he was reflecting on his experience, he stated, "As soon as I left the [opening ceremony] with the heels, I knew it was gonna be . . . a struggle." Continuing, he said:

> And I was telling . . . some of the friends I was walking with [that] I'll never ever talk about girls in their heels again. . . . I now understand [that] sometimes my friends will be walking around and . . . the girl friends will be . . . in heels [and] sometimes they'd be behind . . . So walking around like, to do this event, you know, it was all in good character, it was fun, challenging, especially when we got to the hill portion of the event . . . There was a sign that said "feel free to take off your heels for the duration of the hill" and I was like, no, I wanna make it.

Another walker also failed to understand the purpose of the heels beyond the literal experience of walking in high heels: "I can't really criticize anymore 'cause it's like, more power to you for like, stomping up and down the esplanade in those stilettos because I can't do it. You know what I mean?" Participants failed to recognize the high-heeled shoes as a symbol of the gender and sexual inequalities that situate women as more susceptible to sexual violence.

Changing Behavior

WaM is one event, among several educational initiatives (i.e., "Green Dot" bystander training), implemented at GLU to increase awareness and mobilize individuals to take action in preventing sexual violence. Green Dot is a national campaign, with a curriculum built on the premise that individuals can develop the skills to prevent sexual violence. Green dots serve to counter the image of red dots spreading across a map, "symbolizing the spread of some terrible epidemic—each tiny red dot representing an individual case" (Green Dot Overview, 2010). By contrast, green dots represent "any behavior, choice, word, or attitude that promotes safety . . . and communicates utter intolerance for violence" (Green Dot Overview, 2010).

To educate about Green Dot, event-planning staff streamed a PowerPoint slideshow during the pre-event activities. However, attendees were participating in games occurring on stage; men were struggling in heels and few people paid attention to the slideshow. During opening ceremony speeches, two speakers referred to the Green Dot campaign and bystander training, but they failed to explain what Green Dot symbolizes. One speaker concluded her speech stating, "The power of Green Dot is simple, red dots are bad, green dots are good. You decide what you want to do in our community," leaving too much unexplained.

This missed opportunity was even more evident when walkers were asked what they know about bystander training; most reported being completely unfamiliar with the training or its purpose. For instance, walkers said, "I do not know what bystander training is" and "I'm not familiar with this term." A few acknowledged that a training is offered at GLU but were unfamiliar with its purpose.

Discussion and Implications

The findings from this study reveal that walkers were largely motivated to participate in WaM in order to support a worthy cause and have fun. Staff had the objectives of increasing participation and engaging men in preventing sexual violence. However, the overemphasis on having fun and increasing participation left the event falling short on developing feminist activist behaviors. Further, the "fun" involved with wearing heels reduced WaM to a parody of *doing* femininity.

High heels were used in a way that reinforced gender and sexual inequalities, and failed to extend men's awareness of sexual violence beyond a "worthy cause" with which they may have episodic involvement. Men's brief foray into performing femininity did not destabilize hegemonic masculinity. WaM instead situated men's involvement with feminist issues as atypical. In light of our findings, some may argue that WaM events should no longer be implemented. However, consistent with those who suggest that hybrid masculinity holds potential to disrupt hegemonic masculinity (Arxer, 2011; Messner, 2007; Yeung et al., 2006), we believe that WaM could blur gender and sexual boundaries and challenge dominant gender norms. Grounded in that belief, we offer some recommendations for practice.

1. Orient planning team members. Too often event planning groups fall prey to the "tyranny of the immediate" (Schroeder & Pike, 2001); for WaM event planning, organizers were too focused on having sufficient numbers of high heels in size 9 or larger and increasing men's participation in the event. While the logistics of event planning are necessary, event organizers should spend time getting oriented to the larger mission and purpose of the event, and could even be assigned to read an article (e.g., Bridges, 2010) in order to initiate dialogue about intended goals (and risks of unintended outcomes) for WaM.

2. Incorporate reflection and dialogue. Reflection and dialogue are well established as important tools to help students recognize and to make sense of identity intersections (Iverson & Seher, 2014; Seher & Iverson, 2015). Lester and Harris (2015) observe that male students must be afforded opportunities to recognize the effects of traditional male socialization and the ways in which "men are traditionally socialized to believe in hegemonic conceptions of masculinity and to adopt sexist, homophobic, and unhealthy attitudes" (p. 163). Event organizers could draft reflective prompts that would be sent to participants who preregister; they could facilitate dialogue at the concluding WaM ceremony; and they could prepare a discussion guide for coaches, advisors, and others who require men to participate, empowering them to conduct pre- and post-event dialogues. This deeper engagement may lead men to view their involvement in WaM, and thus their role in sexual violence prevention, as more than episodic.

3. In whose shoes? GLU changed the name of its event from Walk a Mile in *Her* Shoes, to Walk a Mile in *Their* Shoes, in an effort to be inclusive of gender nonconforming students and to acknowledge that sexual violence is committed by men and women, and that victims are female- and male-identified. However, the use of this gender-neutral/plural pronoun does not alone disrupt dominant gender constructions. Additionally, it fails to illuminate how intersecting identities contribute to varied lived experiences; for instance, poor women of color are "most likely to be in both dangerous intimate relationships *and* dangerous social positions" (Richie, 2000, p. 1136, my emphasis). Event organizers must (further) complicate identity assumptions about who are victims and perpetrators, as well as interrogate how privilege and advantage operate systemically (i.e., that White victims and perpetrators receive benefits from their White skin privilege).

Limitations

We acknowledge some limitations in this study. First, we are aware that asking participants about their motivations for involvement in WaM could yield socially desirable responses, meaning respondents may exaggerate or inflate their strengths and achievements, or deny or trivialize their deficiencies and failures (Ray, 1984). This reality intersects with another limitation, that the gender of the researcher may affect responses. Having a woman investigate an issue that is often viewed as a woman's issue may impact how men respond. Third, the sample (like the campus and the attendees at WaM) was a predominantly White population. Future inquiry is warranted to investigate how dimensions of identity (e.g., race, social class) intersect with gender. Fourth, this inquiry did not include questions regarding homophobia that might arise from homosocial programming. Finally, this is a case study of one campus and thus provides little basis for generalization (Kohlbacher, 2006); however, Yin (2003) observes that we can realize "analytical generalization" from case study research (p. 10), meaning we intend for our findings to "generalize to a theory [by providing] some evidence that supports a theory but not necessarily proves it" (Perry, 1998, p. 790). These limitations point to the need for further inquiry. Men must be engaged in the prevention of sexual violence, and empowered to engage other men in efforts to interrupt and challenge heteronormative masculinity that contributes to rape supportive cultures.

References

Abbey, A., McAuslan, P., Zawacki, T., Clinton, A.M., & Buck, P.O. (2001). Attitudinal, experiential, and situational predictors of sexual assault perpetration. *Journal of Interpersonal Violence, 16*(8), 784–807.

Ahrens, C.E., Rich, M.D., & Ullman, J.B. (2011). Rehearsing for real life: The impact of the InterACT sexual assault prevention program on self-reported likelihood of engaging in bystander interventions. *Violence Against Women, 17*(6), 760–776.

Allan, E.J. (2004). Hazing and gender: Analyzing the obvious. In H. Nuwer (Ed.), *The hazing reader* (pp. 275–294). Bloomington, IN: Indiana University Press.

Aronowitz, T., Lambert, C.A., & Davidoff, S. (2012). The role of rape myth acceptance in the social norms regarding sexual behavior among college students. *Journal of Community Health Nursing, 29*(3), 173–182.

Arxer, S.L. (2011). Hybrid masculine power: Reconceptualizing the relationship between homosociality and hegemonic masculinity. *Humanity & Society, 35*(4), 390–422.

Atherton-Zeman, B. (2009). Minimizing the damage: Male accountability in stopping men's violence against women. *The Voice: A Journal for Battered Women*, 8–13.

Awards & Honors. (n.d.). Available at www.walkamileinhershoes.org/About/awards.html#.VlymkOLG9pk.

Barber, K., & Kretschmer, K. (2013). Walking like a man? *Contexts, 12*(2), 40–45.

Baum, K., & Klaus, P. (2005). *Violent victimization of college students, 1995–2002.* (NCJ Publication No. 206836). Washington, DC: U.S. Department of Justice, Office of Justice Programs, Bureau of Justice Statistics.

Bird, S.R. (1996). Welcome to the men's club: Homosociality and the maintenance of hegemonic masculinity. *Gender & Society*, *10*(2), 120–132.

Braun, V., & Clarke, V. (2006). Using thematic analysis in psychology. *Qualitative Research in Psychology*, *3*, 77–101.

Bridges, T.S. (2010). Men just weren't made to do this: Performances of drag at "walk a mile in her shoes" marches. *Gender & Society*, *24*(1), 5–30.

Brownmiller, S. (2013). *Against our will: Men, women and rape*. New York: Open Road Media.

Carr, J.L., & VanDeusen, K.M. (2004). Risk factors for male sexual aggression on college campuses. *Journal of Family Violence*, *19*(5), 279–289.

Casey, E., & Smith, T. (2010). "How can I not?": Men's pathways to involvement in anti-violence against women work. *Violence Against Women*, *16*(8), 953–973.

Centers for Disease Control and Prevention (CDC). (2014). National intimate partner and sexual violence survey: 2010 summary report.

Chapleau, K.M. (2015). Using masculinity to stop sexual violence: Must women be weak for men to be strong? *Sex Roles*, *73*(1–2), 86–89.

Chekwa, C., Thomas Jr, E., & Jones, V.J. (2013). What are college students' perceptions about campus safety? *Contemporary Issues in Education Research (CIER)*, *6*(3), 325–332.

Coker, A.L., Cook-Craig, P.G., Williams, C.M., Fisher, B.S., Clear, E.R., Garcia, L.S., & Hegge, L.M. (2011). Evaluation of green dot: An active bystander intervention to reduce sexual violence on college campuses. *Violence Against Women*, *17*(6), 777–796.

Connell, R.W. (1987). *Gender and power*. New York: Polity Press.

Crenshaw, K. (1991). Mapping the margins: Intersectionality, identity politics, and violence against women of color. *Stanford Law Review*, *43*(6), 1241–1299.

Daigle, L.E., Fisher, B.S., & Stewart, M. (2009). The effectiveness of sexual victimization prevention among college students: A summary of "what works." *Victims and Offenders*, *4*(4), 398–404.

Deming, M.E., Covan, E.K., Swan, S.C., & Billings, D.L. (2013). Exploring rape myths, gendered norms, group processing, and the social context of rape among college women: A qualitative analysis. *Violence Against Women*, *19*(4), 465–485.

Flood, M. (2011). Involving men in efforts to end violence against women. *Men and Masculinities*, *14*(3), 358–377.

Flood, M., & Pease, B. (2009). Factors influencing attitudes to violence against women. *Trauma, Violence & Abuse*, *10*(2), 125–142.

Foubert, J.D. (2000). The longitudinal effects of a rape-prevention program on fraternity men's attitudes, behavioral intent, and behavior. *Journal of American College Health*, *48*(4), 158–163.

Foubert, J.D., & Marriott, K.A. (1997). Effects of a sexual assault peer education program on men's belief in rape myths. *Sex Roles*, *36*(3–4), 259–268.

Foubert, J.D., & Perry, B.C. (2007). Creating lasting attitude and behavior change in fraternity members and male student athletes the qualitative impact of an empathy-based rape prevention program. *Violence Against Women*, *13*(1), 70–86.

Fulu, E., Warner, X., Miedema, S., Jewkes, R., Roselli, T., & Lang, J. (2013). *Why do some men use violence against women and how can we prevent it? Quantitative findings from the United Nations Multi-Country Study on men and violence in Asia and the Pacific*. Bangkok: UNDP, UNFPA, UN Woman and UNV. Available at www.partners4prevention.org/sites/default/files/resources/p4p-report.pdf.

Gerson, J.M., & Peiss, K. (1985). Boundaries, negotiation, consciousness: Reconceptualising gender relations. *Social Problems, 32*(4), 317–331.

Gibson-Graham, J.K. (1996). *The end of capitalism (as we know it): A feminist critique of political economy.* Cambridge, MA: Blackwell Publishers.

Gidycz, C.A., Orchowski, L.M., & Berkowitz, A.D. (2011). Preventing sexual aggression among college men: An evaluation of a social norms and bystander intervention program. *Violence Against Women, 17*(6), 720–742.

Green Dot Overview. (2010). *Green Dot Etcetera.* Available at www.livethegreendot.com/gd_overview.html.

Groth, A.N., & Birnbaum, H.J. (2013). *Men who rape: The psychology of the offender.* New York: Springer.

Hamilton, M., & Yee, J. (1990). Rape knowledge and propensity to rape. *Journal of Research in Personality, 24*(1), 111–122.

Hammond, E.M., Berry, M.A., & Rodriguez, D.N. (2011). The influence of rape myth acceptance, sexual attitudes, and belief in a just world on attributions of responsibility in a date rape scenario. *Legal and Criminological Psychology, 16*(2), 242–252.

Hartley, J. (2004). Case study research. In C. Cassell, & G. Symon (Eds.), *Essential guide to qualitative methods in organizational research* (pp. 323–333). Thousand Oaks, CA: Sage.

Hollander, J.A. (2014). Does self-defense training prevent sexual violence against women? *Violence Against Women, 20*(3), 252–269.

Iverson, S., & Seher, C. (2014). Using theatre to change attitudes toward lesbian, gay, and bisexual students. *Journal of LGBT Youth, 11*(1), 40–61.

Karjane, H.M., Fisher, B.S., & Cullen, F.T. (2005). *Sexual assault on campus: What colleges and universities are doing about it?* Washington, DC: Office of Justice Programs, U.S. Department of Justice.

Kaufman, M. (2001). Building a movement of men working to end violence against women. *Development, 44*(3), 9–14.

Kimmel, M. (1995). *Manhood in America: A cultural history.* New York: Free Press.

Kimmel, M. (1986). Introduction: Toward men's studies. *American Behavioral Scientist, 29*(5), 517–529.

Kohlbacher, F. (2006). The use of qualitative content analysis in case study research. *Forum: Qualitative Social Research, 7*(1), Art. 21. Available at www.qualitative-research.net/index.php/fqs/index.

Krebs, C.P., Lindquist, C.H., Warner, T.D., Fisher, B.S., & Martin, S.L. (2009). College women's experiences with physically forced, alcohol-or other drug-enabled, and drug-facilitated sexual assault before and since entering college. *Journal of American College Health, 57*(6), 639–649.

Langhinrichsen-Rohling, J., Foubert, J.D., Brasfield, H.M., Hill, B., & Shelley-Tremblay, S. (2011). The men's program: Does it impact college men's self-reported bystander efficacy and willingness to intervene? *Violence Against Women,* 1–17.

Lazar, M. (Ed.). (2005). *Feminist critical discourse analysis: Gender, power and ideology in discourse.* New York: Palgrave Macmillan.

Lederer, L. (Ed.). (1980). *Take back the night: Women on pornography.* New York: William Morrow Co.

Lester, J., & Harris III, F. (2015). Engaging undergraduate women and men. In S.J. Quaye, & S.R. Harper (Eds.), *Student engagement in higher education: Theoretical perspectives and practical approaches for diverse populations* (2nd ed., pp. 149–170). New York: Routledge.

Lorber, J. (2004). "Night to his day": The social construction of gender. In L. Richardson, V. Taylor, & N. Whittier (Eds.), *Feminist frontiers* (6th ed., pp. 33–51). Boston, MA: McGraw Hill.

McMahon, S. (2010). Rape myth beliefs and bystander attitudes among incoming college students. *Journal of American College Health, 59*(1), 3–11.

McMahon, S., Postmus, J.L., Warrener, C., & Koenick, R.A. (2014). Utilizing peer education theater for the primary prevention of sexual violence on college campuses. *Journal of College Student Development, 55*(1), 78–85.

Macomber, K.C. (2012). *Men as allies: Mobilizing men to end violence against women* (Unpublished doctoral dissertation). North Carolina, NC: North Carolina State University.

Masters, N.T. (2010). "My strength is not for hurting": Men's anti-rape websites and their construction of masculinity and male sexuality. *Sexualities, 13*(1), 33–46.

Messner, M.A. (2007). The masculinity of the governator: Muscle and compassion in American politics. *Gender & Society, 21*(4), 461–480.

Moynihan, M.M., Banyard, V.L., Arnold, J.S., Eckstein, R.P., & Stapleton, J.G. (2011). Sisterhood may be powerful for reducing sexual and intimate partner violence: An evaluation of the bringing in the bystander in-person program with sorority members. *Violence Against Women, 17*(6), 703–719.

Moynihan, M.M., Banyard, V.L., Arnold, J.S., Eckstein, R.P., & Stapleton, J.G. (2010). Engaging intercollegiate athletes in preventing and intervening in sexual and intimate partner violence. *Journal of American College Health, 59*(3), 197–204.

Moynihan, M.M., Banyard, V.L., Cares, A.C., Potter, S.J., Williams, L.M., & Stapleton, J.G. (2015). Encouraging responses in sexual and relationship violence prevention: What program effects remain 1 year later? *Journal of Interpersonal Violence, 30*(1), 110–132.

Muehlenhard, C.L., & Linton, M.A. (1987). Date rape and sexual aggression in dating situations: Incidence and risk factors. *Journal of Counseling Psychology, 34*(2), 186–196.

Murphy, M.J. (2009). Can "men" stop rape? Visualizing gender in the "My Strength is Not for Hurting" rape prevention campaign. *Men and Masculinities, 12*(1), 113–130.

O'Donohue, W., Yeater, E.A., & Fanetti, M. (2003). Rape prevention with college males: The roles of rape myth acceptance, victim empathy, and outcome expectancies. *Journal of Interpersonal Violence, 18*(5), 513–531.

Orchowski, L.M., Gidycz, C.A., & Raffle, H. (2008). Evaluation of a sexual assault risk reduction and self-defense program: A prospective analysis of a revised protocol. *Psychology of Women Quarterly, 32*(2), 204–218.

Paul, L.A., & Gray, M.J. (2011). Sexual assault programming on college campuses: Using social psychological belief and behavior change principles to improve outcomes. *Trauma, Violence, & Abuse, 12*(2), 99–109.

Perry, C. (1998). Processes of a case study methodology for postgraduate research in marketing. *European Journal of Marketing, 32*(9/10), 785–802.

Phipps, A. (2010). Violent and victimized bodies: Sexual violence policy in England and Wales. *Critical Social Policy, 30*(3), 359–383.

Piccigallo, J.R., Lilley, T.G., & Miller, S.L. (2012). "It's cool to care about sexual violence": Men's experiences with sexual assault prevention. *Men and Masculinities, 15*(5), 507–525.

Ray, J.J. (1984). The reliability of short social desirability scales. *The Journal of Social Psychology, 123*, 133–4.

Richie, B. (2000). A Black feminist reflection on the antiviolence movement. *Signs, 25*(4), 1133–1137.

Rosenbaum, A., & O'Leary, K.D. (1981). Marital violence: Characteristics of abusive couples. *Journal of Consulting and Clinical Psychology, 49*(1), 63.

Sawyer, R.G., Thompson, E.E., & Chicorelli, A.M. (2002). Rape myth acceptance among intercollegiate student athletes: A preliminary examination. *American Journal of Health Studies, 18*(1), 19–25.

Schroeder, C.C., & Pike, G.R. (2001). The scholarship of application in student affairs. *Journal of College Student Development, 42*(4), 342–55.

Schumacher, J.A., Feldbau-Kohn, S., Slep, A.M.S., & Heyman, R.E. (2001). Risk factors for male-to-female partner physical abuse. *Aggression and Violent Behavior, 6*(2), 281–352.

Searles, P., & Follansbee, P. (1984). Self-defense for women: Translating theory into practice. *Frontiers: A Journal of Women Studies, 8*(1), 65–70.

Seher, C., & Iverson, S.V. (2015). From dialogue to action: Consciousness-raising with academic mothers. *NASPA Journal About Women in Higher Education, 8*(1), 17–28.

Stake, R.E. (1995). *The art of case study research.* Thousand Oaks, CA: Sage.

Sweetman, C. (Ed.). (1997). *Men and masculinity.* Oxford, UK: Oxfam.

Telch, C.F., & Lindquist, C.U. (1984). Violent versus nonviolent couples: A comparison of patterns. *Psychotherapy: Theory, Research, Practice, Training, 21*(2), 242.

Terry, R.L., & Doerge, S. (1979). Dress, posture, and setting as additive factors in subjective probabilities of rape. *Perceptual and Motor Skills, 48*(3), 903–906.

Tevis, T., & Griffen, J. (2014). Absent voices: Intersectionality and college students with physical disabilities. *Journal of Progressive Policy & Practice, 2*(3), 239–254.

Urback, R. (2013). Theo Fleury's "Victor Walk" brings the silent suffering of male abuse victims into the open. *National Post* [online]. Available at http://news.nationalpost.com/full-comment/robyn-urback-theo-fleurys-victor-walk-brings-the-silent-suffering-of-male-abuse-victims-into-the-open.

Walk a Mile in Her Shoes. (n.d.). Available at www.walkamileinhershoes.org/.

Weitlauf, J.C., Smith, R.E., & Cervone, D. (2000). Generalization effects of coping-skills training: influence of self-defense training on women's efficacy beliefs, assertiveness, and aggression. *Journal of Applied Psychology, 85*(4), 625.

West, C., & Zimmerman, D.H. (1987). Doing gender. *Gender and Society, 1*(2), 125–151.

Wooten, S.C. (2015). Heterosexist discourses: How feminist theory shaped campus sexual violence policy. In S.C. Wooten & R.W. Mitchell (Eds.), *The crisis of campus sexual violence: Critical perspectives on prevention and response* (pp. 33–51). New York: Routledge.

Workman, J.E., & Orr, R.L. (1996). Clothing, sex of subject, and rape myth acceptance as factors affecting attributions about an incident of acquaintance rape. *Clothing and Textiles Research Journal, 14*(4), 276–284.

Yeung, K., Stombler, M., & Wharton, R. (2006). Making men in gay fraternities: Resisting and reproducing multiple dimensions of hegemonic masculinity. *Gender & Society, 20*(1), 5–31.

Yin, R.K. (2003). *Case study research: Design and methods* (Vol. 5, 3rd ed). Thousand Oaks, CA: Sage.

PART III

Ending Rape Culture as a Campus-Wide Mission

6

CREATING A CULTURE SHIFT IN RESPONSE TO SEXUAL VIOLENCE ON COLLEGE CAMPUSES

Matthew R. Shupp, Stephanie Erdice, and Cecil Howard

The "Dear Colleague" Letter by the Office of Civil Rights (OCR) in 2011 to institutions of higher education calling for more effective and efficient handling of allegations of sexual misconduct sent shock waves through institutions of higher education in America, as many had to acknowledge they were nowhere near on par with where they should have been, and felt unprepared to meet even the basic requirements within a reasonable time frame. Financial constraints, lack of intellectual capital, and an overall ignorance to these new mandates contributed to institutional paralysis across most college campuses. Over five years later, the U.S. Department of Education has sent out several more guiding documents, has initiated investigations against hundreds of institutions, and, likewise, has resolved many complaints via resolution agreements for those institutions found to not be in compliance with federal mandates.

Unfortunately, many institutions still feel overwhelmed, understaffed, and under-resourced, and, as a result, dread the thought of an OCR review. Some institutions have enacted innovative collaborative measures to address their Title IX responsibilities, and yet continue to feel underprepared to adequately respond in a swift and decisive manner should an OCR investigation occur. Compliance with federal mandates is essential to ensuring campus safety for all students. The OCR has provided campuses with clear guidelines and resources to reach that goal, and administrators must use those directives to develop comprehensive sexual misconduct policies and resources that reflect their own campuses' mission and culture.

This chapter highlights how one institution's use of federal laws, regulations, and guidelines provided by Title IX, the Violence Against Women Act (VAWA), and the Clery Act guides its campus beyond compliance toward a cultural shift where students have equal access to education without fear of sexual violence. It is broken up into three distinct, yet interconnected, parts. We first share a brief overview and historical context of how colleges and universities arrived at our current state of affairs. This is accomplished by providing a brief historical overview of the OCR's Dear Colleague Letter, federal mandates imposed through stricter interpretation of Title IX as it relates to institutions' responses to alleged cases of sexual misconduct, as well as other mandates that guide institutional practice.

Next, we discuss Shippensburg University of Pennsylvania's efforts to maintain compliance and, most importantly, establish a proactive call to action as well as what it takes to ensure its success. This 7,000-student university has, through a combined effort involving representatives from across campus, built a campus engagement program designed to end sexual assault and domestic violence on our campus. Different perspectives from areas such as campus activities, the Women's Center, the faculty union, Dean of Student's office, athletics, residence life, facilities, information technology, and many other areas helped strengthen the program and give the success of its implementation to the campus in general and not a specific area. Although Title IX oversight is the obligation of one person or office, we focus on the strategy of adopting a holistic approach to eradicating sexual misconduct through collaborative efforts throughout the campus.

The final section builds upon Shippensburg's best practices where the authors share recommendations for other universities to implement a proactive approach and to move beyond compliance. We challenge staff, faculty, and administrators to create an ethos of collaboration where members are dedicated to shifting their campus culture through educating and empowering their community to end sexual misconduct.

The content of this chapter is presented though three lenses: the Director of Social Equity and Title IX Coordinator, a faculty member and college student affairs educator, and the Director of the Women's Center. The Director of Social Equity discusses his background in practicing law in the public sector and the importance of having a "legal mind" on a college campus. The faculty member, an Assistant Professor in a CACREP[1]-accredited Counseling and College Student Personnel graduate counseling program, highlights "theory to practice" in action, including inviting guest speakers to class to discuss the lived experience and "real-world" implications of law and campus policy. Finally, the Director of the Women's Center highlights her work as a victim advocate and campus-wide educational coordinator.

A campus that cares about preventing campus sexual assault will develop a holistic approach toward education. Our chapter explores such campus-wide initiatives and collaborations at a macro level as well as at the department and individual (micro) level.

Shippensburg University of Pennsylvania: One University's Approach

Benefits of Legal Expertise for Title IX Compliance

In light of the Department of Education's enhanced enforcement of Title IX and sexual harassment complaints, Shippensburg University of Pennsylvania, a mid-sized, public institution and member of Pennsylvania's State System of Higher Education (PASSHE), assigned its Title IX responsibilities to its Office of Social Equity, and recently appointed an experienced civil rights attorney as the executive director of that office. Job announcements for Title IX Coordinator positions on college and university campuses rarely, if at all, limit the qualifications to law graduates exclusively. In fact, many will require Masters, PhDs, or other terminal degrees. Over the past few years, however, several colleges and universities have begun the practice of indicating a preference for the Juris Doctorate degree in their job announcements. In some instances, the Title IX Coordinator's role is held by attorneys in the universities' general counsel office. Shippensburg University of Pennsylvania's Title IX Coordinator holds a 30-year license to practice law, has litigated many civil rights cases, teaches civil rights courses, and develops and conducts trainings for investigating civil rights cases.

The move to assign an attorney over Title IX allegations and other instances of sexually harassing behavior places the university in a position for an immediate preliminary review of alleged sexual misconduct—from a legal perspective—of not only Title IX matters, but also matters arising under other federal law such as Clery and the VAWA. Because Title IX is a legal provision and is impacted almost exclusively by legal principles, the assignment of Title IX duties to a legally trained professional on the part of the institution was intentional and provides the necessary lens upon which to examine whether or not the university is in full compliance with the mandates set forth by the OCR.

Hiring Practices for Title IX Coordinators

Although the core of Title IX is a mere 37 words, "No person in the United States shall, on the basis of sex, be excluded from participation in, be denied the benefits of, or be subjected to discrimination under any education program or activity receiving federal financial assistance" (20 U.S.C. §1681[2]), its impact has spawned many Dear Colleague letters and substantial guidelines from the OCR that have attempted to explain various provisions of the law, as well as extensive case law that has resulted from numerous court challenges. Additionally, OCR's enhanced enforcement of this area deems it essential that institutions carefully dot all I's and cross all T's. This need for constant legal attention to Title IX concerns has set off a trend with major institutions across the country hiring attorneys to fulfill the role of Title IX Coordinator.

Recently, Florida State University hired an attorney with an extensive background in sexual harassment, sexual assault, and domestic violence in the wake of rape allegations made against a prominent football player. Similarly, UCLA hired an experienced civil rights attorney and litigator to handle its Title IX functions. Brown University did the same with the hiring of an attorney with substantial victim advocacy and Title IX compliance experience. Edinboro University of Pennsylvania, a sister campus to Shippensburg University of Pennsylvania and member of PASSHE, hired a former judge to handle its Title IX responsibilities. Shippensburg University of Pennsylvania followed suit with the hiring of its new Title IX Coordinator who has extensive legal training, not only in the various federal civil rights laws such as Title VI, Title VII, Title IX, ADA, etc., but also with litigating civil rights complaints and advising boards and senior officials.

These attorneys not only attend conferences and trainings relative to Title IX and Title VII of the Civil Rights Act, but they also attend law-related conferences and engage in discussions of these federal laws with practicing attorneys outside of the higher education environment. They then return to their respective campuses armed with not only the administrative and regulatory knowledge of what the law requires, but also with a good understanding of critical nuances and salient legal distinctions of how the laws are applied. This extensive level of legal background only adds to the degree of protection an institution affords its students, staff, and faculty. Additionally, that level of experience affords great protection for the institution from potential liability.

Interestingly, it appears that attorneys hired as Title IX Coordinators across the country are not coming from within the ranks of higher education. Instead, it appears that many, like Shippensburg University of Pennsylvania's Title IX Coordinator, are leveraging extensive civil rights experience within government, judicial, and administrative bodies, and transferring this knowledge to higher education. This approach to Title IX Coordinator hiring could factor heavily in effective disposition of claims and other matters arising under Title IX. Legal-minded Title IX Coordinators can apply their training and skills, and work in conjunction with other entities on campus such as student affairs offices, women's centers, and residence hall staff to effectively resolve matters.

Cross-Campus Collaborations

A prime example of efficiency and the effectiveness of this collaborative relationship between the Title IX Coordinator and other campus entities was seen when Shippensburg University of Pennsylvania's Title IX Coordinator, in conjunction with the university's faculty union and ad hoc committee members, spearheaded an effort to address faculty reporting concerns of alleged Title IX offenses. The committee began by reviewing the basics of the Title IX reporting requirements and expressed the important goals of this policy. The purpose of the committee was not to undermine Title IX's importance, but rather to share information and develop questions that would help faculty navigate classroom assignments and curriculum issues related to Title IX.

To our campus community, OCR's directives appeared clear and direct. Yet, confusion abounded when nuanced situations presented themselves. Several questions emerged that required investigation: When, specifically, must past sexual misconduct or child abuse be reported? Would class assignments fall under the "public awareness events" criteria for not reporting? What is the most appropriate response when a student discloses experiences with sexual assault or domestic violence as part of a self-reflective assignment? Campus faculty ruminated on the importance of explicitly sharing our role as mandated reporters with students; yet, it was equally difficult and confusing to balance the reporting requirements with the important goal of helping students engage in self-awareness and self-expression.

After addressing the interests of many entities, the university, as well as the other PASSHE institutions, received legal clearance from the PASSHE legal office to proceed with potential solutions. One of these solutions was the inclusion of a syllabi statement for all faculty members to include in their course syllabi and review at the beginning of each semester. Shippensburg University of Pennsylvania's collaborations resulted in greater transparency between all members of the campus community, including the institution's students gaining a firmer grasp on faculty members' responsibility to campus safety both inside and outside of the classroom.

Training Future Student Affairs Practitioners from a Social Justice Framework

ACPA-College Student Educators International, a leading higher education organization, identified sexual violence on college campuses as a social justice issue (ACPA, 2015a, b). In complementary fashion, the counseling profession cites social justice as an emerging societal concern within the profession (Gladding, 2013). Student affairs professionals must be acutely aware of salient laws and policies that guide their practice, especially as it relates to sexual violence on college campuses. Shippensburg University of Pennsylvania's Department of Counseling and College Student Personnel's curriculum emphasizes a social justice framework. For example, the program requires all graduate students enrolled in the college student personnel specialization to complete an institutional environmental assessment assessing campus safety. This approach follows the program's guiding philosophy of training our students as helping professionals and educators from a student development perspective.

Our graduate counseling program utilizes an approach where faculty synthesize and integrate overarching practical concepts into every dialogue rather than treating practical application of the material as a separate, limited component of the program experience. In other words, faculty do not address sexual violence on college campuses on special days. Rather, concepts of safety, social justice, and inclusion are infused across our curriculum. In this way, students are encouraged to think critically and identify how these concepts factor into their lived experience. For example, all students within our graduate program must accumulate 700 hours of practical experience in the form of three separate internships (Practicum in Counseling, Field I, Field II). The first experience, Practicum in Counseling, is a 100-hour field-based placement in an institutional setting providing in-depth supervised professional experiences. Field I and II serve as the culminating practical experience where students spend 600 hours (over two, 15-week semesters) in a professional setting appropriate to their career interests. The supervision of these student interns is deliberate, intentional, and shared between faculty and site supervisors, where each student is evaluated on appropriate technical skills. Student learning outcomes, cocreated between site supervisor and student, are grounded in the ACPA Professional Competencies (2015a, b), most specifically the competency of Pluralism and Inclusion. This competency is described as the professions' need for increased levels of multicultural competency, specifically where "all views are valued" so as to create a pluralistic campus valuing "the importance of culture" (2015a, p. 14).

The concept of utilizing a social justice framework also extends to content classes. Last summer, the department of Counseling and College Student Personnel offered an elective entitled Current Issues in Higher Education. The course focused "on the identification and analysis of contemporary issues, innovations, and trends facing student personnel administrators in higher education," where high impact practices and considerations for student success were discussed (Course Outlines Website, n.d.). Further, the course discussed current issues practitioners face in the field. The course was intentionally designed in a seminar format, where every other week featured a guest speaker. The class content for the prior week was student-driven based upon current issues impacting higher education. Topics included enrollment trends, campus safety and concealed weapons, Fraternity and Sorority Life, and campus climates including social justice issues in relation to Title IX and sexual assault. Guest speakers included the Associate Vice President for Enrollment Management, a member of the university's Campus Police, the Director of Fraternity and Sorority Life, co-chair of the university's LGBTQ+[3] Concerns Committee, Director of the Women's Center, and Director of the Office of Social Equity, both coauthors of this article. In this format, students were able to derive meaning of the class content by hearing the lived experience from the guest speakers, helping each student understand the role these positions play in campus safety and ending interpersonal violence on college campuses. By infusing campus culture challenges into the higher education curriculum, we are broadening their concept of sexual misconduct and advancing the skills of future higher education practitioners.

From Compliance to Culture Change

The key to ending the epidemic of sexual violence on college and university campuses is creating a culture shift, moving from reacting to federal mandates to creating a proactive campus culture focused on student education, wellness, and overall safety. We espouse that a large majority of campus constituents care about the issue of sexual assault and domestic violence. Many faculty and staff understand the impact interpersonal violence can have on a student, both in their personal life and in their ability to succeed academically. Therefore, everyone has a stake in reducing the numbers of incidents of interpersonal violence on college campuses. However, because of the complicated nature of these crimes and violations of university codes of conduct, few people feel adequately prepared to help victims of sexual assault or domestic violence. In addition, many persons do not have a visible way to show their support for ending these crimes.

Evaluating your Sexual Misconduct Adjudication Process

Before the release of the Dear Colleague Letter in 2011, Shippensburg University of Pennsylvania had a long history of supporting victims of sexual misconduct and adjudicating these breeches through their Student Code of Conduct. Although our processes were rooted in equality for both parties, one significant flaw was that sexual misconduct incidents were adjudicated through the same means as other cases, like alcohol violations or incidents of academic dishonesty. Special consideration was not always given to the complexities of sexual misconduct, its disproportional effect on cisgender, heterosexual women, and women of color, and the barriers present for victims who were cisgender, heterosexual men, and members of the LGBTQ+ community.

Over the last 5 years, trainings, seminars, and national resources have informed many of Shippensburg University of Pennsylvania's new procedures and policies for adjudicating these specific violations, allowing for a thorough process that respects the healing practice of the victim, while, at the same time, granting adequate due process for all parties. The new sexual misconduct adjudication process was crafted primarily by the Dean of Students, the Director of Student Conduct, the Director of the Women's Center, and the university's general counsel. Input was also sought from the Director of Social Equality, victims, respondents, and faculty and staff members. The expertise of these parties, coupled with additional trainings and resources, allowed the university to create a process trusted by the campus community. Support from the president and his cabinet as well as from governing boards of the institution, including student senate and the university forum, paved the way for change in our process. With a foundation of a fair and thorough sexual misconduct adjudication process, the campus community is empowered to swiftly and effectively address sexual misconduct.

The most significant change to the method of adjudicating sexual misconduct cases was the addition of an independent investigator to compile the facts of the alleged incident. This step sets this procedure apart from other conduct violations. In the past, the complainant—the university's terminology for a student alleging a sexual misconduct violation—was asked to recount their story in front of a three-person code of conduct board with the respondent—the terminology for a student accused of a code of conduct violation—present. This created an intimidating environment for the victim and a "he said/she said" dynamic. In these situations, it was often hard for victims to tell a complete story and, many times, they were revictimized. In the new process, instead of directly meeting with a board of three strangers, the complainant meets with trained investigators. These investigators are members of the faculty and staff that have volunteered for this position and undergo special training on appropriate questioning, trauma, sexual misconduct, and due process. After hearing the student's story, they begin to mine the story for more facts and details. These crucial details may lead investigators to speak with students, staff, and other pertinent witnesses that interacted with the student before or after the incident. This approach creates an environment that is much more conducive for creating a complete story from the complainant.

The investigators' interview with the respondent mirrors this process. The role of the investigators is to be fair and impartial. They are compiling a comprehensive document that includes facts of the incident that is passed onto the Student Code of Conduct Board. Before the hearing with the board, members of the board review the entire document, which may include witness statements, copies of pictures, videos, and social media posts. As a result, the students directly involved in the alleged incident do not have to retell their stories; they only have to answer the board's questions. This process has significantly reduced the length of time of hearings, resulting in swift and efficient resolutions, and relieves, at least partially, the pressure placed on the complainant.

The process respects the healing process of the victim, primarily by making it his or her choice to participate in the proceedings. In addition to this important step, the process creates a comfortable environment for the victim throughout the process. Scheduling meetings in a place the victim feels comfortable, accommodating his or her schedule, taking special care to make sure the victim does not come in contact with the respondent, and using technology to accommodate the needs of either party are just a few of the ways that Shippensburg University of Pennsylvania seeks to be sensitive to the victim's healing process. It is inevitable that the complainant will come in contact with several people throughout the investigation. Working to minimize that number and ensure those persons, Student Code of Conduct Board Members, investigators, office managers, the Director of Student Code of Conduct, among others are well trained in the effects of sexual misconduct and trauma are an important part of the new process.

After receiving feedback from victims on this new process, the Office of Student Conduct inserted several steps in the process, which included updating the students involved in what was happening with their case. The new process includes several face-to-face meetings with a member of the Student Code of Conduct staff to explain and prepare the students for a hearing. These meetings are optional, but allow both the complainant and respondent a chance to ask questions about the process and review material that will be submitted to the hearing board.

Reflecting upon Shippensburg University of Pennsylvania's approach to investigation and adjudication of sexual misconduct cases, we encourage institutions of higher education to continually evaluate their own practices. This process begins by continually asking reflective questions such as "Why are we doing X a certain way?" and "Might there be a better approach to X?" The faith your campus community has in your investigation and adjudication policies and procedures is key to creating an effective culture shift on your campus. Not only does the process need to comply with the laws and guidelines for the OCR, but it is also essential that faculty, staff, and students trust the process.

Using a Messaging Campaign to Unite Your Institution's Language

Students not only need to know if institutions of higher education are compliant with the regulations set forth by the OCR, but they also need to know faculty, staff, and administration care about their safety, well-being, and academic success. Shippensburg University of Pennsylvania engages in a variety of practices that illustrates our ethic of care. How will your students know that you care about sexual assault and violence prevention? Answering this question is the first step in shifting your campus culture and working toward eliminating sexual misconduct from your campus community.

One of the questions Shippensburg University of Pennsylvania struggled with was how to convey that the university took the issue of campus sexual violence seriously. Many people in our campus community felt and continue to feel strongly about advocating for an end to sexual assault and domestic violence. Athletic administration, facilities staff, professors, deans, student government officers, fraternity men and sorority women, department chairs, and many more were speaking out about these crimes, but often only in low, rumbling murmurs. What we needed was a rallying cry—a way to unite our voices.

Whether it is a national or international campaign customized to fit your campus, or a program designed and implemented by your own students, its effectiveness will hinge on campus advocates' ability to take a close look at your own campus and match it with a public awareness effort that will be accepted by your community. We found our voice through the national "No More" campaign.

The national No More campaign began in 2013 as an effort to bring global attention to the issues of sexual assault and domestic violence. A website, public service announcements featuring popular celebrities, and a social media campaign quickly spread this simple and effective message. The symbol and slogan were adopted by states and other organizations to help spread the word about resources and the No More mission (No More, n.d.). Shippensburg University's Women's Center Director contacted the No More campaign in 2014 shortly after its own launch and asked permission to adopt it on our campus. With an enthusiastic "yes" from their headquarters and a small group of advocates on our campus, Shippensburg University of Pennsylvania launched this program at its annual Take Back the Night Rally in April of 2014.

Take Back the Night is the cornerstone event of Shippensburg University of Pennsylvania's Sexual Assault Awareness Month Programming. It's a rally, march, and speak-out. Each year at the rally, administrators, students, and community members pledge their commitment to ending sexual assault and intimate partner abuse on our campus. We then march across campus chanting antisexual assault mantras and waving rally signs. We conclude the night with a speak-out, allowing anyone to speak about their experience with and survival of violence. Beginning in 2014, we introduced the campus to the Ship Says No More. One year later, the entire rally was dedicated to this theme and we were able to report on the progress the campaign made in just 12 months, including debuting our own Ship Says No More video.

This approach imparted to our university two important educational features. First, it gave us a visible avenue to show current and future students and their families that we care about this issue. It also allowed us to centralize all of our information pertaining to sexual misconduct in one easily accessible and understandable website. Information about resources, both on campus and off campus, reporting procedures, definitions, how to help a friend, and our code of conduct procedure are all outlined on this site. We have also included pictures of students, faculty, and staff holding Ship Says No More signs and taking the pledge to be a part of ending violence in our community. In the spring of 2015, we created our own Ship Says No More video with the help of our campus newspaper. This video features faculty, staff, and students from around campus, including the Dean of Students and the President of the University. This video is the opening page of the website and is used in all our prevention and education programs. These primary prevention methods assist us in intervening before the violence occurs and help us address the underlying causes that contribute to sexual misconduct (OAESA, 2014). Using tools like these to boost primary prevention efforts can have a solid impact on shifting the culture of a campus, eradicating rape culture and sexual assault myths, and empowering the campus with an educated perspective on how to prevent sexual misconduct.

The Ship Says No More program originated in our Women's Center, but it quickly became an education and prevention tool available to the entire campus. For example, the Student Activities Office bought 2,000 cellphone wallets with our Ship Says No More graphic to distribute during welcome fairs and other events around campus, so members of our campus community could show their support for the program. Another important example centers on the faculty union. The social justice faculty union subcommittee was responsible for the design of the syllabi statement mentioned earlier in this article. Though not mandatory to include in course syllabi, many faculty have included it in their syllabi and added it to their checklist of items to review during their first class. Within the first few weeks of the launch of the program, Ship Says No More posters were distributed to every corner of campus, including on bulletin boards, faculty and staff office doors, the entrance to the Dean of Student's office, residence halls, and dining service facilities.

The Ship Says No More campaign proved and continues to prove to be an effective pedagogy for sexual misconduct education. It integrates the message throughout students' campus experience and is inclusive of intersecting identities. The campaign is simple and can be easily adapted to target specialized student groups. These are all recommendations and best practices for prevention education learning goals (Beyond Compliance, ACPA, 2015a, b). Shippensburg University of Pennsylvania is a place where sexual assault and domestic violence are not accepted and this message has been infused into the fabric of the institutional culture. Before students arrive for classes in the fall, during orientation and fall welcome week, when they join a sports team or fraternity or sorority, and during their first day of class are all times they are hearing the message that Shippensburg University of Pennsylvania says no more to violence and sexual assault.

Despite the OCR's guidance to help institutions of higher education create safe and inviting places for their campus communities, sexual assault and violence continues to exist in record high numbers. This chapter addressed sexual misconduct education through the lens of creating a culture shift through campus collaborations. Eradicating sexual violence on college campuses cannot rest solely on one administrator or office. In order to affect long-lasting and systemic change, all members of the campus community have a responsibility of creating a safe learning environment for all members. There is much work to be done and the stakes are simply too high not to come together to end sexual violence on our campuses.

Notes

1   Council for the Accreditation of Counseling and Related Educational Programs.
2   Title 20 U.S. Code Chapter 38—Discrimination Based on Sex or Blindness.
3   LGBTQ+ (lesbian, gay, bisexual, transgender, and queer) as an initialism is an attempt at recognizing myriad of complex and intersecting identities within this diverse population. Yet, it is not an entirely-inclusive term. Individuals with a spectrum of additional identities may feel further marginalized with the singular, overarching usage of LGBTQ+. The authors' choice in language throughout this article is not meant to be intentionally exclusionary.

References

ACPA. (2015a). *Beyond compliance: Addressing sexual violence in higher education.* Washington, DC: ACPA College Student Educators International.

ACPA. (2015b). *Document of professional competencies.* Washington, DC: ACPA College Student Educators International.

Gladding, S. (2013). *Counseling: A comprehensive profession* (7th Ed.). Upper Saddle River, NJ: Merrill/Prentice Hall.

No More. (n.d.). *About section.* Retrieved from http://nomore.org/about/.

OAESA (2014). *Creating change together: A guide for rape crisis centers partnering with colleges & universities.* Ohio Alliance to End Sexual Assault.

Shippensburg University Department of Counseling and College Student Personnel Course Descriptions (n.d.). Available at www.ship.edu/Counsel/Current/Course_Outlines/.

7

THE ROLE OF CAMPUS-BASED ADVOCACY AND PREVENTION PROFESSIONALS IN CAMPUS CULTURE CHANGE

Lauren (LB) Klein, Jill Dunlap, and Andrew Rizzo

Gender-based violence (GBV)[1] is an endemic societal issue, including on college campuses. While the campus context for GBV has received increasing national attention over the past few years, professionals trained in GBV prevention and survivor advocacy have been present on some campuses for over 30 years. Due to their positions within university bureaucracy, however, the voices of campus-based experts are rarely heard on a national level. With an administrative emphasis on compliance and lawsuit aversion, their recommendations are often not implemented on their own campuses, leading to strategies aimed more at reputation management than supporting GBV survivors or taking meaningful steps toward building a culture of prevention.

This chapter will explore the characteristics of campus-based prevention and advocacy programs and the needs of affiliated professionals. While programs addressing GBV issues have existed on campuses for over 30 years, there has been no published systematic review or even basic national data on such programs published to date. This chapter is based on findings from the first national study of campus-based GBV programs, utilizing a sample of 286 such programs as well as in-depth consultation interviews with campus-based advocates and prevention professionals, community-based professionals, and national experts. This not only elucidates trends and gaps in training and services nationwide, but also amplifies the voices of these subject matter experts who are often absent from national conversations on GBV issues on campus. This chapter strives to identify challenges in addressing campus GBV. Professionals working to prevent GBV and support survivors are often unable to articulate these challenges without significant career risk. By providing a broader picture, we hope this study is a start toward elevating the marginalized voices of these professionals so their critical perspectives can become more central to the national conversation. Practical implications as well as recommendations for future research based on the perceptions of these professionals are also provided.

Gender-Based Violence on Campus

GBV is a pervasive global public health problem (World Health Organization, 2014). Estimates suggest that 20 to 25% of women are raped during their college career (Fisher, Cullen, & Turner, 2000). While other forms of GBV are understudied in the campus context, 20 to 25% of women experience physical dating or domestic violence in their lifetime and 20- to 24-year-olds are most vulnerable to nonfatal relationship abuse (Banyard, 2014; Catalano, 2007). Nonphysical violence is also prevalent, with 15% of women and 6% of men having been victims of stalking in their lifetime (Breiding, 2014).

Campuses provide a crucial and challenging environment for GBV prevention and intervention, due to the insular and dense nature of the campus population and environment along with increased dating and alcohol and other drug use, strong peer group socialization risk factors, and a substantial population of students who are in the highest risk age group, 16- to 24-year-olds (Abbey, 2005; Bachar & Koss, 2001; Black et al., 2011; Carmody, Ekhomu, & Payne, 2009). The vast majority of college student survivors do not label what happened to them as rape and do not report to campus administrators or the police (Boundurant, 2001; Gerstein & Gerstein, 2015; Peterson & Muehlenhard, 2011). Finding themselves on campuses with compliance-oriented emphases on reporting and adjudication, survivor advocates are challenged to cultivate more survivor-centered, comprehensive approaches.

Program Proliferation

While efforts to address GBV on campus have existed since the 1970s, the number of programs and positions has increased steadily since 1998 when the Office on Violence Against Women (OVW) began providing specific grants to reduce sexual assault, domestic violence, dating violence, and stalking on campus. Over the past 4 years, there has been significantly more national attention to issues of gender violence on campus including: the "Dear Colleague Letter" from the Department of Education in 2011 explicitly connecting GBV to Title IX; the Campus Sexual Violence Elimination Act (Campus SaVE) within the Violence Against Women Act (VAWA) Reauthorization in 2013; updates to the Clery Act; 124 institutions of higher education facing investigations by the Office of Civil Rights; and major attention from the White House Task Force to Protect Students from Sexual Assault (Cantalupo, 2015). This has led to a second surge in the creation of campus programs to address GBV.

Program Impacts

These campus-based programs, ranging from a single position serving the entire institution to offices with multiple staff, share similar missions to community-based domestic and sexual violence programs: to address GBV through prevention and advocacy (Payne, 2008). Many studies have indicated that the presence of survivor advocates and coordinated community response within communities enhance survivor safety and reduce the impact of trauma (Campbell et al., 2004; Campbell & Wasco, 2005). Survivors are also more likely to seek support from stand-alone centers that have multiple roles and respond to multiple forms of GBV (O'Sullivan & Carlton, 2001). Providing sustainably funded programs specific to addressing GBV can help survivors navigate systems while providing prevention programs across the social environment and improving communication across the community (Koss, Bachar, & Hopkins, 2004; Rucinski, 1998).

As Carmody et al. (2009) mention, campus-based advocates and prevention professionals, while understudied, are a crucial source of information because they are in the prime position to identify campus needs, are subject matter experts, and are working most closely with students and survivors (p. 507). Campuses are interdependent, complex environments that also intersect with their local communities; campus-based professionals are well suited to coordinate efforts for advocacy, prevention, and education (Danis, 2006; Payne, 2008). While significant anecdotal evidence exists for campus-based program successes, there is a dearth of peer-reviewed studies pointing to the positive impact of such programs and their efforts.

Program Challenges

Increasingly, state and federal legislative efforts are designed with the goal of increasing official reporting by survivors (S. 590, 2015; CA SB 967, 2014). Additionally, VAWA regulations require campuses to provide prevention education programs that in part raise awareness of services available to survivors of sexual assault (79 FR 62752). Despite all of these efforts, however, service utilization and formal disclosure by students still tend to be far lower than the prevalence rates of victimization (Gerstein & Gerstein, 2015; Sabina & Ho, 2014).

Some students do seek services on campus, but little research to date has focused on the professionals providing those support services to survivors. There are very few studies of campus advocacy programs. Further, because little research has focused on campus programs, the needs of campus-based program staff have rarely been assessed. Payne (2008) investigated the difference between campus and community-based advocate needs. While campus and community programs share similar missions and philosophies, the researcher found that the challenges of campus-based professionals were rooted in collaboration difficulties with both internal and external constituents.

In addition, prevention efforts are challenging to assess for effectiveness at the community level (Chamberlain, 2008; Lee, Guy, Perry, Sniffen, & Mixson, 2007). Previous studies indicate the need for campus-based programs to consist of well-trained, highly visible accessible staff members who are supported by all levels of administration and institutional stakeholders (Cares, 2013; Gillum, 2014; Gerstein & Gerstein, 2015). Only 52% of campuses of the over 400 campuses surveyed in one study had a response protocol for sexual violence (Gerstein & Gerstein, 2015). Even if resources do exist, it does not mean students are aware of these programs or are utilizing them (Hayes-Smith & Levett, 2010).

Both advocacy and prevention efforts are also often grossly underfunded, a concern cited frequently by participants in the few available studies of campus-based professionals (Carmody et al., 2009; Payne, 2008). As Potter et al. (2015) mention, institutions are not fulfilling researcher recommendations for "strategic planning and resource allocation for multiple prevention and response strategies that reach students, faculty, and staff in ongoing ways throughout each student's years on campus" (p. 4). Studies have attributed this lack of change to insufficient institutional buy-in, focus on university image over actual practice, lack of clear policies or accessible resources, insufficient training of campus employees, and schools focusing on legal mandates rather than best practices (Carmody et al., 2009; Gerstein & Gerstein, 2015; Hayes-Smith & Hayes-Smith, 2009; Hayes-Smith & Levett, 2007). These challenges, however, have mostly been gleaned from studies of students and not of university professionals themselves who are working in the fields of advocacy and/or prevention. This study fills a critical gap in the research, illuminating the greatest perceived needs of campus-based GBV prevention and advocacy programs.

Methods

Guiding Philosophy

Prior to undertaking this research project, the authors heard from many frontline campus advocates and prevention educators that they felt marginalized and left out of important conversations on their campuses about how best to prevent and respond to GBV at their institutions. Indeed, the research described here was very much inspired by those informal conversations that the authors had with countless colleagues across the country. It is important to note that the methodology of this study was deliberately designed to both amplify the voices of the marginalized frontline workers on campus and to protect the privacy of respondents who otherwise might not have felt safe sharing the successes and challenges in their work.

Participants

Recruitment

Upon undertaking this survey of prevention professionals and campus advocates, it was clear that no national data on prevention education and advocacy programs or personnel existed. Some campus prevention and advocacy programs have existed since the late 1970s, around the same time that many women's centers were also created at institutions across the country. In fact, many prevention and advocacy positions are located within campus women's centers today. Yet, there was no identifiable list of campus prevention and advocacy programs or personnel that would easily serve as a study population. In order to create a list of campus programs, the authors worked with long-time leaders in the field to compile a list of universities that belonged to a national listserv of prevention educators. The Sexual Assault Program Coordinators (SAPC) listserv served as the starting point for the creation of a national data set of campus prevention and advocacy programs. There were 719 members of the SAPC listserv as of June 2015, which include community-based prevention educators as well as some high school prevention programs. The authors removed any non-higher education institutions or agencies, and completed a Google search of each remaining institution for identifiable personnel or programs specific to either GBV education or response. The Google search resulted in a list of approximately 185 campus prevention and advocacy programs. The authors then cross-referenced that original database with a list of 116 campuses that had received a Department of Justice, OVW campus grant between 2010 and 2014. The final combined data set included 272 institutions of higher education with either an identified prevention education program or campus advocacy program. A campus was considered to have a campus program for purposes of inclusion in the data set if the campus had at least one full-time, identifiable person listed on the institution's website with a title indicating prevention educator or survivor advocate or an office with a title indicating either of those two focus areas.

The recruitment strategy for the survey was designed to be institution-specific. Because many campuses have prevention education efforts separated from advocacy and response efforts, or multiple educators or advocates within a single department, it was likely that an open solicitation or recruitment strategy would lead to duplicate responses from some campuses. The survey was approved by the Institutional Research Boards at both Northern Illinois University and the University of Colorado at Denver. As approved, the survey was designed to solicit confidential, though not anonymous, data from respondents. In a careful effort to ensure confidentiality, data on respondents' institutions were not collected. Without this information, removing duplicate institutional responses would not have been possible, which is why recruitment was designed to occur through institution-specific recruitment e-mails.

Institution Characteristics

The survey received responses from campuses across the country, with 34 states represented. There were between one and eight institutional respondents per state, with an average of approximately two institutions per state. The state with the highest number of responses had eight institutions that responded to the survey. The overwhelming majority of respondents were from public 4-year colleges or universities with only 27% of respondents coming from private institutions. While 9% of respondents indicated that their institutions were religiously affiliated, another 9% indicated that their campuses were Hispanic-serving institutions; 3% indicated representing Historically Black Colleges and Universities (HBCUs). The greatest number of respondents came from institutions with 25,000 or more students with 17% coming from campuses with populations ranging between 5,000 and 9,999, and another 15% coming from campuses with 10,000 to 16,999 students.

Materials

In searching for extant data on the work of interpersonal violence prevention educators and advocates, it was clear that little existed. The perspectives of this population are absolutely invaluable to campus administrators, legislators, student activists, and researchers, and yet rarely are these professionals asked to share their experiences. The majority of research on campus prevention education focuses on the efficacy of program content rather than the educators and professionals themselves (Bannon, Brosi, & Foubert, 2013; Coker et al., 2011; Hollander, 2014; McMahon, Lowe-Hoffman, McMahon, Zucker, & Koenick, 2013). Very few studies in any discipline are focused on the work or perspectives of advocates in general, or on that of campus advocates more specifically (Carmody et al., 2009; Coker et al., 2012; Maier, 2008; Strout, Amar, & Astwood, 2014).

This study was developed in collaboration with prevention education professionals and campus advocates across the country. In particular, members of the leadership council of the newly formed Campus Advocates and Prevention Professionals Association (CAPPA) were continually asked for input and feedback. The CAPPA leadership council consists of 17 campus prevention educators and advocates from a range of institutions across the country. Fifteen key stakeholder interviews with campus, state, and national experts also informed instrument development. Additionally, authors solicited feedback during survey development from approximately 10 other campus professionals who piloted the survey using the Qualtrics survey platform. Pilot survey respondents indicated that some data, such as salary ranges and departmental budgets, would likely discourage participants from responding and so those items were removed. Additionally, some questions were altered to include multiple responses because single answer responses were not capturing the data accurately, according to pilot respondents.

Procedure

Data Collection

The survey was disseminated in early October with an original deadline of two weeks for completion. The authors identified either a department e-mail address or a specific department contact person for the survey solicitation, and from the original data set, surveys were sent to 256 institutions of higher education. Upon receiving fewer responses than anticipated, the response deadline was extended by two weeks and a reminder e-mail was sent to those who had not yet opened or completed the survey. Of the 256 campuses e-mailed, 87 full responses were received for a response rate of 34%. However, only 149 e-mails were opened, which may have been the result of incorrect contact information.

In addition to the e-mail solicitation sent to the specific combined data set, an e-mail solicitation was sent to two national listservs after the survey launched, the SAPC listserv and the newly formed CAPPA listserv. The SAPC listserv reaches approximately 700 members and the CAPPA listserv reaches approximately 200 members. The purpose of the e-mail was to notify the listserv members that either they or someone on their campus should have received the survey and that if they did not, they were welcome to notify the authors to receive a link to the survey. The survey link was not sent as part of the additional recruitment in order to avoid duplicated responses.

Data Analysis

Of the 35 survey items, 10 provided an opportunity for respondents to provide their own responses. Seven of those questions asked respondents' comments on training for advocates and prevention professionals and one asked for any additional comments. Of particular interest for this chapter, respondents were asked to identify the greatest needs of campus advocacy and prevention programs.

Respondents' answers were downloaded from Qualtrics into the Microsoft Excel spreadsheet program. The items were analyzed using an iterative qualitative content analysis process (Lieblich, Tuval-Mashiach, & Zilber, 1998). First, the authors read each respondent's answer to each of the three questions and then repeatedly read the collective responses to each question to establish themes. Second, the data was uploaded into QDA Miner Lite, a computer-assisted qualitative analysis software. The text of the responses was then coded according to the identified themes and reviewed through three rounds of reading, coding, rereading, and recoding. Third, the coding themes were combined into categories, discussed, and refined. Throughout this process, both representative and compelling responses were noted as they related to emerging themes.

Findings

Program Characteristics

Staffing

Survey questions relating to program staff included a question regarding prevention education and a question regarding advocacy. Participants were instructed to answer both questions in terms of full time equivalent (FTE), or the number of hours dedicated to prevention or advocacy in terms of full-time workers. For example, 1.5 FTE for advocacy would indicate that the equivalent of one and a half full-time employee's worth of time is dedicated to providing advocacy services. To be considered a campus-based GBV program (and therefore qualified to be contacted for this study), an institution needed to have at least 1 FTE dedicated to either prevention education or advocacy.

Prevention education

A total of 74 respondents indicated the number of staff, in FTE, that are dedicated to providing GBV prevention education at their institutions. The number of staff ranged from 0 to 6 staff members, with the most frequent response (41%) indicating that the campus had one full-time prevention educator.

Advocacy

A total of 76 respondents indicated the number of staff, in FTE, that are dedicated to providing direct advocacy support services to survivors of GBV at their institutions. Again, the number of advocacy staff ranged from 0 to 6 staff members, with the most frequent response (37%) indicating that the campus had one full-time advocate (Table 7.1).

TABLE 7.1 Descriptive Statistics of Staffing for Prevention and Advocacy

Statistic	Prevention (n = 74)	Advocacy (n = 76)
Mean	1.72 FTE	1.60 FTE
Mode	1.00*	1.00**
Standard Deviation	1.25	1.21
Minimum	0***	0****
Maximum	6	6
Skew	Positive	Positive

* This answer was given by 41% of respondents (n = 30).
** This answer was given by 37% of respondents (n = 28).
*** This answer was given by 4% of respondents (n = 3).
**** This answer was given by 9% of respondents (n = 7).

Institutional Position

Survey questions relating to institutional position included whether a respondent's program included a position with a director level title, what larger unit supervised their program, and from which sources their program receives funding.

Director Level Title

A total of 76 respondents responded to the question about having a Director level position. The majority (55.3%) of respondents indicated that their GBV program did not include a position with a director level title, while the remaining respondents (44.7%) indicated that their office did include a position with a director level title.

Program Supervision

A total of 75 respondents indicated which larger unit their GBV program was supervised by within the institution; 3% by Academic Affairs, 9% by Counseling Center, 8% by Health Promotion, 33% by Student Affairs/Life, 8% by Student Health Services, 1% by Title IX Coordinator, and 7% by Women's Center. As respondents could indicate supervision by more than one of the options listed, a total of 25% indicated their GBV program is supervised by two or more units. These results come with a word of caution, however, since many student health services, women's centers, and counseling centers also fall within divisions of student affairs.

Program Funding

A total of 77 respondents indicated how their GBV program is funded; 42% from University Funds, 10% from Student Fees, 5% from OVW Campus Grants, 1% from Rape Prevention/DELTA Grants, and 3% from Other Grants. Several respondents (3%) indicated sources other than those listed. As respondents could indicate funding from more than one source, a total of 38% indicated their program received funding from two or more sources.

Program Needs

The iterative qualitative analysis process leads to the identification of representative responses to three open-ended questions (Table 7.2). Five overarching categories emerged from response themes: financial, professional, buy-in, philosophical, and policy and procedural needs (Table 7.2).

TABLE 7.2 Frequencies of Identified Program Need: Themes & Categories

Category	Themes	n	%
Financial		46	33
	Lack of staff	21	15
	Lack of budget	21	15
	Lack of space	2	1
	Lack of visibility	2	1
Professional		37	27
	Lack of evidence-based practices	8	6
	Lack of respect for professionals in the field	8	6
	Lack of professionalization of the field	7	5
	Lack of national support for the work	6	4
	Burnout	3	2
	Work not sustainable when national attention dissipates	3	2
	Difficult to know if the work is effective	1	1
	Lack of campus-specific training	1	1
Buy-In		32	23
	Institutions do not support the work	13	9
	Students are not engaged	6	4
	Staff do not have a "seat at the table"	6	4
	Lack of participation by faculty/staff	4	3
	Advocates not seen as essential	3	2
Philosophical		17	12
	Lack of understanding of GBV issues	6	4
	Prevention is not prioritized	4	3
	Compliance focus	3	2
	Program is not inclusive of marginalized groups	3	2
	Lack of discussion of dating/domestic violence	1	1
Policy & Procedure		7	5
	Programs do not have confidentiality	4	3
	Lack of trauma-informed approaches	1	1
	Unfunded state mandates	1	1
	Lack of relationships with community organizations	1	1
Total		139	100

Financial

The most frequently mentioned needs directly or indirectly pertained to budget allocations and fiscal prioritization of the GBV program's work by the institution. Participants pointed most often to an inadequate staffing level to achieve institutional goals or federal mandates or to a lack of program budget. Related issues included a lack of a physical location or separate office and a lack of visibility due to an inability to afford marketing materials or branding assistance.

Professional

Respondents also indicated needs related to the broader profession. Some concerns were related to a lack of available practices such as evidence-based practice, a lack of campus-specific capacity building opportunities, or insufficient metrics to measure success. Other professional concerns related to a lack of cohesion in the field including a lack of national support for the work or a concern that once the issue falls off the national radar that support will dissipate. Respondents also indicated a lack of respect for GBV advocates and prevention professionals' expertise or perceiving them as biased. A related concern was that there is currently no certification program or professionalization of the field. The need to address burnout was also named as a salient professional need.

Buy-In

Respondents also highlighted a need for added buy-in. They perceived that institutions often did not support their work or were not truly invested in taking the steps necessary to end GBV. On a related note, several respondents indicated that they did not have a "seat at the table," often mentioning that key decisions were made without their input as content experts. Some cited student disinterest while others expressed concerns with engagement from faculty and staff. Others felt as though advocates are no longer seen as essential to responding to GBV and have been replaced by investigatory models and "neutral" confidential advisors.

Philosophical

Other expressed needs were more philosophical in nature. Respondents felt that there needed to be greater capacity built around understanding of GBV issues. Constituents were often formulating strategies that came from an uninformed or reactionary place. Others stated a lack of prioritization of prevention, some believing that prevention and compliance have become synonymous. Compliance culture was mentioned as an impediment to the more long-term and comprehensive goals of prevention and advocacy. In addition, a need to center marginalized groups was the focus of several responses, including specific mentions of racial and ethnic minorities and lesbian, gay, bisexual, transgender, and queer students. One respondent indicated a need to stop treating dating and domestic violence like an add-on to sexual violence.

Policy and Procedure

A handful of respondents expressed concerns with policies and procedures. Several respondents indicated a concern that programs do not have confidentiality, lost their confidentiality, or felt the confidentiality of their communications with survivors was constantly at risk. Additional concerns in this area included a lack of trauma-informed approaches, an issue with unfunded mandates from state government, and the institution not having close relationships with community organizations or the state sexual assault coalition.

Discussion

The goal of this study was to nationally survey the structure of college and university campus-based programs for GBV prevention and advocacy, and to explore the needs of professionals working in those programs. We not only identified diverse program characteristics such as organizational structure, institutional positionality, staff sizes, and funding sources, but also five major categories of need based on qualitative responses from professionals at 87 campuses across the United States. Taken together, these findings provide three main areas of greatest need for campus-based advocates and prevention professionals: institutional respect, institutional authority, and professional identity and cohesion. The mixed-method approach of this study allows for a nuanced discussion of these needs, which are in-line with previous findings about GBV work in other environments (Payne, 2008). We conclude with recommendations for future investigations of campus-based programs.

Limitations

As the first systematic study of campus-based GBV programs, the authors needed to overcome a number of obstacles. First and foremost, there is no national dataset or register of GBV programs on college or university campuses. Therefore, it is difficult to generalize this data as representative of all programs that address GBV in a higher education context. The program database formed for this study relied heavily on programs' visibility on the web. Not only did this limit the number of total programs identified, but this may also have impacted the study response rate. Slightly more than half of the programs contacted opened the e-mail, suggesting that a large number of programs' online profiles were not up-to-date. Given the high intensity and emotionality of the work of GBV advocates and prevention professionals, it is possible that website maintenance is frequently deprioritized and inaccurate information remains online for a long period of time.

Another limitation of the database inclusion criteria is that a program is defined to have a minimum of 1.0 FTE dedicated to GBV prevention education or advocacy. This study does not identify needs of institutions without any staff dedicated to this issue, although institutions looking to create programs would benefit in using this study to guide the creation, funding, and supervision of such a program.

Areas of Concern for Campus Programs

Respondents frequently emphasized both the challenges and opportunities of the current cultural moment, including a shift to all prevention and intervention efforts on GBV being subsumed under Title IX. Elevated attention to GBV issues coupled with a Title IX focus on adjudication and compliance have made institutions of higher education challenging landscapes to navigate for prevention and advocacy professionals.

Lack of Institutional Respect

Despite increased media attention to the high prevalence rates of GBV on college campuses, these findings indicate that campus GBV programs are still misunderstood and marginalized within their own institutions. This marginalization was exemplified in a number of statements regarding a lack of institutional buy-in. In addition, respondents indicated knowledge gaps and inadequate policy that fails to prioritize the work of GBV professionals. As one interviewee put it, "I was often told to 'stay in my lane,' to 'know my role,' when ending sexual assault is in our office's mission statement!"

A lack of acknowledgement by institutional leadership of the necessity of campus-based advocates was specifically mentioned in several comments. As one respondent said:

> Right now advocates are still see[n] as "optional" or an added bonus rather than an essential component of any campus program, so it would be nice to see that to be as much of an expectation as having a Title IX Coordinator or offering a bystander intervention program.

The comparison to Title IX is a particularly salient issue, given that the specialty profession of Title IX Coordinator has only existed for a few years compared to the decades-long work of campus-based advocates and prevention professionals. These two topics are fused into single areas by some institutions, as one professional interviewed noted:

Sexual violence is being treated like a new epidemic taking campuses by storm rather than the endemic societal issue it is. On campuses in particular, there is an increased challenge in separating prevention programming from policy programming. They are being conflated in our educational programs, but the pedagogy should not be the same for both. "Because the policy says so" does not change attitudes or culture.

Institutional focus on policy and compliance can also minimize the true amount of work needed to truly eradicate GBV.

In addition to the necessity of professionals addressing GBV on campuses, the true scope of the work is not recognized when institutions make staffing decisions. One professional interviewed regarding their greatest needs highlighted this ignorance:

> I think there is the obvious issue with resources: time, staff, [and] money to do the work. There are unrealistic expectations. I'm a one-person center tasked with preventing sexual assault and intimate partner violence from happening on the entire campus.

In addition to unrealistic staff decisions and policy implementations, it may also be the case that other campus staff are barriers to effective prevention and advocacy work. One respondent highlighted that, "supervisors and other campus stakeholders' [need to build] capacity in knowledge and understanding in this field." Barring an increase in knowledge generally about this issue, other solutions that would alleviate the lack of understanding and centering of this issue were mentioned. In particular, respondents said they need "inclusion at the table," when discussion and decisions about GBV responses are happening.

Lack of Institutional Authority

Campus-based GBV professionals typically do not find themselves in positions with much institutional authority or resources at their disposal. The strongest theme regarding the needs of campus-based programs was financial-needs based. Twenty-one respondents specifically mentioned a lack of personnel and staffing as the greatest need facing programs; as one interviewee summed up the problem, "I felt alone most days, especially as the only campus advocate. . . . I wasn't going to end violence by just talking to one student at a time." A need for greater financial investment in campus-based programs is not new (Carmody et al., 2009). Our findings suggest several possibilities for why funding continues to elude campus-based programs.

Adequate institutional position and authority is still withheld from campus-based programs. Only about half of respondents reported having a staff person at the director level within the institution. This finding resonates with concerns from many frontline-level staff who feel that their position or programs are buried within existing institutional structures. This means that many campus GBV programs likely do not have a dedicated individual advocating for them when institutional decisions regarding budget and personnel allocation are made. Several respondents identified this need, referring to it as a need for "institutional legitimacy" or "institutional support" of their program, or a need for more "leadership buy-in." One respondent further critiqued, "[We need] access. Every university probably has subject matter experts on sexual assault prevention, but they are usually low level employees."

Slightly more than half of campuses surveyed reported that all of their funding came from either university funds or student fees. The remainder indicated that some or all of their funding came from grant-based sources such as the OVW or the Centers for Disease Control and Prevention. While this might be a temporary solution, the work of locating and competing for external funds can add considerable strain to already emotionally draining and work-intensive jobs. Additional anxiety can come from a lack of job security, as grant-funded positions can expire at the end of the grant period. Once funding is received, staff is further saddled with not only their normal reporting structures but must complete external reports to agencies from which they receive funds. While not insurmountable by themselves, when considered in light of the many comments on understaffing and burnout these findings converge to indicate a lack of sustainability of this work on campuses. As one respondent pointed out, "[we have] need of additional funding, proper space allocation, and sustainability of program (after it no longer receives national attention)." Locating external funding is further complicated by the disparate fields and educational backgrounds of professionals in this field, as one interviewee highlighted, "Our OVW funding ran out and [my institution] expects me to find new money to replace it. I'm not even sure where to look. There's a real lack of cohesion in our field."

Lack of Professional Identity and Cohesion

More than a quarter of respondents identified their greatest need as lying outside of the institution itself. A significant number of respondents articulated the need for a professional identity as being the greatest need they have, and one that is a need of the entire profession of campus-based GBV programs and their staff. Recent institutional focus on compliance with federal regulations has served to highlight this issue, as one interviewee pointed out, "Title IX [Adjudication] Coordinators did not really exist a few years ago. Now they are considered a powerful specialty field. This has further marginalized advocates and prevention professionals who do not even have a professional home." This lack of professional identity is exacerbated by the high variation in where programs are housed within institutions. In other words, it is difficult to build colleague networks across campuses when the variance in size and type of program at each institution is so great.

Several respondents spoke specifically to a need for clearer professional standards. Determining the exact roles and capacities of advocates was highlighted by two respondents. "I think it would be extremely helpful for Campus Advocates to have a shared set of resources and guidelines of what services the position offers," offered one respondent. Another echoed that sentiment, saying, "[we] need reasonable guidelines for how many professionals are needed to adequately serve each campus (ex. If you have a population of X, you should have Y advocates and X prevention professionals in order to appropriately serve your community)."

Although the field of campus GBV work draws frequently from community-based programs and models, respondents also reported that the differences between services in each setting need to be recognized. "While skills from community advocates are transferable to campus advocacy, we need to see more resources directed at campus interpersonal violence [prevention]." Community-based programs have statewide, regional, and national coalitions that promote standards of practices and metrics for assessing advocacy work. Similar structures are needed for work within institutions of higher education, as one respondent noted. "[We need] national best practices for campus advocacy programs." A critical obstacle to creating these standards is the unpredictable location of GBV programs within campuses.

Another obstacle that arose that impacts the ability to build a professional identity is the wide range of campus departments to which GBV programs report. Respondents identified eight different units that supervise their programs, including counseling, student affairs, Title IX, academic affairs, health promotion, and student health services. Each of these reporting structures may be accompanied by an affiliation with a different national professional association. For example, the accreditation process for a health services facility is very different from the guidelines for health educators or the certification process for clinical psychologists or counseling center staff. Some national organizations standards apply only to individual-level staff member training, whereas other professional standards apply to entire offices and their policies. A review and systematization of job responsibilities or governance structures for these individuals and their programs would do a great deal to alleviate some of these issues.

Recommendations

While this study provides an initial foray into understanding the needs of campus GBV advocates and prevention professionals, some of the methodological limitations could be improved by future studies. Further research on the web presence and accuracy for campus GBV programs should be done, to build upon this study and work such as Hayes-Smith and Hayes-Smith's (2009) analysis of sexual assault web content from institutions of higher education. Particularly given new federal requirements relating to transparency and survivor resource aware-ness raising, this area is ripe for further research. The methodology utilized here represents just the beginning of a much-needed exploration of the work of prevention professionals and advocates in higher education.

To date, there is no nationally representative set of campus GBV programs with which to compare our dataset. While we utilized a comprehensive database constructed using various methods for campus program identification, we are unable to determine if our set of respondents represents the larger field. Only a quarter of campuses who participated are private, even though in the United States there are approximately equal numbers of private institutions (1,730) and public institutions (1,644) of higher education (Carnegie Foundation for the Advancement of Teaching, 2015). Furthermore, a comprehensive evaluation comparing campuses with programs to campuses without programs may shed light on the ways in which programs come to exist. Exploring this process is crucial to ensuring that when new programs are created, they are intentionally designed and sustainable.

Several conclusions within this study warrant specific, targeted inquiry. Investigations of program staffing in particular would be fruitful. The past few years have seen a sharp increase in attention to the issue of GBV on college campuses. Are the current program characteristics collected by this study a result of very recent additions in staff FTE, or promotions that elevate a program position to a director level title? Future investigations should examine the exact timing and motivations for increases in program staffing and institutional authority, with consideration of national events such as the Dear Colleague Letter or grant time periods. Organizational structure is also an area that remains largely obscured. Future studies should not only be cognizant of where a GBV program lies within the larger campus, but also consider how that placement might affect the delivery of prevention education and advocacy services.

An area of inquiry not considered by this first study is program assessment. Although we provide descriptive statistics and remarks from professionals around the country, it is difficult to say whether the campus programs examined in this study are successful or not. Although a frequent concern that we identified was understaffing, we can offer little guidance on how much staff would be enough to adequately address prevention education or advocacy on a single campus. Future research is needed on how, and with what metrics and considerations, campus GBV programs could be evaluated for performance and success.

We hope this study can serve as an initial portrait of the needs and challenges facing work on GBV within college campuses. Our findings present more questions than answers, and this field is one largely unexamined despite existing for decades. As one interviewee stated:

> We're having a cultural moment right now. Expectations have fundamentally shifted in the past five years around campus sexual violence. It's possible to use this energy as a lever for broader change. I don't think we'll ever go back to the way that things were in 2010.

Timely and critical explorations are needed to fully understand why professionals working to end GBV on campus are so frequently disrespected, relegated to ineffectual ranks, and left without a professional home or identity.[2]

Notes

1   Gender-based violence (GBV) is used herein as an umbrella term for multiple forms of violence such as sexual assault/harassment, dating/domestic violence, and stalking. While this term is used for the sake of consistency, the authors recognize other practitioners may use myriad terms including interpersonal and power-based violence to describe similar forms of abuse.
2   Thank you to Rebecca Woofter for her contributions to this research.

References

Abbey, A. (2005). Lessons learned and unanswered questions about sexual assault perpetration. *Journal of Interpersonal Violence, 20*(1), 39–42.

Bachar, K., & Koss, M.P. (2011). From prevalence to prevention: Closing the gap between what we know about rape and what we do. In C.M. Renzetti, J.L, Edleson, & R.K. Bergen (Eds.), *Sourcebook on violence against women* (pp. 117–142). Thousand Oaks, CA: Sage Publications.

Bannon, S.R., Brosi, M.W., & Foubert, J.D. (2013). Sorority women's and fraternity men's rape myth acceptance and bystander intervention attitudes. *Journal of Student Affairs Research and Practice, 50*(1), 72–87.

Banyard, V.L. (2014). Improving college campus-based prevention of violence against women: A strategic plan for research built on multipronged practices and policies. *Trauma, Violence, and Abuse, 15*(4), 339–351.

Black, M.C., Basile, K.C., Breiding, M.J., Smith, S.G., Walter, M.L., Merrick, M.T., & Stevens, M.R. (2011). *National intimate partner and sexual violence survey (NISVS) 2010* (Summary Report). Atlanta, GA: National Center for Injury Prevention and Control, Centers for Disease Control and Prevention.

Boundurant, B. (2001). University women's acknowledgement of rape: Individual, situational, and social factors. *Violence Against Women, 7*(3), 294–314.

Breiding, M.J. (2014). Prevalence and characteristics of sexual violence, stalking, and intimate partner violence victimization: National Intimate Partner and Sexual Violence Survey (NISVS) 2011. *Morbidity and Mortality Weekly Report, 63*(8), E11–E12.

Bronfenbrenner, U. (1979). *The ecology of human development.* Cambridge, MA: Harvard University Press.

Campbell, R., Dorey, H., Naegelli, M., Grubstein, L.K., Bennett, K.K., Bonter, F., Smith, P.K., Grzywaz, J., Baker, P.K., & Davidson, W.S. (2004). An empowerment evaluation model of sexual assault programs: Empirical evidence of effectiveness. *American Journal of Community Psychology, 34*(3), 251–262.

Campbell, R., & Wasco, S. (2005). Understanding rape and sexual assault. *Journal of Interpersonal Violence, 20*(1), 127–131.

Cantalupo, N.C. (2015). *Five things student affairs professionals should know about campus gender-based violence (Issue Brief).* Washington, DC: NASPA Research & Policy Institute. Retrieved from www.naspa.org/images/uploads/main/5Things_Gender_Based_Vio lence.pdf.

Cares, A.C. (2013). What is the role of college faculty in stopping sexual assault? *The Resource: Newsletter of the National Sexual Violence Resource Center*, Spring Summer 16–30. Enola, PA: National Sexual Violence Resource Center.

Carmody, D., Ekhomu, J., & Payne, B.K. (2009). Needs of sexual assault advocates in campus-based sexual assault centers. *College Student Journal, 43*(2), 507–513.

Carnegie Foundation for the Advancement of Teaching. (2011). *The Carnegie Classification of Institutions of Higher Education* (2010th ed.). Menlo Park, CA: Center for Postsecondary Research.

Catalano, S. (2007). *Intimate partner violence in the United States. U.S. Department of Justice, Bureau of Justice Statistics.* Retrieved from http://bjs.ojp.usdoj.gov/content/pub/pdf/ipvus.pdf.

Chamberlain, L. (2008). *A prevention primer for domestic violence: Terminology, tools, and the public health approach.* Retrieved from www.vawnet.org/applied-research-papers/print-document.php?doc_id=1313.

Coker, A.L., Cook-Craig, P.G., Williams, C.M., Fisher, B.S., Clear, E.R., Garcia, L.S., & Hegge, L.M. (2011). Evaluation of Green Dot: An active bystander intervention to reduce sexual violence on college campuses. *Violence Against Women, 17*(6), 777–796.

Coker, A.L., Smith, P.H., Whitaker, D.J., Le, B., Crawford, T.N., & Flerx, V.C. (2012). Effect of an in-clinic IPV advocate intervention to increase help seeking, reduce violence, and improve well-being. *Violence Against Women, 18*(1), 118–131.

Danis, F.S. (2006). In search of safe campus communities: A campus response to violence against women. *Journal of Community Practice, 14*(3), 29–46.

Fisher, B.S., Cullen, F.T., & Turner, M.G. (2000). *The sexual victimization of college women (Research Report).* Washington, DC: Department of Justice, National Institute of Justice.

Gerstein, R., & Gerstein, L. (2015). Sexual violence on campus: Survey results reveal "insufficient progress" being made in sexual violence reporting. *Campus Safety and Student Development, 16*(3), 53–56.

Gillum, T.L. (2014). Reconceptualizing prevention of violence against women on college campuses: Response to Victoria Banyard's actualizing the potential of primary prevention: A research agenda. *Trauma, Violence, and Abuse, 15*(4), 352–357.

Hayes-Smith, R.M., & Hayes-Smith, J. (2009). A website content analysis of women's resource and sexual assault literature on college campuses. *Critical Commentary, 17*(2), 109–123.

Hayes-Smith, R.M., & Levett, L.M. (2010). Student perceptions of sexual assault resources and prevalence of rape myth attitudes. *Feminist Criminology, 5*(4), 335–354.

Hayes-Smith, R.M., & Levett, L.M. (2007). *Sexual assault resources on campus: Availability and adequacy.* Paper presented at the 59th annual meeting of the American Society of Criminology, Atlanta, GA.

Hollander, J.A. (2014). Does self-defense training prevent violence against women? *Violence Against Women, 20*(3), 252–269.

Koss, M.P., Bachar, K., & Hopkins, C. (2004). Expanding a community's justice response to sex crimes through advocacy, prosecutorial, and public health collaboration. *Journal of Interpersonal Violence, 19*(12), 1435–1463.

Lee, D.S., Guy, L., Perry, B., Sniffen, C.K., & Mixson, S.A. (2007). Sexual violence prevention. *The Prevention Researcher, 14*(2), 15–19.

Lieblich, A., Tuval-Mashiach, R., & Zilber, T. (1998). *Narrative research: Reading, analysis, and interpretation.* Thousand Oaks, CA: Sage Publications, Inc.

McMahon, S., Lowe-Hoffman, M., McMahon, S.M., Zucker, S., & Koenick, R.A. (2013). What would you do: Strategies for bystander intervention to prevent sexual violence by college students. *Journal of College and Character, 14*(2), 141–151.

Maier, S.L. (2008). "I have heard horror stories . . .": Rape victim advocates' perceptions of the revictimization of rape victims by the police and medical system. *Violence Against Women, 14*(7), 786–808.

O'Sullivan, E., & Carlton, A. (2001). Victim services, community outreach, and contemporary rape crisis centers. *Journal of Interpersonal Violence, 16*(4), 343–360.

Payne, B.K. (2008). Challenges responding to sexual violence: Differences between college campuses and communities. *Journal of Criminal Justice, 36*(3), 224–230.

Peterson, Z., & Muehlenhard, C. (2011). A match-and-motivation model of how women label their nonconsensual experiences. *Psychology of Women Quarterly, 35*(4), 558–570.

Potter, S.J., Banyard, V.L., Stapleton, J.G., Demers, J.M., Edwards, K.M., & Moynihan, M.M. (2015). *Informing students about campus policies and resources: How they get the message matters (Research Report).* Durham, NH: Prevention Innovations Research Center; White House Task Force to Protect Students from Sexual Assault. Retrieved from http://cola.unh.edu/sites/cola.unh.edu/files/departments/Prevention%20Innovations%20Research%20Center/White_Paper_87367_for_web.pdf.

Rucinski, C. (1998). Transitions: Responding to the needs of domestic violence victims. FBI Law Enforcement Bulletin, 67, 15–19.

Sabina, C., & Ho, L.Y. (2014). Campus and college victim responses to sexual assault and dating violence: Disclosure, service utilization, and service provision. *Trauma, Violence, & Abuse, 15*(3), 201–226.

Strout, T., Amar, A.F., & Astwood, K. (2014). Women's center staff perceptions of the campus climate on sexual violence. *Journal of Forensic Nursing, 10*(3), 135–143.

World Health Organization (WHO). (2014). *Violence against women: Intimate partner and sexual violence against women.* Retrieved from www.who.int/mediacentre/factsheets/fs239/en/.

8

A COMMUNITY APPROACH TO SUSTAINABLE SEXUAL ASSAULT PREVENTION STRATEGIES

Mary Geller and Lori Klapperich

The College of Saint Benedict (CSB), a residential liberal arts college for women, and Saint John's University (SJU), a residential liberal arts college for men, were founded by Benedictine monastic communities. The Rule of Benedict, a guiding treatise advocates a balanced life of service, inclusiveness, worship, hospitality, and community living. The campuses sit adjacent to their respective founding monasteries, and Sisters and Monks are highly engaged with both student populations.

Today, we have one academic program and faculty that enrolls 3,800 undergraduate students. The institutions are located six miles apart in central Minnesota. Students take classes together on both campuses with busses running continuously between the two. CSB/SJU have separate student development and residential programs that intentionally attend to gender-specific developmental needs of women and men. Examples include but are not limited to: the Institute for Women's Leadership and Men's Development Institute focusing on issues and leadership opportunities specific to women and men, as well as the CSB Health Advocates, looking at health through the lens of women and the SJU Health Initiative, doing the same through the male lens. Both institutions have a four-year residency requirement with approximately 10% of students per institution living off-campus.

CSB/SJU as Catholic, Benedictine, liberal arts colleges, are academic communities dedicated to the intellectual, spiritual, and ethical formation of all their members, and to academic excellence in the search for truth. The founding and ongoing inspiration of these institutions is the Catholic intellectual tradition, in the context of Benedictine values and spirituality.

The intellectual life of these campuses embodies and affirms the harmony of faith and reason in addition to the dignity of each person, both of which are central to the Catholic tradition. There is a profound commitment to exploring how faith and reason are mutually enriching and challenging in understanding the human condition and in the full development of the human person. As Catholic and Benedictine institutions, we support the development of the whole person and teach our students both inside and outside the traditional classroom. Members of the two learning communities are challenged and encouraged to integrate the skills of the academic life with a life of faith.

Some may think that as Catholic institutions, it would be difficult to address issues of sex, physical intimacy, and sexual violence, when in fact that has been the impetus and foundation for our work. The opening to our sexual misconduct policy impresses these principles upon the reader and supports the Catholic mission of the institutions:

> In institutions such as ours, which espouse Catholic and Benedictine values, every community member's awareness of and respect for the rights and human dignity of all persons undergirds community life. These values demand that we strive to create an environment where the sacredness of each person is honored. Sexual assault conduct violates the sacredness of the person, weakens the health of the community, and is antithetical to the mission of these institutions. (College of Saint Benedict and Saint John's University, 2016)

A sexual misconduct policy can be strengthened for both religious and secular institutions when it is framed within the institutional mission as a moral imperative and not solely a legal obligation.

In this chapter, we will discuss our policy, process, and assessment work to address sexual misconduct. More importantly, we will address community-based education/prevention strategies to mitigate risk within our community. It is our hope that by sharing our data and our work we can, in some small way, help others who are struggling to reduce the risk of sexual misconduct on their own campus.

History and Grounding Philosophy

In the spring of 2007, sexual assault education and prevention was moved to the work of health promotion staff when the Office of Student Human Rights was eliminated and the duties reassigned. The work being done out of that office was grounded in feminist theory and thus programmatically limited in scope. The office did have student worker hours that health promotion staff was able to secure. Since the rest of the health promotion work was grounded in population-based public health and local assessment, it was important to frame sexual assault similarly to those other issues. The work undertaken was basically what would happen with a new issue being addressed or a new program being put into place.

Staff began researching the topic, including risk and protective factors, best practices, and what other schools and community organizations were doing regarding this issue.

What was found was that sexual assault was primarily in the domain of women's centers and community sexual assault centers, and was considered a women's issue. Efforts centered on either how to help the potential victim to be safer or how to help the survivor heal. Some discussion could be found in the literature about what was important for all students or community members to know, do, or say but applications were limited. Although helping the survivor heal is extremely important work, it was the belief of health promotion staff that addressing sexual assault only in this way would do nothing about the number of victims/survivors. That number would just continue to increase. The focus needed to move more upstream—what was happening in the environment that might encourage, condone, or tolerate sexual activity without consent? What could all members of the community do to build an environment that encouraged behaviors, attitudes, and beliefs that not only supported victims and allowed them to thrive and heal but also made sexual assault and other acts of sexual violence less likely to occur? There were articles on bystander intervention coming out around this time as well, which caught the eye of the staff and contributed to the programming efforts in our campus communities.

It was through presenting the results of the literature review, what other schools and communities were doing, and CSB/SJU local data that staff and upper administration came to an understanding that there was a need to meet students where they were and help them understand the issues they faced from a health and safety perspective. It was also understood that a need existed to examine the environments of the two campuses, and begin a process much like was done for alcohol in the early 2000s to identify and reduce and/or eliminate practices, policies, attitudes, beliefs, and actions that might encourage, condone, or tolerate sexual activity without consent. This was the beginning of the first sexual violence education and prevention plan. Implementation began the following fall. Student workers were hired and a basic plan developed that included defining the issue, defining consent, and illustrating what consent was, and why it was important to all as well as identifying the myths and realities of sexual violence. This plan grew each year as student and professional staff were better able to plan and implement strategies from a public health approach, involving more and more community constituents.

Health promotion staff has not had this plan questioned, interfered with, or had any attempts at silencing due to Catholic teaching. In fact, our Catholic, Benedictine heritage was looked to for inspiration and language to form our philosophy and approach for addressing sexual violence and creating culture change. Upper administrators have been kept informed of any new research and trends, and how they affected the ongoing work. We struggle at times with how to deal with overall sexual health, but have not waivered on the need to address sexual violence. When the 2011 Dear Colleague Letter came out and more national attention was focused on sexual violence on college campuses, health promotion staff felt quite confident that the work being done at CSB/SJU on the education/prevention side met all recommendations.

At CSB/SJU, we define our desired community as built on individuals who demonstrate through their deeds and actions: respect for persons, truthful living, deep listening, justice, and the common good. Community living is at the core of Benedictine values. It is in community that we learn who we are and what we have to offer each other and the world. It is in community that we learn how to listen and respect one another. It is in community that we continue to work on being and remaining safe, and creating adaptive environments that welcome all and exclude none, truly embracing diversity in all of its myriad presentations including culture, ethnicity, race, religion, beliefs, abilities, socioeconomic status, gender, gender identity, sexual preference, and language proficiency.

Sexual assault has no place in this defined community. We believe everyone has the right to be in relationships (family, friends, work, and intimate partner) that are safe and respectful. We approach sexual assault as a community public health issue within a social-ecological framework with strategies that acknowledge stages of change and address knowledge, attitudes, beliefs, and practices. We identify behaviors that help create and sustain this definition of community as well as behaviors that detract from this community. We devise interventions that lead to an increase in the practice of positive behaviors and a decrease in the practice of negative behaviors. The methods we utilize include policy development and enforcement, social marketing, media outreach, peer education, and community engagement. Our ultimate goal is sustained community culture change that truly represents our community definition.

We *cannot* predict who will become a victim of sexual violence or who will perpetrate sexual violence. We *can* address the risk and protective factors on individual, relational, and campus community levels. We *can* design interventions that move students from awareness to action. We *can* design interventions that strengthen faculty and staff capacity to contribute to a positive, supportive environment and to respond to sexual assault situations. We *are* committed to breaking down cultural norms that support sexual violence related behaviors as well as fortifying cultural norms of an inclusive, respectful community.

Areas of Action

1) Making Health a Shared Value

This Area of Action focuses on engaging communities, providers, and advocates in understanding social and economic determinants of health. When people join forces and place a high value on health, they are more likely to demand health-affirming policies and practices. Many of our current partners and grantees are likely to find their work falls within this Area of Action, including healthy communities, providers, and organizations who are trying to reduce chronic illness in underserved communities, and advocates for local policy and environmental changes to prevent childhood obesity.

2) Fostering Collaboration to Improve Well-Being

Let's face it, the United States has some serious health issues, and we can't rely on any one sector to solve them alone. Leaders across sectors, including health professions, academia, business, and government, must bring their skills to the table and work together to improve health in communities and across the nation. In this Action Area, an activity might bring policymakers, school health officials, local businesses, and parents together to achieve healthy weight for children. In others, employers and health insurers might team with community partners on wellness programs to improve both worker and broader community health.

3) Increasing Equity in Healthy Community Environments

Your ZIP code should not negatively determine your health status—nor should your race, income, or level of education. All residents deserve to live in neighborhoods that are safe and free from environmental threats. They should have access to nutritious and affordable food, recreational facilities, healthy school environments, and access to bike trails and sidewalks. This Area of Action focuses on interventions that promote health through equal access in all communities to activities and conditions that promote wellbeing where we live, work, and play.

4) Re-Envisioning Health and Health Care

The current health care system remains too fragmented, too costly, and too out of reach for too many people. This Action Area focuses on improving access to high-quality, effective, prevention-focused, and affordable health care, for everyone around the country. Specific activities will include reducing overuse or misuse of services, increasing cost transparency, and improving care coordination and prevention strategies. Collaboration will be a key focus. For example, when providers are linked with community partners, they can better address the complex health and socioeconomic factors affecting many lower-income people with chronic disease.

Goals

The set goals prioritized risk factors described in our Interventions section. Programming is designed to be layered—awareness, education, engagement, and action. Our idealized community is one:

1. Whose members acknowledge and integrate into their lives, healthy, caring sexual attitudes and practices;
2. Whose culture reflects civility, respect, and nonviolence;
3. Whose members conceptualize sexual activity as an individual choice, where yes *or* no is an accepted and respected response to someone asking;
4. Where all understand sexual activity between people needs to be consensual without the influence of alcohol or other drugs or the presence of pressure, force, threat, manipulation, or intimidation;
5. Whose members understand that sexual assault is about power and control;
6. Where all are ready, willing, and able to intervene in language and behaviors that support, endorse, or tolerate sexual activities without the affirmative consent of those involved;
7. That prioritizes accountability for perpetrators and enablers;
8. Where survivors feel safe to report;
9. Whose members support survivors' healing process and work to understand how sexual assault happens here; and
10. Whose members understand that sexual assault and intimidation are real and they can and should play a role in prevention and intervention.

We provide educational opportunities, information, and dialogue designed to engage students in learning more about sexual violence as an issue and understanding the terms related to sexual violence; debunking the myths of sexual violence and helping students understand the realities including red flags and contributing factors; and understanding that community does make a difference and there is a role for students, faculty and staff, including intervening.

We believe these interventions will:

1. Increase community understanding of why this is a community issue and how individuals can identify high-risk situations as well as develop community norms and values that could have a positive effect;
2. Increase all students' capacity to understand and confront gender-based stereotypes, jokes, songs, comments, and actions that might enable attitudes, beliefs, and behaviors that could lead to or normalize sexual violence;
3. Increase bystander capacity to understand, recognize, and intervene in high-risk situations;
4. Increase potential perpetrators' capacity to understand what sexual assault is, what healthy relationships are, what actions are appropriate, and what actions are not appropriate as well as what is expected by our communities; and
5. Increase potential victim capacity to understand what sexual assault is, recognize risks and red flags, understand and implement safety tips, and identify and avoid high-risk situations.

Policy

A strong sexual misconduct policy is not only an intervention in itself but is at the heart of a community public health approach. Policy is key to laying out acceptable and unacceptable community standards and behaviors, and influences how community members view sexual violence within the campus community. There are four key areas to policy, including: development, accessibility, implementation, and assessment. All four are necessary for a successful policy.

It is imperative that a sexual misconduct policy is clear, comprehensive, and user friendly. Clear policies and definitions lead to effective adjudication (implementation) and can serve as key tools for sexual violence prevention. The following components are included in our policy:

I   Purpose, Scope, and Definitions (including a clear definition of affirmative consent)
II   The Law
III   Reporting Sexual Misconduct
IV   Fair and Equitable Treatment of the Parties
V   Complaint Procedure
VI   Confidentiality
VII   Retaliation
VIII   Sanctions
IX   External Complaints

At CSB/SJU, we work very hard to consistently review our policy for our communal moral imperative, legal compliance, effectiveness, and the ability for it to be as accessible as possible to all. As such, we have created a team of individuals including Title IX coordinators from both campuses as well as all deputy Title IX coordinators and the Director of Security/Life Safety. This group meets monthly to address issues and questions that arise as we put our policy into practice. We work closely with our legal counsel, who have been key advisors in federal and state legislative interpretation and compliance.

There have been several benefits in working with this team approach when it comes to policy development, implementation, and evaluation. First, while the Title IX Coordinator holds ultimate responsibility, it is the collective that carries the weight and responsibility for compliance. Therefore, even though we are a small institution, our bench is deep because of the number of staff highly trained, knowledgeable, and up-to-date in this work. Our team consists of the Executive to the President, whom also serves as our Title IX Officer, Vice President for Student Development, Dean of Students, Human Resource Director and Associate Director, and the Provost.

Second, we have several colleagues with whom we can confer to double-check our work and ensure that we are following our policy and remain in compliance with state and federal regulations. For example, Minnesota has recently passed some additional requirements for colleges and universities regarding sexual assault and sexual violence. Our campus team is working together to make sure that we will meet the deadline for compliance. In addition, we have multiple perspectives around the table so when we are revamping policy, we can approach it simultaneously from both a depth and breadth perspective.

Finally, it is critically important to promulgate the policy readily and consistently to all campus constituents on an annual basis since the nature of our campuses have new people constantly arriving. Here at CSB/SJU, new students, during orientation, receive a packet of material and attend a session co-developed by a professor of theology and orientation staff. Included in this information is:

1. Characteristics of healthy and unhealthy relationships
2. Confidential reporting
3. Definition of consent (what it is and what it is not)
4. Frequently asked questions
5. How to make a campus report
6. How you can help
7. Reporting to law enforcement and the court
8. Sexual misconduct policy and procedures
9. Website resources

In addition, all returning students in the fall receive a letter within the first week of class that points them to our sexual misconduct policy and resource website. We have recently added an annual online training for all faculty, staff, and students that reviews our policy and community standards.

Assessment and Evaluation

The first campus-wide survey conducted that included sexual assault-related questions was in 2005. We have evolved from being more concerned with sexual practices and number of partners to sexual violence-related attitudes, beliefs, and behaviors, as well as readiness to address sexual violence issues and bystander-related beliefs and actions. Sexual assault questions have been included in our general health survey and have been asked every three years, including the 2015 general health survey. We will be moving current questions to a stand-alone campus climate survey that will be launched in 2017. That will complete the three-year assessment rotation: general health survey, alcohol and other drug survey, and campus climate survey. We are currently gathering faculty, staff, and students to help develop the balance of the survey. We will have an opportunity to ask more about incidents of assault, harassment, partner violence, and stalking. But, we will also take this opportunity to search for questions and/or scales that will help us gather more information about how the culture change process is progressing and to ensure we are meeting our student learning goals.

The data in the tables and figures in the next section show results of questions already being asked on the general health survey. They certainly contribute to an understanding of our community and students, but we will need to develop other more broad-based questions if we are to look at culture change from the framework described here, adapted from culture change literature. We also need to test our working theory that providing more opportunities for engaged discussion focusing on sexual violence-related, as well as inclusivity-related, issues is key to moving culture change forward.

Culture Change Stages

Much of the culture change literature contained examples of projects done in worksites. We adapted the stages used to work toward culture change in the work environment to a process that made sense to us in our community. We continue to search the literature to help us evolve our understanding of the process and how to assess and evaluate.

The first stage seems quite clear in the literature. We need to **understand the community as it is now**. We are searching for questions and scales that we can use in our campus climate survey to assist us in this first step. We will also use a less structured strategy of facilitated dialogue. The most recent research from Krebs et al. (2016) on campus climate validation includes some questions and scales that appear relevant. Next, we need to **create a shared vision of community**. As stated earlier in this chapter, the definition of our community has been developed. Now we need to identify opportunities to share with faculty, staff, and students, and build support. Then, **define the change strategy**. We need to identify, define, and disseminate what is needed to be the community we envision, the behaviors we need to increase, and the behaviors we need to decrease or eliminate. This change strategy needs **faculty, staff, and students' buy-in and commitment**. All constituents must understand this community vision, want this community, understand they contribute to this community, and be willing to make changes in their own behavior and intervene with others, in order to be this community. That will allow us to **implement the change strategy and build self-efficacy** through engaging opportunities to learn, develop, and practice skills and actions needed to create the change. Another important aspect is **institutionalizing the change to ensure sustainability**. We need to determine what we can put into institutional practices, policies, and training in order to sustain the change.

We have already witnessed some positive changes happening in our campus communities. There has been a significant shift in how sexual assault is viewed on our campuses. As seen in Table 8.1 below, the most significant move is away from thinking sexual assault is not a problem at all. The data in Table 8.2 indicates that for the first time since we have been surveying students about these topics, sexual assault moved into the top five problem issues. This information coupled with the readiness to address data in Figure 8.1 indicates CSB students are firmly in the contemplation stage of readiness to address sexual violence issues, while SJU students are emerging into the contemplation stage. Understanding this, we need to provide students with ideas and opportunities for action. Sexual assault myths continue to be rejected by the majority of students, as shown in Figures 8.2 and 8.3. As Figure 8.4 illustrates, we have work to do on bystander intervention regarding verbal comments or jokes, regardless of the issue. This key information gathered from our surveys helps us customize and enhance the work we are doing to address sexual violence on our campuses.

We also have a qualitative research project that is being conducted on our campuses. This research project focuses on the following question: How do Title IX and sexual misconduct issues on campus reflect a gendered campus environment? The researcher will review institutional policies and language shared widely on campus (such as the Sexual Misconduct Policy and Procedure, the Title IX website, and health promotion materials), observe institutional trainings and events designed to raise campus awareness of these issues, conduct interviews with CSB and SJU students about their perceptions about Title IX and sexual misconduct issues on campus, and collect course papers related to the topic. Using a feminist research lens and drawing on national literature about sexual assault on college campuses that focuses on the relationship between sexual violence and sexism, hegemonic masculinity, and patriarchy (Angelone, Mitchell, & Grossi, 2015; Armstrong,

TABLE 8.1 "Have you thought any of the following were problems during the last school year at CSB, at SJU?"—Sexual Assault

1 Not at All a Problem	2 Small Problem	3 Some Problem	4 Great Problem	5 Very Great Problem
CSB-2012	*at CSB		**at SJU	
*69.7%	20.8%	8.1%	1.1%	0.3%
**68.9%	19.8%	8.6%	2.3%	0.4%
CSB-2015				
*16.3	23.3	34.4	6.0	10.0
**18.3	27.9	29.8	15.5	8.4
SJU-2012	*at SJU		**at CSB	
* 66.1%	25.7%	6.9%	1.0%	0.3%
**65.1%	21.5%	10.5%	2.1%	0.8%
SJU-2015				
29.0%	29.6%	25.8%	11.1%	4.4%
30.3%	26.2%	27.1%	11.2%	5.3%

TABLE 8.2 Top Five Problems Reported by Students at CSB/SJU

2015	2012	2009	2005
Stress	Stress	Stress	Stress
Alcohol	Alcohol	Alcohol	Eating Disorders
Depression	Nutrition	Nutrition	Alcohol
Sexual Assault	Depression	Depression	Nutrition
Sexual Harassment	Eating Disorders	Eating Disorders	Depression

CSB students thought were problems at CSB (some problem to very great problem) (Top 5)

2015	2012	2009	2005
Alcohol	Alcohol	Alcohol	
Stress	Stress	Stress	
Marijuana	Marijuana	Marijuana	
Sexual Harassment	Gaming	Tobacco	
Sexual Assault	Tobacco	Gaming	

CSB students thought were problems at SJU (some problem to very great problem) (Top 5)

2015	2012	2009	2005
Stress	Stress	Stress	Stress
Alcohol	Alcohol	Alcohol	Gaming
Sexual Assault	Nutrition	Nutrition	Alcohol
Depression	Gaming	Gaming	Nutrition
Nutrition	Marijuana	Tobacco	Sexual Orientation

SJU students thought were problems at SJU (some problem to very great problem) (Top 5)

2015	2012	2009	2005
Stress	Stress	Stress	
Depression	Nutrition	Alcohol	
Sexual Assault	Eating Disorders	Nutrition	
Nutrition	Alcohol	Eating Disorders	
Alcohol	Depression	Depression	

SJU students thought were problems at CSB (some problem to very great problem) (Top 5)

Agree/Strongly Agree

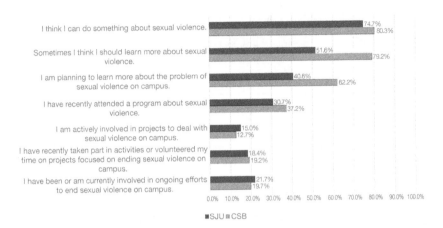

Disagree/Strongly Disagree

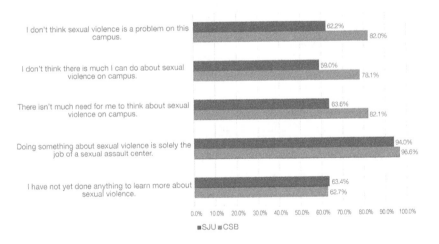

FIGURE 8.1 Readiness to Address Sexual Assault

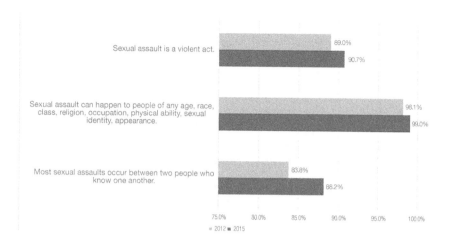

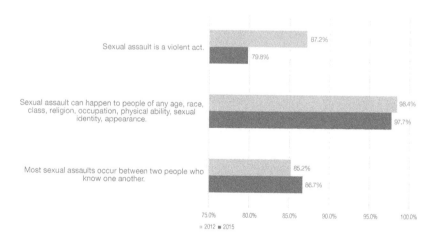

FIGURE 8.2 Sexual Assault Myths, Agree/Strongly Agree (CSB/SJU)

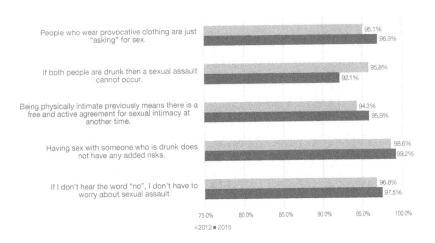

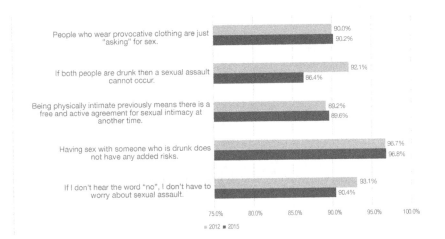

FIGURE 8.3 Sexual Assault Myths, Disagree/Strongly Disagree (CSB/SJU)

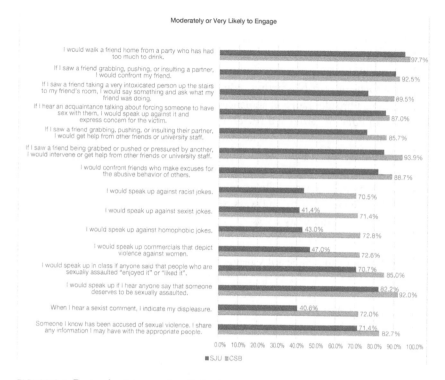

FIGURE 8.4 Bystander Intervention Behaviors

TABLE 8.3 Top Reasons for Answering "never or rarely" to Above Issues

CSB	SJU
Don't want to make the situation worse	None of my business
None of my business	Don't see it as a problem
Fear	Don't want to make situation worse

Hamilton, & Sweeney, 2006; Kilmartin & Berkowitz, 2005; Jozkowski, 2015; Rhode, 1999; Wooten, 2016), the researcher will analyze the ways that campus discourse around Title IX and sexual misconduct reflects a gendered campus environment. We hope this project as well as other research projects in progress or being discussed by faculty will assist us in determining where we are as a community and what we need to do to keep moving toward our end goal.

Specific Interventions

Although a strong policy that is fairly, justly, and consistently enforced is foundational to our work on issues related to sexual violence, it cannot be the be all and

end all of a campus prevention strategy. We acknowledge that currently the reality of what we know about sexual violence is limited, that there are few thoroughly evaluated best practices, and that many strategies remain unevaluated. But, we believe that by bringing together multiple philosophies and perspectives, moving beyond a focus on variables within individuals, addressing broader social norms, and reaching a broader range of audiences, we can create an empowering climate based on an ethic of caring and responsibility and increased contextual thinking which will rewrite the script of sexual violence in our campus communities.

In examining the environments, populations, practices, beliefs, and attitudes of our campus communities, we identified the following risk factors for sexual violence perpetration from Tharp et al. (2013) that guide our efforts (see Table 8.4). We endeavor to find ways to address these factors on the individual, relationship, and community levels.

TABLE 8.4 Risk Factors for Sexual Violence Perpetration

DOMAIN	FACTOR
Peer attitudes & behavior	Peer sexual aggression Approval for forced sex Pressure for sexual activity
Hyper masculinity/all male peers	Sports participation
Intimate partner processes & characteristics	Relationship process More casual relationship status
Sexual behaviors & other noncognitive sex-related factors	Impersonal sex Exposure to sexually explicit media Sexual risk taking Motivation for sex
Sex-related cognitions	Victim blaming Rape & knowledge of sex
Interpersonal factors	Empathic deficits Cue misinterpretation
Gender-based cognition	Rape myth acceptance Traditional gender role adherence
Violence-related cognitions	Acceptance of violence Dominance Competitiveness
Substance use	Alcohol use

Adapted from Tharp, A.T., DeGue, S., Valle, L.A., Brookmeyer, K.A., Massetti, G.M., Matjasko, J.L. (2013). A systematic qualitative review of risk and protective factors for sexual violence perpetration. *Trauma, Violence & Abuse, 14*(2) 133–167.

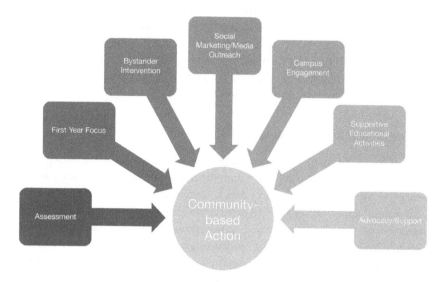

FIGURE 8.5 CSB/SJU Model for Sexual Violence Interventions

Figure 8.5 is the model developed by health promotion staff that guides our intervention design.

First Year Focus

There is research that indicates first-year students (women) are targeted more heavily than returning students and that the first six weeks on campus are the most vulnerable (Kimble, Neacsiu, Flack, & Horner, 2008). The most recent research conducted by Cantor, et al, (2015) for the "Report on the AAU campus climate survey on sexual assault and sexual misconduct" indicated that the risk of the most serious types of non-consensual sexual contact, due to physical force or incapacitation, decline from freshman to senior year. This decline is not as evident for other types of nonconsensual sexual contact. Although we do not have any hard data providing evidence of that on our campuses, we can assume that the youngest and newest students on campus are the most vulnerable. We believe vulnerability is a key component to victimization. We have some anecdotal evidence, through student discussion, that first-year students are looking to find their place here, to fit in, and this search influences their vulnerability and thus, their risk of sexual assault.

With the potential of added vulnerability of first-year students and the desire of our institutional leaders to make clear from day one that sexual violence has no place in our communities, these institutions want to send a clear, consistent message early in students' academic careers. This makes programming around sexual assault and alcohol issues essential for incoming students. With new federal guidelines and regulations, the legal imperative has become a broader requirement. Although we have been doing first year programs for many years, they have evolved to become more local, more interactive, and intentionally more engaging and thought-provoking. The following are some of the comprehensive strategies we are deploying to reach incoming students.

Online Sexual Assault Course

We first began requiring incoming students to complete an on-line alcohol course (MyStudentBody) in 2006. This requirement did not have any consequences associated with it, but we had very good compliance. Over 95% of all first-year CSB and just under 95% of all first-year SJU students completed the course. When online sexual assault courses also became available, we switched to Student Success (2009) and had incoming students complete both their online alcohol and sexual assault courses before coming to campus. We typically reevaluate programs that are available when our contract is going to expire, and upper administration liked the format of the Campus Clarity "Think About It" program that encompasses both alcohol and sexual assault. We switched to Campus Clarity in 2014. At this point, we do not have any assessment data on student perception or any evaluative data on learning measures. Compliance has remained high when done early in the academic year, so there has not been the need to implement any type of consequences such as registration holds. We have offered incentives in the form of bookstore gift cards to early completers.

Orientation Speaker

The H.O.U.S.E. program—which stands for Harm no one; Own your actions; Use common sense; Speak up; and Everybody matters—is designed to introduce first-year college students to the topic of sexual assault within the framework of healthy personal relationships. This 70-minute program that occurs during Orientation and encompasses most if not all first years and their Orientation Leaders begins by talking openly with incoming students about the college "social scene" present on most campuses today (i.e., the "hookup culture"). The program transitions into naming and defining key concepts associated with Title IX regulations regarding sexual assault. Attendees of the H.O.U.S.E. program leave with a clear understanding of sexual assault, the nature of consent, and what they can do to prevent the threat of sexual assault both personally and within the wider campus community.

Dr. Kari-Shane Davis Zimmerman is a Catholic moral theologian who designed the H.O.U.S.E program as a way to educate first-year students on the topic of sexual assault from the unique perspective of the Catholic moral tradition.

The program serves as a complement to the courses she teaches and the more general healthy personal relationships programming she offers each academic year for upper-class students, full-time faculty and staff, Resident Assistant (RA) training, student development leaders, and campus ministry staff.

Residential Life Programs

A discussion-based presentation titled "Healthy Personal Relationships" facilitated by Dr. Kari-Shane Davis Zimmerman and conducted in the residence halls talks openly about the hookup culture present on the CSB/SJU campus and what that means for young women's sense of self, understanding of CSB/SJU "social scripts," and ways to avoid the "whoever cares less game," as well as positive ways to think about healthy personal relationships (friendships and romantic) in the midst of a hookup culture. A similar program has been developed and implemented for first-year men in their residence halls that serves as a platform for future discussions on the topic. In this manner, CSB/SJU is able to have gender-focused discussions based on what our research tells us are gaps in students learning and development around these issues. Students report having more open and honest discussions and women report being more comfortable asking questions in single sex groups, particularly in first-year areas.

Bystander Intervention

Bystander intervention programs are derived from work done in a number of academic disciplines but most notably social psychology and criminology. Theories that have influenced and guided the development of bystander intervention efforts include diffusion of responsibility, theory of planned behavior, and more broadly based social norms theories from social psychology, as well as routine activity and rational choice theories from criminology (examples include Armitage & Conner, 2001; Berkowitz, 2003; Cohen & Felson, 1979; Darley & Latane, 1968; Dovidio et al., 2006; Dyson & Flood, 2008; Sutton, 2008). The program described below is grounded in this research. Evaluation research on bystander intervention programs has indicated that programs can significantly decrease participants' rape myth acceptance, increase their knowledge of sexual violence, significantly increase their pro-social bystander attitudes, increase bystander efficacy, and increase self-reported bystander intervention behavior. Engaging in these programs appears to benefit students of all genders and affects participants over a somewhat longer period of time than some other programs (Banyard, Moynihan, & Plante, 2007).

CSB and SJU describe themselves as communities that are caring, hospitable, and welcoming. And still, even in these communities, we have language, attitudes, actions, and behaviors that can lead to or possibly cause problematic, if not dangerous, situations. To truly be campuses with healthy and caring attitudes and practices and have a culture that is civil, respectful, and nonviolent, we need community members who are ready, willing, and able to intervene in inappropriate, high-risk, or problematic situations. Engaging community members in intervening is the goal of bystander training programs. That is true in implementing our bystander intervention program as well but equally true is that our two-hour programs are opportunities to dialogue with students, engaging with them on who we are as a community, who we want to be, and what actions are necessary on the part of all of us to be the community we envision. Bystander intervention offers us a way to operationalize our culture change efforts. We take information gathered from our survey (e.g., being less likely to intervene on verbal comments or jokes), and discuss with students about why that may be and how they might be able to intervene in simple, everyday ways. We also test out theories and assess anecdotal information we get from more casual conversations with faculty, staff, and students. We are able to customize the conversation to our communities as our number of programs has increased.

Bystander Intervention Program

The goal of the two-hour program is to increase motivation, skills, and confidence in responding to behaviors that threaten a person's health, safety, and well-being through:

1. Awareness/education
2. Dialogue
3. Intentional thought and action

We want to encourage/acknowledge prosocial, helping behaviors; increase and optimize decision-making steps; reduce inhibiting factors (pluralistic ignorance, conformity, diffusion of responsibility, etc.); increase awareness and identification of risk factors; make "in-group" more inclusive; and practice perspective taking.

The program draws its participants from several areas of campus. The largest sector is student employees of student development departments including Residential Life, Intercultural and International Student Services, Campus Ministry, First Year Forward Mentors, Peer Health Promotion groups, and Orientation Leaders. Scholarship and classroom groups like Bonner Scholars and Education Ethics have helped us move into the academic side. Some years, CSB Athletics has a strong presence. They are working on a plan to institutionalize some form of bystander intervention within the athletic department. It is important on a male campus with a strong athletic presence to get buy-in by coaches and student athletes. We continue to strategize on how best to achieve this. We focus our marketing efforts on faculty and staff who work directly with students. Most students still do not understand why a program of this nature would be valuable for them but most, after attending, have only positive reactions.

Currently, we have a goal of 25% of the campus population having attended a bystander intervention program some time in their four years. It is an arbitrary goal at this point as we assess where the tipping point is to improving in our campus culture. In the past two academic years (2014–15 and 2015–16), just over 20% of the student population participated in a bystander intervention program. We are developing our campus climate survey to help inform our efforts and the modification of our goals.

We have also developed a three-hour bystander intervention program facilitator training that covers the research and theoretical underpinnings of bystander intervention programs, what our program goals, strategies, and methods are, and a deconstruction of our actual program, so facilitators understand why each segment is done and how it relates to the theoretical base. Trainees (faculty, staff, and students who have gone through a program and wish to take on a leadership role) also learn about how students respond to various sections and what we have learned about our own communities through this customized program. Tips are provided on how to engage students in a dialogue that is more than superficial. Trainees then shadow a program before they facilitate themselves. Even if all current trained facilitators do not facilitate a program, it is another way to educate faculty and staff about our efforts and build support and buy-in for our defined community and overall efforts, an essential component to culture change. It is also the next step to integrating bystander intervention programming into the classroom.

Campus Engagement

We tend to lay the groundwork of sexual violence by defining the terms through posters and ads. However, the bulk of the health communication work is in the form of social marketing. In line with social marketing research, we (1) involve the target market through assessment, conversation, and product development; (2) segment our audience when needed—by gender, class level, athletes, etc.; (3) treat the environment and behavior we are seeking as products, outlining the benefits and costs related and helping our audience understand product desirability; (4) identify and address the competition—media, alcohol culture, etc.; (5) and meet the audience where they are at, both physically and intellectually. We utilize a variety of approaches and seek partnerships to further the buy-in within the community. All of this is done in an effort to create actual behavior change that benefits all community members.

Multilevel communication strategies and interventions are necessary to ready target audiences to understand the issues; understand their roles regarding the issues;

understand the actions they can take; encourage and motivate them to take action; and maintain the attitudes and beliefs necessary to sustain any changes resulting from their actions.

The CERTS Team (promoting Consent, Equality, Respect, Talking, & Safety) is a small group of student employees that addresses sexual violence utilizing social marketing techniques and practices—developing population-based media products to address the definitions of sexual violence-related terms, myths and realities, alcohol risks, bystander intervention, as well as empathy and healing for survivors.

CSB/SJU have a bus system to take students back and forth from each campus. There are poster holders on each bus that only Health Promotion is allowed to use. Posters developed by the CERTS team are placed on the busses, as well as at key locations throughout both campuses and in residential halls. Other media-based products this group develops and distributes including water bottles, notepads, and t-shirts are for branding purposes.

We also develop more educationally based media products, primarily posters and advertisements for the school newspaper that address:

1.   Definitions
2.   Myths/realities
3.   It's On Us (community-based themes)

Student-Developed Sexual Assault Initiatives

Upper class are hired as student employees, complete training in sexual assault, and lead this initiative, which is designed to bring student workers from various departments, student organizations, clubs, and student volunteers at large, to form a constituency group. These students connect departments and student organizations across both campuses, to streamline and build on independent efforts to address sexual assault. By becoming knowledgeable in the issues related to sexual assault through training (e.g., bystander intervention, trauma, policies, and legislation), they are able to provide others with opportunities to learn about sexual assault. A critical benefit of student-developed sexual assault initiative is that they offer students buy-in for creating change on their campus. They can provide the needed resources, activities, events, and tools to support healing for their classmates who are survivors and foster an environment that does not tolerate, condone, or enable sexual activity without consent.

Part of the responsibilities of the co-coordinators described above is to facilitate the development of a first-year student discussion program. They worked with the initial group of trained, volunteer, upper class facilitators to develop a curriculum to be used as a guide for these discussions. The program is designed to be conducted over two 90-minute gatherings and covers personal values and college expectations in the first session, and a discussion of what sex is and breaking down consent in the second meeting. The facilitators conducted one pilot for the program in the spring of 2016. Recruitment and training of facilitators for the next academic year has begun with a goal of partnering with Residence Life to implement more broadly in the fall of 2016.

Faculty/Staff Initiative

In May of 2014, between 50 and 60 faculty and staff were identified as potential allies to sexual assault education and prevention efforts, and were invited to come to a kick-off breakfast in September of 2014 to discuss sexual violence as it relates to our campus initiatives and how they could be involved. The goals were to have a common understanding of the related issues, to understand the laws and recommendations, and to get people to volunteer to go through a community process in order to identify interventions that could be worked on from a faculty/staff perspective. This community process was based on the public health model and included conducting a literature review to understand sexual assault issues in a more broad-based way, identifying risk and protective factors that relate to these campus communities, prioritizing risk and protective factors on which our interventions should be based, brainstorming potential interventions, and identifying the top interventions on which to focus. The top focus that came out of the work was to help faculty and staff better understand the issue and their responsibilities to the issue and have a common language in order to better serve victim/survivors and to engage a broader audience in cultural, institutional, and practice changes.

Currently, the Human Resources department manages staff education and prevention efforts. The Human Resources Director and Associate Director serve on the Title IX team. Campus Clarity conducts staff and student training programs. The two online programs are similar in content and customized to each audience in providing education and guidance on how to recognize and report sexual misconduct. The program content includes case studies, videos, and quizzes to test understanding. The training program was implemented in fall 2014 with a completion rate of over 70% in the first academic year. This training is now included in new hire orientation requirements for all faculty and staff.

Supportive Educational Activities

This is the catchall for activities that include speakers and other performers brought to campus to address sexual violence-related issues as well as homegrown activities. One of these activities is "Journey through Healing," a walk-through interactive display featuring stories of sexual assault survival, support, and stepping in, as well as facts and statistics, short videos on specific issues such as consent and victim blaming, scenarios and bystander intervention strategies, and activities such as "Unpacking the Misconceptions" of sexual assault and victim empathy. This activity is typically offered for a full day and professors are asked to encourage their students to go through the display, sometimes providing extra credit to attend. Survivor stories from students on these campuses are featured in the display. These types of activities are considered supportive in nature and may not be the same each year.

Looking at This Approach and the Broader Conversation

The bottom line is that sexual violence is a very complex issue. There are no quick fixes to changing the status quo and society's harmful gender scripts. Although we are very proud of how we approach sexual violence as a health, safety, and cultural issue, how our programs have evolved and grown in complexity, and how the members of our community have begun to seek out their roles and responsibilities, we know we are just at the beginning of understanding what is needed. To truly address sexual violence in any meaningful way requires engaged efforts by a broad constituency over time. The national attention has brought institutions of higher education, including ours, to the table. It has helped members of these communities to understand that sexual violence is an issue here and that each of us has a role to play. We are capitalizing on that attention by creating more opportunities for dialogue and critical analysis. However, we know national attention is fickle. In an effort to show strength on this topic, will laws and policies be put into place that will make addressing sexual violence a legal burden that overwhelms the moral imperative? Will the waning attention allow campus administrators' attention to also wane? Will we be able to build the infrastructure needed to sustain our current efforts and build and evolve our approaches and programs—research-based surveys, data repositories, and research-based programs and best practices—before the attention moves on to another issue of concern?

While we believe in and are currently utilizing a team approach, we also acknowledge every one of our team members have other responsibilities unrelated or not directly related to sexual violence. Will this team be able to sustain the energy necessary to move this effort forward and who will direct, guide, facilitate, and lead as we move into the future?

As the landscape of federal legislation shifts and more education and attention is being paid to sexual violence on college campuses, institutions have to shift more time, more personnel, and more fiscal resources toward legal counsel on policy and case review. These cases can also take an immense personal toll on the staff who work with these students and see them struggle through the process. How do we sustain this new caseload without burning out staff? And what will we need to strategically abandon in order to afford the cost of this work both fiscally and in human resources? These are questions we are pondering as we watch the landscape continue to shift around these issues. The fact that we have a strong policy, a campus-wide community education initiative, and quality assessment in place will help us navigate the white water around us.

The good news is we are seeing markers of success in our work via increased reporting, increased institutional support, and increased faculty, staff, and student engagement in our efforts to mitigate sexual violence. We have also experienced an increased number of those involved in bystander training. We have better defined interventions, we see success in strengthening the community's capacity, and we are beginning to see students more aware of and better responding to sexual assault situations. It truly does take a broad-based community approach to combat the social bombardment of sexual exploitation and sexual violence so prevalent in today's mass media. Here at CSB/SJU, we have corralled the energy across campus toward eradicating through community education, sexual violence on our campuses.

References

American College Health Association (ACHA). (2012). *ACHA guidelines: Standards of practice for health promotion in higher education* (3rd ed.). May 2012. Retrieved from www.acha. org/documents/resources/guidelines/ACHA_Standards_of_Practice_for_Health_Promotion_in_Higher_Education_May2012.pdf.

American College Health Association (ACHA). (2011). ACHA position statement on preventing sexual violence on college and university campuses. Retrieved from www.acha.org/documents/resources/guidelines/ACHA_Statement_Preventing_Sexual_Violence_Dec2011.pdf.

Angelone, D.J., Mitchell, D., & Grossi, L. (2015). Men's perceptions of an acquaintance rape: The role of relationship length, victim resistance, and gender role attitudes. *Journal of Interpersonal Violence, 30*(13), 2278–2303.

Armitage, C.J., & Connor, M. (2001). Efficacy of the Theory of Planned Behavior: A Meta-analytic Review. *British Journal of Social Psychology, 40*(4), 471–499.

Armstrong, E.A., Hamilton, L., & Sweeney, B. (2006). Sexual assault on campus: A multilevel, integrative approach to party rape. *Social Problems, 53*(4), 483–499.

Banyard, V.L., Eckstein, R.P., & Moynihan, M.M. (2010) Sexual violence prevention: The role of stages of change. *Journal of Interpersonal Violence, 25*(1), 111–135.

Banyard, V.L., Moynihan, M.M., & Plante, E.G. (2007). Sexual violence prevention through bystander education: An experimental evaluation. *Journal of Community Psychology, 35*(4) 463–481.

Berkowitz, A (2003b). Applications of Social Norms Theory to Other Health and Social Justice Issues. Chapter 16 in H.W. Perkins (Ed.). The Social Norms Approach to Preventing School and College Age Substance Abuse: A Handbook for Educators, Counselors, Clinicians. San Francisco, CA: Jossey-Bass.

Bernhardt, J.M. (2004). Communication at the core of effective public health. *American Journal of Public Health, 94*(12), 2051–2053.

Berkowitz, A.D. (2010). Fostering healthy norms to prevent violence & abuse: The social norms approach. In K.L. Kaufman (Ed.), *The prevention of sexual violence: A practitioner's sourcebook* (pp. 147–172). Holyoke, MA: NEARI Press.

Burnett, A., Mattern, J.L., Herakova, L.L., Kahl, D.H. Jr., Tobola, C., & Bornsen, S.E. (2009). Communicating/muting date rape: A co-cultural theoretical analysis of communication factors related to rape culture on a college campus. *Journal of Applied Communication Research, 37*(4), 465–485.

Campbell, R., Sprague, H.A., Cottrill, S., & Sullivan, C.M. (2011). Longitudinal research with sexual assault survivors: A methodological review. *Journal of Interpersonal Violence, 26*(3), 433–461.

Cantor, D., Fisher, B., Chibnall, S., Townsend, R., Lee, H., Bruce, C., & Thomas, G. (2015). *Report on the AAU campus climate survey on sexual assault and sexual misconduct.*

Cohen, L.E., & Felson, M. (1979). Social Change and Crime Rate Trends: A routine activity approach. *American Sociological Review, 44*(4), 588–608.

College of Saint Benedict and Saint John's University. (2016). *Student Handbook.* Retrieved from www.csbsju.edu/student-employment/student-handbook.

Cox, P.J., Lang, K., Townsend, S.M., & Campbell, R. (2010). The rape prevention and education (RPE) theory model of community change: Connecting individual and social change. *Journal of Family Social Work, 13*(4), 297–312.

Dahlberg, L.L., & Krug E.G. (2002). Violence—A global public health problem. In E. Krug, L.L. Dahlberg, J.A. Mercy, A.B. Zwi, & R. Lozano (Eds.), *World Report on Violence and Health* (pp. 1–56). Geneva, Switzerland: World Health Organization.

Darnton, A. (2008). *Reference report: An overview of behaviour change models and their uses.* Centre for Sustainable Development, University of Westminster. Retrieved from www.peec works.org/PEEC/PEEC_Gen/01796129–001D0211.0/Darnton%202008%20Overview%20of%20behavior%20change%20models%20and%20uses.pdf.

Darley, J. M., & Latané, B. (1968). Bystander intervention in emergencies: Diffusion of responsibility. *Journal of Personality and Social Psychology,* 8, 377–383.

Dovidio, J.F., Pilavin, J.A., Schroeder, D.A., & Penner, L.A. (2006). The Social Psychology of Pro-social Behavior. Mahwal, NJ: Erlbaum

Dyson, S., & Flood, M. (2008). Building Cultures of Respect and Non-Violence: A Review of Literature Concerning Adult Learning and Violence Prevention Programs with Men. Prepared for Australian Football League by Australian Research Centre in Sex, Health & Society at LaTrobe University.

Foubert, J.D., Brose, M.W., & Bannon R.S. (2011). Pornography viewing among fraternity men: Effects on bystander intervention, rape myth acceptance & behavioral intent to commit sexual assault. *Sexual Addiction & Compulsivity: The Journal of Treatment & Prevention, 18*(4), 212–231.

Gidycz, C.A., Orchowski, L.M., & Berkowitz, A.D. (2011) Preventing sexual aggression among college men: An evaluation of a social norms and bystander intervention program. *Violence Against Women, 17*(6), 720–737.

Heward, S., Hutchins, C., & Keleher, H. (2007). Organizational change—key to capacity building and effective health promotion. *Health Promotion International, 22*(2), 170–177.

Holt D., Armenakis A., Field, H., & Harris, S. (2007). Readiness for organizational change: The systematic development of a scale. *The Journal of Applied Behavioral Science, 43*(2), 232–255.

Jessup-Anger, J., & Edwards, K. (2015). Comprehensive sexual violence prevention education. In J. Jessup-Anger & K. Edwards (Eds.), *Beyond compliance: Addressing sexual violence in higher education* (p. 7). Washington, DC: ACPA-College Student Educators International.

Jozkowski, K.N. (2015). "Yes means yes"? Sexual consent policy and college students. *Change, 47*(2), 16–23.

Kaplin, W.A., & Lee, B.A. (2009). *A legal guide for student affairs professionals* (2nd ed.). San Francisco, CA: Jossey-Bass.

Kilmartin, C., & Berkowitz, A.D. (2005). *Sexual assault in context: Teaching college men about gender*. Mahwah, NJ: Psychology Press.

Kimble, M., Neacsiu, A.D., Flack Jr., W.F., & Horner, J. (2008). Risk of unwanted sex for college women: Evidence for a red zone. *Journal of American College Health, 57*(3), 331–336.

Krebs, C., Lindquist, C., Berzofsky, M., Shook-Sa, B., & Peterson, K. (2016). *Campus climate survey validation study: Final technical report*. Washington, DC.: Bureau of Justice Statistics. Retrieved from www.bjs.gov/content/pub/pdf/ccsvsftr.pdf.

Lake, P.F. (2011). *Foundations of higher education policy: Basic legal rules, concepts, and principles for student affairs*. Washington, DC: National Association of Student Personnel Administrators.

Langhinrichsen-Rohling, J., Foubert, J.D., Brasfield, H.M., Hill, B., & Shelley-Tremblay, S. (2011). The men's program: Does it impact college men's self-reported bystander efficacy and willingness to intervene? *Violence Against Women, 17*(6), 743–759.

Lisak, D., & Miller, P.M. (2002). Repeat rape and multiple offending among undetected rapists. *Violence and Victims, 17*(1), 73–82.

Lonsway, K. (2009). *Rape prevention and risk reduction: Review of the research literature for practitioners*. Harrisburg, VA: VAWnet, a project of the National Resource Center on Domestic Violence/Pennsylvania Coalition Against Domestic Violence. Retrieved from www.vawnet.org/applied-research-papers/print-document.php?doc_id=1655.

McMahon, S. (2010). Rape myth beliefs and bystander attitudes among incoming college students. *Journal of American College Health, 59*(1), 3–11.

Prochaska, J.O., & DiClemente, C.C. (1982). Transtheoretical therapy: Toward a more integrative model of change. *Psychotherapy: Theory, Research and Practice, 19*(3), 276–288.

Rhode, D.L. (1999). *Speaking of sex: The denial of gender inequality*. Cambridge, MA: Harvard University Press.

Schensul, J. (2009). Community, culture and sustainability in multilevel dynamic systems intervention science. *American Journal of Community Psychology, 43*(3–4), 241–256.

Sutton, R.M., Douglas, K.M., Wilkin, K., Elder, T.J., Cole, J.M., & Stathi, S. (2008). Justice for whom, exactly? Beliefs in justice for the self and various others. *Personality and Social Psychology Bulletin, 38*, 528–541.

Tharp, A.T., DeGue, S., Valle, L.A., Brookmeyer, K.A., Massetti, G.M., & Matjasko, J.L. (2013). A systematic qualitative review of risk and protective factors for sexual violence perpetration. *Trauma, Violence & Abuse, 14*(2) 133–167.

Weiner, B.J., Amick, H., & Lee, S.D. (2008). Conceptualization and measurement of organization readiness for change: A review of the literature in health services research & other fields. *Medical Care Research & Review, 65*(4), 379–436.

Weinreich, N.K. (1996). Integrating quantitative and qualitative methods in social marketing research. *Social Marketing Quarterly, 3*(1), 53–58.

Wooten, S.C. (2016). Heterosexist discourses: How feminist theory shaped campus sexual violence policy. In S.C. Wooten & R.W. Mitchell (Eds.), *The crisis of campus sexual violence: Critical perspectives on prevention and response* (pp. 33–52). New York: Routledge.

Websites

www.csbsju.edu/human-rights/human-rights/csbsju-human-rights-policy
www.notalone.gov
www.asaccu.org/index.php?option=com_content&view=article&id=54&Itemid=368

9

BUILDING A COMPREHENSIVE VIOLENCE PREVENTION PROGRAM

Five Lessons Learned While Striving for Success

Jennifer L. Graham, Melissa D. Gerrior, and Carrie L. Cook

Though violence on college campuses has increasingly become an issue of public concern, it emerged predominantly in the 1990s, when incidents of violence became widely publicized. The passing of the 1990 Campus Security Act (now known as the Jeanne Clery Disclosure of Campus Security Policy and Crime Statistics Act) solidified federal concern about campus crime disclosures, and required mandatory reporting of criminal incidents on campus and neighboring property (The Cleary Center, 2012). Yet regardless of mandated disclosure laws, campus crime victimization remains a critical concern for scholars, campus officials, and students. Government officials have renewed their focus and a recent White House task force report calls attention to the issue and challenges institutions of higher education to more effectively understand and prevent sexual assault on college campuses (White House Task Force to Protect Students from Sexual Assault, 2014).

What we currently know about power-based interpersonal violence (PBIV)[1] on college campuses illustrates a few key findings. First, female college students stand relatively moderate to high risks of sexual assault (Fisher, Cullen, & Turner, 2000; Sinozich & Langton, 2014; Wilcox, Jordan, & Pritchard, 2007). Some of the higher estimates suggest that up to 20–25% of female[2] college students have experienced sexual assault during their college careers (Anderson & Clement, 2015; see also Fisher, Daigle, & Cullen, 2010, for a review). The high rate of sexual victimization among young women in general is consistently supported in research (Fisher et al., 2000; Tjaden & Thoennes, 2000). Even surveys targeting national populations (rather than limited to college samples) support that risk for sexual assault is highest for women who are relatively young, under 25 years of age (Breiding et al., 2014). Sexual victimization is not limited to women on campus; a recent poll found that 7% of men reported sexual victimization while in college (Anderson & Clement, 2015).

Second, both college women and men suffer high rates of intimate partner violence. One study found that during college, between 19–27% of women were victims of intimate partner violence (Smith, White, & Holland, 2003), while up to 28–32% of college women and 31–39% of college men reported this type of victimization in the past year (Sabina & Straus, 2008; White & Koss, 1991).

Third, the variation in empirical studies on the prevalence of stalking perpetration and victimization among college students indicates these estimates are uncertain. These studies suggest that between 10 and 20% of college women reported recent (in the last 6 months or while enrolled at the university) stalking victimization (Buhi, Clayton, & Hepler Surrency, 2009; Fisher, Cullen, & Turner, 2002; Jordan, Wilcox, & Pritchard, 2007; Mustaine & Tewksbury, 1999). Other studies show estimates of lifetime stalking victimization for combined male and female samples to include 25–27% of sample respondents (Fox, Gover, & Kaukinen, 2009; Nobles, Fox, Piquero, & Piquero, 2009).

Finally, victimization is often not limited to one type; much of this research illustrates the presence of co-victimization or poly-victimization: a combination of physical, sexual, and other types of victimization, such as psychological, economic, or academic abuse (Amar & Gennaro, 2005; Sabina & Straus, 2008; Wilcox et al., 2007). Additionally, even if college students did not experience their victimization while enrolled in college, the lifetime estimate studies suggest that previous victimization experiences can certainly impact their experiences and behavior during college. These statistics are difficult to summarize and generalize because of varying sampling and measurement methodologies, yet the conclusions we can draw from them remain consistent. It is evident that college students are at risk of experiencing PBIV, although the level, type, and context may vary. It seems very apparent, however, that female college students are at a high risk of suffering sexual assault during their college years. There have also been recent calls for increased research focusing on under-examined samples of students, including, but not limited to, LGBTQ populations (Rankin, 2005).

While the exact picture of college student victimization surrounding PBIV is still somewhat unclear, its existence establishes the importance of programs and resources geared toward prevention education and intervention of campus violence and victimization. The purpose of this chapter is to provide information about the initial efforts surrounding prevention and intervention on one college campus, Georgia College (GC). These are continuous efforts, so we urge caution when interpreting these experiences as final or generalizable. Regardless, we believe it is imperative to be reflective and transparent about our experiences, as we also look to other campuses for information about how to best improve our own practices.

Campus, Program, and Funding Background

GC is Georgia's designated public liberal arts university. It is situated in a rural area of middle Georgia. The undergraduate population is slightly below 6,000, with just under 1,000 graduate students. The college is one of two public institutions in the state with a Women's Center, which was founded in 2005 by a group of passionate students. Since its origination, the Women's Center has focused on comprehensive violence prevention efforts as well as overall issues of gender equity on campus. Until 2013, the Women's Center had one professional staff member; after receiving federal grant funding (described below), the staff increased to two and a half professional staff. While the Women's Center primarily serves students on campus, it also serves faculty and staff.

The GC Women's Center staff unsuccessfully applied for the "Grants to Reduce Domestic Violence, Dating Violence, Sexual Assault, and Stalking on Campus Program" from the Office on Violence Against Women (OVW) in 2009. However, OVW provided valuable insight as to why the proposal was rejected. The application experience created an opportunity for collaborative assessment of campus strengths as well as gaps related to the issue of PBIV. Over the next few years, the Women's Center coordinator slowly began addressing OVW's comments through building bridges between the Women's Center and additional campus departments such as Campus Police, Counseling Services, Housing, and Campus Life. These collaborations facilitated opportunities for individuals across various functional areas to discuss violence on campus in a meaningful way. For example, in collaboration with campus officials, the Women's Center coordinator began work on creating a campus sexual misconduct policy. She increased advocacy efforts on campus by implementing a menu of advocacy options for students, such as accompaniment to the hospital, law enforcement interviews, judicial proceedings, etc. She began conversations on campus around issues such as victim confidentiality and providing accommodations to victims following an assault. Under her leadership, the Women's Center mission shifted from solely providing awareness programming to also providing preventative educational programming. Through these activities, campus officials and stakeholders began thinking and working on violence prevention on campus in strategic and collaborative ways, rather than in silos as institutions often do.

GC applied again for this grant in 2013 and was successfully funded. One of the reasons we believe the 2013 application was successful is because it went beyond the four mandatory focus areas (mandatory prevention education, campus law enforcement training, campus judicial board training, and creation of a coordinated community response team, or CCR) to include expanded services for victims and Sexual Assault Nurse Examiner (SANE) training for Emergency Room (ER) nurses.

Project BRAVE (Bobcats Rising Against Violence Everywhere)[3] is the campus's comprehensive PBIV prevention education program funded primarily through OVW grant dollars. Project BRAVE takes a primary prevention approach. Primary prevention focuses on addressing the root causes of violence rather than ways potential victims may be able to reduce their risk of being victimized (Curtis & Love, n.d.). Therefore, at the foundation of Project BRAVE, one finds the core tenets of the Socio-Ecological Model (Centers for Disease Control, 2004), the Spectrum of Prevention (Davis, Fujie, Parks, & Cohen, 2006), and the Social Change Model (Higher Education Research Institute, 1996). Each of these theories and practical frameworks inform the scope, goals, and implementation of Project BRAVE. By centering our work through the multiple levels of prevention, we keep at the forefront the understanding that violence cannot be eradicated by a one-time program, a speaker, a policy, a marketing campaign, or any other singular component. Violence prevention can only be achieved when we strategically plan how to engage our community at multiple levels: the individual (awareness and knowledge acquisition), the relationship (bystander intervention education), the community (increasing education of first responders, establishing a CCR team), and the society (policy or legislative changes). It is when each of these levels is impacted that we will begin to see the fruits of our efforts.

Specifically, Project BRAVE hones in on the importance of community and societal level interventions through the establishment of a CCR team and through the implementation of policies and procedures on campus that establish a framework for responding to victims of PBIV. When a college establishes a CCR, a multidisciplinary team with representatives from across the campus and community, it speaks volumes to the community about the importance the institution places on violence prevention; it communicates that violence prevention is everyone's responsibility and while particular individuals or departments may have specific roles in addressing violence, it does not lie solely with those units to solve the issue of campus PBIV (Garner & Maxwell, 2008).

As we continue with this chapter, the purpose of which is to discuss the lessons, successes, and challenges we have encountered throughout the process of creating our comprehensive program, the authors would like to acknowledge that two of us approach this work from victim advocacy and student affairs backgrounds, and the third approaches this work from the perspective of being a faculty member in criminal justice. While our backgrounds inform our approach and perspectives, they do not preclude us from hearing the other perspectives at the table and considering multiple approaches. Diverse perspectives lead us to value the multiple approaches present across our campus and community. These perspectives help us keep the focus on survivor-centered[4] programs and services, create educational programming that utilizes student development theory as well as appreciate the critical need for evaluating these programs and services.

Lesson 1: Building Strategic Partnerships Early is Key to Successful Implementation

A central theme throughout the building of our comprehensive PBIV prevention program has been one of partnerships. We have found partnerships to be a critical piece of the puzzle on our campus. Effective, long-term partnerships rely on early and ongoing relationship building (Leiderman, Furco, Zapf, & Goss, 2002). Building partnerships also lays the groundwork for a comprehensive program, one that recognizes that one entity cannot effectively address violence or victimization (Barry & Cell, 2009). Partnerships allow everyone to have a voice at the table to ensure their needs are being addressed.

One of the benefits of a multidisciplinary team is the multiple perspectives (even those that do not share the same vision) that are brought to the table. The Women's Center views the issue of PBIV differently than Campus Police may, who view it differently than Legal Affairs may, etc. However, when everyone is present and participating in prevention conversations, it becomes more difficult to ignore those singular perspectives. It is important to strategically invite entities who may not share your vision or understanding of PBIV to be part of your CCR. Only when institutions recognize these differences and address them can they be effective in moving forward with their mission with respect to their PBIV initiative.

When campuses take the time to build a CCR, they are able to lay the foundation for their future endeavors. Establishing such a group presents an opportunity to move away from the silos that often define our work and into collaborative partnerships (Barry & Cell, 2009; Shepard, Falk, & Elliott, 2002). Entities on campus begin using a shared language, consistent messaging, and work together to create a shared vision for what violence prevention on campus will look like. A CCR offers a dedicated space to discuss the intersectionality of violence prevention work, where the perspectives of advocates, conduct board officers, general counsels, housing staff, faculty, campus police, Title IX officials, administration, and the multitude of other voices on campus can be heard with equal weight. For example, a piece of shared language that we have established is the survivor-centered nature of our work; we encourage appreciation of the victim/survivor perspective. Coordination between entities and agencies has shown promise in uniformly and effectively addressing domestic violence in some communities (Garner & Maxwell, 2008; Robinson, 2006). Bringing everyone to the table gives us an opportunity to see where the gaps are in our services as well as our partnerships, to determine who and what is missing, and to begin to address those missing pieces. For example, when creating our campus's new sexual misconduct policy, we were able to hear perspectives from diverse voices including advocates, legal counsel, risk mitigators; what emerged was a policy that was survivor-centered but also ensured fairness and due process for involved parties. We still grapple with answering some of these questions as the work is in constant motion, but we know we have the time and space to carefully consider these questions.

The intersectional lens that a CCR brings a campus helps to ensure the needs of underrepresented populations on campus are integrated. It allows us to consider how violence prevention might look different for different groups of students, or for faculty and staff. This lens also requires examination of how to effectively communicate our message to different populations. When members of under-represented populations are already at the table, they are not an afterthought but are valued members of the work in progress. Meeting the needs of underrepre-sented populations becomes integrated into the work from the beginning. That is not to say that specific outreach or attention will not be needed to ensure the prevention work is inclusive and meaningful to all. On our campus, we plan to hold a series of focus groups with several underrepresented groups, such as students with disabilities, LGBT, and students of color, to improve our response to their needs.

We faced very little resistance on campus and initially in our community when we set out to apply for the grant in 2013, likely because we had sought to establish a wide range of partnerships. However, during the application process, challenges arose. A local regional governmental entity was applying for a different grant from OVW and expressed concern that our application to the Campus Grant program would mean that they could not apply for the Rural Grant program. They were concerned enough to approach some of our community partners and asked them to refuse to sign a memorandum of understanding (MOU) with us. This was very troubling, as we had worked very hard on establishing these partnerships. The first thing we did was sit down with our campus partners and explain what was going on and that we could both apply for the different grant programs, that they would not be in competition with one another. Afterwards our campus partners helped us communicate this message with the community partners with whom they worked closely. For example, Campus Police helped explain this to our local police force and were able to help us secure a MOU with that agency. For some partners (both internal and external), we initially failed to develop these strong relationships early on, despite eventual agreements about responsibilities as indicated in the MOU. We remain concerned about whether this precludes a culture of real collaboration, trust, and cohesion between partners—something scholars warn can threaten sustainability and goal realization (Leiderman et al., 2002). By leveraging our existing positive partnerships, we were able to better communicate with our community partners and address their needs and concerns. We continue to use this approach when we are faced with resistance or challenges. We do not always see eye to eye, but being able to see the bigger picture of our primary goal allows us to continue with forward movement.

Another challenge we faced was determining how to best use the talents of the partners we had identified. Our first task force meeting had an attendance of over 40 people, which was promising. The next challenge came in trying to figure out how to mobilize people and work on key areas of the project mission. After much trial and error, and frustration on the part of our partners, we determined we needed two groups: a smaller "core" group who would meet on a monthly basis and a larger group that would meet on a quarterly basis. This allowed our core team to focus more directly on challenges in implementation, without overburdening our community partners with the minutiae of the campus-specific activities.

One of the areas where we still face challenges is the process of bringing new partners on board. We love that new partnerships and collaborations are being forged, but we have found that when these partners join the CCR it has the potential to create confusion in roles and responsibilities. Often in the work of PBIV prevention, roles overlap and the boundaries between responsibilities become obscure. When we overlay the differing reporting processes for victims the boundaries are even more confused. This is one of the primary reasons a CCR team is critical. These meetings present the opportunity to hash out roles and responsibilities in safe and self-reflective ways. We have found these meetings helpful in moving us beyond ambiguity, and we hope they will continue to be useful in planning and implementing PBIV.

As mentioned above one of the strategies that proved most effective was calling on our campus and existing community partnerships when we experienced roadblocks. During the five years between grant applications, we had successfully built partnerships with many campus departments, including Housing, Campus Police, Counseling Services, Student Affairs, Title IX investigator, Legal Affairs, and Campus Life. We also formed relationships with Crisis Line and Safe House of Central Georgia as well as Georgia Network to End Sexual Assault (GNESA). Both Crisis Line and GNESA are nonprofit organizations. Crisis Line is the closest nonprofit victim service provider to GC and GNESA is our state's sexual assault coalition. We developed a partnership with Crisis Line through use of their advocacy trainings and assisting their implementation of a Clothesline Project.

Our partnership with GNESA was slower to develop. Women's Center professional staff received sexual assault advocacy training from them in 2009 and were in sporadic communication with GNESA staff afterwards. Communications amped up as we began working on our second grant attempt. As our statewide coalition, GNESA offered tremendous resources that were largely untapped by our campus. We began the work of intentionally cultivating this relationship, seeking to understand how each organization could work to assist the other. We were able to partner with GNESA on training for law enforcement on sexual assault investigations. GNESA was able to use space on our campus for free and our officers were able to attend training locally. GNESA also offers SANE training that nurses from our local hospital were able to attend. In return, GNESA was seeking to understand campus processes and help local rape crisis center staff build partnerships with their local campuses. Our Women's Center staff was able to provide presentations around partnering with college campuses to rape crisis staff in the state as well as join a statewide expert committee as the sole college representative. This partnership has been especially meaningful because it is reciprocal: both entities are actively having their needs met and both programs grow as a result.

Lesson 2: Gaining Buy-In From Administrators Further Legitimizes the Program

The second lesson we learned centers on the importance of gaining buy-in from campus administration. We have worked to develop a strong relationship with our campus administration that has resulted in tremendous benefit to our campus. Forging this type of partnership is not without roadblocks or setbacks—as working with administration is often a very bureaucratic process. It is key to know who those key stakeholders are, to identify the individuals you need to have sitting in your CCR meetings. Those are the individuals who can help further develop administrative partnerships.

By meeting with several members of the administration early on in the process, we were able to share our vision of PBIV prevention on campus as well as hear the concerns of our administrators. Members of our campus administration sit on the CCR and contribute in creating the shared vision of Project BRAVE. One of the things we were able to do in those initial meetings was discuss how building a PBIV prevention program would likely cause the number of reported sexual assaults to increase on campus as more students were aware of the resources and services at their disposal. We discussed that this was not to be a cause for concern, that it would not necessarily mean there was increase in PBIV on campus, but rather that more individuals were receiving support. When this happened, our administration was not shocked or surprised, but was able to join us in articulating to concerned stakeholders that this was a byproduct of increased education on campus.

Some of the difficulties faced in gaining administrative buy-in are that administrators are busy. As a result, sometimes it can take a while for their support to trickle down, which can cause a disconnect between the administrative thirty-thousand-foot view and the on-the-ground work. One of the ways we were able to address this challenge was to include representatives from a wide range of institutional positions on our CCR. We have members from administration, mid-level managers, and on-the-ground staff all working together.

Another challenge is that while we have gained buy-in and support, we are still unsure about the long-term institutional commitment. We are currently having conversations about institutionalizing positions to ensure their longevity after grant funds have left our institution, and while those positions have made it through one round of the budget process we are left with uncertainty as to how that process will end. In the meantime, we continue to advocate at all levels for the added value these positions bring to our campus.

One of the ways we have found to be most beneficial in building partnerships with our administration centers on communication. We have sought out ways to intentionally be in communication with our President and Vice-Presidents, as it is difficult for them to be present at CCR meetings; therefore, we ensure we have a representative of their choosing on our communication list. We prepare regular updates and send them even when not requested. We have found our administration appreciates being kept in the loop. Increasing their knowledge about our prevention efforts has enabled them to be able to inform others on campus, steer questions and concerns to the appropriate places, as well as invite Project BRAVE staff to present to cabinet and expanded cabinet meetings regarding Project BRAVE's progress.

Lesson 3: Creating Campus-Wide Synergy

Creating campus-wide synergy has proven to be one of the most crucial pieces of our implementation. At the outset, we had no idea how important this piece would be. Creating synergies and a shared sense of ownership in Project BRAVE has allowed partners and allies to speak up and share the vision at sometimes-critical moments throughout the last few years. There have been a few instances where individuals have tried to start new educational campaigns on campus, but, because of the buy-in on campus, our partners have emphasized the importance of keeping messaging consistent with Project BRAVE. Again, the shared vision created by the CCR proved vital.

When we talk about having a shared vision, we are addressing issues such as ensuring our work is survivor-centered and creating a sense of what prevention work will look like on our campus. It also includes understanding that students' lives are varied and our work needs to be intersectional to address their various needs, keeping in mind that our students come to us with various identities and often face oppression due to race, class, ability, gender identity/expression, and/or sexual orientation (Collins, 2009). This shared vision has led to a broad sense of ownership on our campus, and by including diverse membership within our CCR, we hear from the various voices that help to ensure our work is intersectional in nature.

When we bring multiple constituencies together to do this work, we each bring a different set of words and meanings to the table. When discussing involved parties in a sexual assault, for example, advocates use words like victim and survivor; police use words like alleged victim and accused or perpetrator; and student judicial and Title IX investigators use words like complainant and respondent. We have to be intentional in discussing what we mean when we say these words and decide as a group what language will be used on our campus. For example, in our CCR, we regularly use the term victim/survivor in an effort to keep them at the center of our work, and this terminology may be used when discussing educational programs or advocacy services. Yet, during campus judicial processes we acknowledge that the correct terminology is complainant. Similarly, we have had discussions about the meaning of prevention, as we see it as different than risk reduction. On our campus we have defined prevention as educational programming or activities that are focused on primary prevention (the prevention of PBIV before it ever occurs), for example, focusing on bystander intervention.

Consistent messaging has become an even more important piece of the conversation as we implement Project BRAVE. Coincidentally, the launch of Project BRAVE on our campus coincided with the release of the White House's "It's On Us" campaign. While the White House initiative is an excellent resource for campuses that lack a comprehensive campus-specific campaign, it has proved problematic at times. This dissonance has emerged when certain student groups have pushed to do It's On Us activities in a very surface level way, thereby ignoring the intentional and strategically developed Project BRAVE campaign. As a result, we had to take the time to determine how to meld the It's On Us campaign into the messaging and marketing of Project BRAVE to ensure that the overall message did not get lost in the confusion of what could have seemed like two different initiatives. Project BRAVE has adopted programming that intentionally moves beyond awareness-based campaigns. For example, our BRAVE trainings are informed by evidence-based research (Banyard, Plante, & Moynihan, 2004; Berkowitz, 2013), and incorporate an emphasis not only on the importance of being an active bystander, but on the skills necessary to overcome obstacles to intervening and be successful in intervening. Additionally, BRAVE incorporates marketing and social norming programs that reinforce the knowledge acquisition received through trainings. It's On Us is a social media and event-based awareness campaign and very useful as a beginning point or part of a more comprehensive PBIV initiative, because it lacks components that would move beyond merely creating awareness of a problem and pledging to oppose it.

Another area in which synergy is important is between individual campus initiatives and federal law and policy. This work is inclusive of Title IX, the Clery Act, the Violence Against Women Act (VAWA), law enforcement investigations, campus judicial processes, victim advocacy, academic needs, housing structures, risk mitigation on campus, fraternities and sororities, and athletics, among other departments. Each piece of legislation or regulation imposed from federal or state levels may present a quagmire, as they may be asynchronous with campus policies and campus climate. The result is messy. Campuses across the United States are wrestling with these issues, detangling the many tentacles of law, regulation, policy, and campus climate. Our campus is no different.

As we have grappled with the sheer volume of work and the multiple ways they intersect and overlap, it has become crucial for us to fully define our roles and responsibilities. On our campus, this has become known as "Stay in Your Lane." We often use a car/driver metaphor when discussing how we are survivor-centered on campus: the victim/survivor is in the driver's seat and decides who gets in the car, where it stops, who gets out, and how fast it goes, and we have expanded that to include our roles on campus. For the process to work best, we each have to stay in our lane, staying cognizant of our areas of expertise; the advocate needs to advocate, the police investigate, the DA's office/student judicial process adjudicate. When these roles overlap, when we swerve into someone else's lane, we blur the lines for the victim/survivor who is trying to navigate the car, as well for ourselves as we shape the process for our campus. For example, prior to receiving Project BRAVE grant dollars, many offices on campus were actively working toward reducing incidents of PBIV. However, these units were not always talking with one another and while there were many programming efforts, they were not coordinated nor were they collaborative, which lead to a duplication of efforts and at times mixed messaging for the students. This resulted in uncertainty about what was PBIV, where to go for help, how to report violations of policy, and even whether or not we had a policy. By applying our "stay in your lane" metaphor, we have allowed campus partners to refine their expertise and focus on what they do best allowing others to do the same, which has led to synergies in processes, policymaking, and educational programming.

It has been necessary for us to prioritize our work. We have needed to be strategic in what we will address first as a campus. What we found to work best was to establish our CCR first and foremost, so that we could take the time to create shared vision and language around PBIV on our campus. We created the time and space for multiple perspectives to be heard and incorporated into the larger body of work. Next we implemented our primary prevention education program as we improved our secondary and tertiary prevention methods through increasing advocacy efforts and awareness on campus, while continuously ensuring that federal law and policy are interwoven throughout our initiatives.

Lesson 4: Developing and Sustaining Community Partnerships

Our goals are not achievable without community partners and several rely on strong collaborations with other agencies. Though Project BRAVE is largely student-centered, there are some unique characteristics of the program goals and student population that necessitate the need for strong community partnerships. First, the community will be directly benefitted through several of the program's initiatives (e.g., through available local SANE trained nurses and a community SART (Sexual Assault Response Team)). Second, the university and students contribute to the community population, with about 6,800 enrolled students and over 1,200 faculty and staff. This population also necessitates a need for services from community agencies (i.e., hospital, police, etc.). In other words, the members of the university and community overlap and are not mutually exclusive. What we know about community-university partnerships encompasses several types of collaborative structures across multiple disciplines; yet recent efforts by universities to "engage" with the community have often been justified as initiatives that foster student learning (often via service learning), rather than as purposes of otherwise serving student and community populations (Bringle & Hatcher, 2002; Sandy & Holland, 2006). These efforts have led to the recognition of some features that contribute to sustainable, successful partnerships (Holland & Gelmon, 1998; Torres & Schaffer, 2000).

First, effective and sustainable partnerships must recognize mutual goals (Baum, 2000; Holland & Gelmon, 1998; Leiderman et al., 2002). For example, early discussions with our health partner revealed the current lack of SANE trained nursing staff; yet, we also asked health administrators to reveal specific challenges to achieving this goal (scheduling training, availability of SANE trained nurses, etc.). This conversation helped us understand why it would be difficult to send a nurse to training, even if this initiative was immensely beneficial to both the community and the university. Still, it took over a year after receipt of our grant funding for the training of one nurse to be achieved, and we have not yet assessed the impact on the health partner in terms of covering staffing shifts for the duration of training.

Second, reciprocity and mutual dependency within collaborative relationships are necessary for effective and sustainable partnerships (Bringle & Hatcher, 2002; Bushouse, 2005; Holland & Gelmon, 1998; Leiderman et al., 2002; Scheibel, Bowley, & Jones, 2005). Each partner should see the possibility of achieving their own goals while working together, and outcomes for each partner should be recognized. This is especially critical as higher education has been criticized for treating its surrounding community partners as novices in need of scholarly expertise or as "laboratories" instead of equitable partners (Bringle & Hatcher, 2002; Bushouse, 2005; Cone & Payne, 2002).

Our challenges, as referenced above, lie in continuing to develop and maintain effective partnerships with our community collaborators. Some elements recognized as important to sustainability discussed above are missing in our collaborations with our community partners; for example, in terms of reciprocity, we have not discussed non-program needs or outcomes for our community law enforcement partner. In fact, some community partners agreed to the collaboration (i.e., signed the MOU) without first thoroughly discussing their role. Additionally, we have not yet assessed the barriers our partners may have to collaborate with us. In a qualitative analysis of community partner experiences, scholars have found that community partners value early inclusion in agenda-setting and increased communication (Bushouse, 2005; Vernon & Ward, 1999). Community partners often have to commit scarce resources (e.g., staff) to these endeavors, and failing to recognize and accommodate these resource restraints may prevent the partnership from evolving (Bushouse, 2005; Leiderman et al., 2002). Scholars suggest that unequal, or relative, levels of dependency between partners may also threaten successful or long-term collaboration (Bringle & Hatcher, 2002; Leiderman et al., 2002). We have since developed solid relationships with some of our community partners, but others are precarious, ill defined, or nonexistent. This is evidenced by the absence of some of our local partners at our regular meetings, even if some have participated in extensive training with us. It behooves us to open the lines of communication to see what challenges exist for partners in fulfilling these collaborations, and begin working toward resolution.

Finally, a partnership or collaboration must be defined and communicated in terms of the meaning and responsibilities for each partner; otherwise, it faces risk of dissolution (Bringle & Hatcher, 2002; Bushouse, 2005; Leiderman et al., 2002). Well-defined and openly communicated partnerships move beyond buy-in from the few towards philosophical shifts around mutually agreed upon goals (Bushouse, 2005). For example, a continuous concern for our advocates is that constituencies within our CCR define the issue of false reporting as problematic as a result of anecdotal experience carrying more weight or meaning than empirical data would support. This challenge may be present with our community healthcare partner as well, as we understand that they value SANE-trained staff, but we have failed to make inquiries about other goals we may mutually share. Additionally, although we have "defined" our individual responsibilities (through MOUs), we have failed to engage in continuous communication with some partners about reaching these goals. These areas will continue to require our deliberate and strategic attention as our program develops.

Lesson 5: Student Involvement

The importance of student buy-in and overall involvement in Project BRAVE is perhaps the most integral piece of our program development. Students are at the heart of what we do. Student victim/survivors have been essential across the nation in bringing attention to campus response to PBIV. Our program first and foremost must center the experiences of victim/survivors to be effective. Therefore, our program must center the experiences of students.

Students also fill other vital roles, such as members of organizations, leadership positions, and educators to their peers. On a basic day-to-day level, they are a part of each other's support system. In the development of Project BRAVE, it has been important that we consider all of these roles in order to create a comprehensive program. Early on in its development, Project BRAVE was focused on getting all the "right" individuals at the table. Anecdotally, working with students through the Women's Center's various programs (e.g., Clothesline Project and support groups), we knew that services and programming for victim/survivors on campus were limited.

Since those early stages, students have become an even larger part of our program in many ways. Midway through the fall semester of 2014, a small group of students who were passionate about PBIV approached our office wanting to create a registered student organization with the purpose of raising awareness about the issue as well as help Project BRAVE in any way they could. Due to their dedication and intentional planning with the Project BRAVE professional staff, they became an established student organization by the name of BRAVEheart by the end of that same semester. We recognize that a student organization has a different reach to our overall student population than professionals might; therefore, we work closely with BRAVEheart to ensure all messaging and program content is in line with that of Project BRAVE.

Also drawing on the impact that we know students can have on other students (Banyard et al., 2004), we utilize trained peer facilitators to help educate our student population. By utilizing students in this manner, we present our peer facilitators with opportunities to gain greater understanding of the issues surrounding PBIV, while at the same time leveraging the students' social capital to better spread the message of Project BRAVE (Edwards, 2014). We have focused our training and educational efforts on our fraternity and sorority population on campus during the past year to maximize the impact on campus. By focusing our efforts during this one specific year and using the Diffusion of Innovation (Rogers, 1995), we aim to create behavioral changes in this population that will then lead to behavior changes in our greater campus population. We are halfway through this year of focused trainings and are already beginning to see the fruits of our efforts. The majority of our peer facilitators are affiliated, students who complete the trainings consistently voice the opinion that though the training is long, it is important for all the students on campus to complete it, and they regularly send their friends to trainings. Furthermore, we have seen an increase in reporting and there has been some link to Project BRAVE training in each of the reports (i.e., they themselves or a friend went to training and they knew the Women's Center was a resource for advocacy).

The biggest struggles that we have and currently face regarding students are continuous turnover and consistent messaging. While we have reached a large group of our students with our trainings and programs, there are those pockets of students we have yet to reach. Additionally, as we are situated in a university, student turnover is inevitable, which means an ever-present necessity to recruit and train new groups of students in our programs such as peer facilitation.

Project BRAVE strives to be the known resource and program on our campus surrounding PBIV. However, several times we have encountered students who have just become aware of this issue and want to do something and are not knowledgeable about the work that we are already doing. One example of this is the one-off programming many fraternity's and sorority's national offices mandate campus chapters to do. While this programming is often timely and factually based, it does not often link students to active campus programs and resources and is often quite short, leaving out crucial information and linkages. This creates difficulties in a number of ways. One, when presented with our (longer) training, students feel they have already attended the same training from their national office, despite that our program is campus specific, comprehensive, and intersectional. Two, it increases the difficulty in connecting students for whom this work is meaningful with opportunities to dive deeper into their own knowledge and understanding through mechanisms such as becoming a peer facilitator. Luckily, we have reached a point of prominence on our campus where someone usually encounters said student and points them in our direction for collaboration. However, there have been a few occurrences where students were, for one reason or another, not connected with us and have attempted campus-wide programming that is incongruent with Project BRAVE messaging. Additionally, we acknowledge that we could improve student involvement more continuously throughout the development of trainings and other educational pieces, such as marketing campaigns and programming.

As we move forward, we are in the beginning stages of involving students more in their roles of support systems through the development of Ally and Student Advocate programs. Our Ally program is centered on the idea that students tend to look first to their peers in times of distress. Therefore, the goal of this program is to enable students to respond with empathy to their peers as well as be knowledgeable about campus and community resources in order to connect victim/survivors with further support. We are piloting this program mainly with our sorority women on campus, and these students will be identified within their organization as someone who can support a victim/survivor.

The Student Advocate program is being developed in response to a need for more individuals to be on-call for crisis response beyond the two Project BRAVE professional staff. Our current campus advocates have confidentiality, and we want any future advocates to have confidentiality as well. Therefore, due to reporting mandates required of other university employees, we want to bring students into the process that will work closely with the two Project BRAVE victim advocates as part of the process.

Conclusion

In many ways, this work has been three steps forward, two steps back. We have experienced times of tremendous growth and progress followed by periods of resistance. There are no easy answers in this work as we strive to create an environment that provides the highest level of services to our students while balancing the real or perceived risk to the institution.

We have learned through the process of applying for external funding and implementing the funded activities the importance of building partnerships, gaining administrative buy-in, building campus synergies, forging community partnerships, and gaining student involvement, but perhaps the greatest lesson learned is that the work is never over. As soon as we have reached what we think is a point of success, we realize there is still a kink in the knot that needs to be worked out. However, it is only through this continuous process of untangling knots that we gain a clearer picture of our campus, our community, and the needs of our students as we work to create a campus free of PBIV.

There is tremendous value to approaching this work strategically; this work is not one size fits all. It is crucial to know the culture of your campus and surrounding community. As we look toward the future, we will be focusing on our own unresolved issues: being intentionally more inclusive of all students and all of their identities, strengthening our community partnerships, continuing strong, consistent messaging, and identifying new stakeholders.[5]

Notes

1 The authors would like to extend our gratitude to members of the Project BRAVE CCR, BRAVEheart, and Project BRAVE peer facilitators for their critical work on this initiative. We would also like to thank Andy Lewter and Amber Wilson for their thoughtful comments on earlier drafts of this chapter. We would also like to thank Georgia College and the Office on Violence Against Women for funding Project BRAVE.
2 Power-based interpersonal violence refers to sexual assault, other forms of sexual misconduct, intimate partner violence, and stalking. The umbrella term was intentionally adopted by our campus because of its inclusivity that centers the conversation around power and control.
3 We use the terms women and female and men and male interchangeably throughout to mirror the current body of research, however, we recognize that most research fails to consider non-binary samples and does not include gender expression and identity as separate from biological sex.
4 When we use the phrase "survivor-centered" we are talking about a framework that places a priority on the rights, needs, and wishes of the survivor (UNICEF, 2010).
5 Correspondence concerning this chapter should be addressed to Jennifer Graham, Women's Center, Georgia College, Milledgeville, GA 31061. Contact: jennifer.graham@gcsu.edu.

References

Amar, A.F., & Gennaro, S. (2005). Dating violence in college women: Associated physical injury, healthcare usage, and mental health symptoms. *Nursing Research, 54*(4), 235–242.

Anderson, N., & Clement, S. (2015, June 12). One in five college women say they were violated. *The Washington Post.* Retrieved from www.washingtonpost.com/sf/local/2015/06/12/1-in-5-women-say-they-were-violated/.

Banyard, V.L., Plante, E.G., & Moynihan, M.M. (2004). Bystander education: Bringing a broader community perspective to sexual violence prevention. *Journal of Community Psychology, 32,* 61–79.

Barry, D.M., & Cell, P.M. (2009). *Campus sexual assault response teams: Program development and operational management.* Kingston, NJ: Civic Research Institute.

Baum, H.S. (2000). Fantasies and realities in university-community partnerships. *Journal of Planning Education and Research, 20*(2), 234–246.

Berkowitz, A.D. (2004). *The social norms approach: Theory, research and annotated bibliography.* Retrieved from www.alanberkowitz.com/articles/social_norms.pdf.

Breiding, M.J., Smith, S.G., Basile, K.C., Walters, M.L., Chen, J., & Merrick, M.T. (2014). Prevalence and characteristics of sexual violence, stalking, and intimate partner violence victimization: National Intimate Partner and Sexual Violence Survey, United States, 2011. *Center for Disease Control: Division of Violence Prevention, National Center for Injury Prevention and Control. Surveillance Summaries, 63,* 1–18.

Bringle, R.G., & Hatcher, J.A. (2002). Campus-community partnerships: The terms of engagement. *Journal of Social Issues, 58*(3), 503–516.

Buhi, E.R., Clayton, H., & Hepler Surrency, H. (2009). Stalking victimization among college women and subsequent help-seeking behaviors. *Journal of American College Health, 57*(4), 419–425.

Bushouse, B.K. (2005). Community nonprofit organizations and service-learning: Resource constraints to building partnerships with universities. *Michigan Journal of Community Service Learning, 12*(1), 32–40.

Centers for Disease Control and Prevention. (2004). Sexual violence prevention: Beginning the Dialogue. Atlanta, GA: Centers for Disease Control and Prevention.

Collins, P.H. (2009). *Black feminist thought: Knowledge, consciousness, and the politics of empowerment.* New York: Routledge.

Cone, D., & Payne, P. (2002). When campus and community collide: Campus-community partnerships from a community perspective. *The Journal of Public Affairs, 6,* 203–218.

Curtis, M., & Love, T. (n.d.). *Tools for change: An introduction to the primary prevention of sexual assault.* Austin, TX: Texas Association Against Sexual Assault.

Davis, R., Parks, F.L., & Cohen, L. (2006). *Sexual violence and the spectrum of prevention: Towards a community solution.* Enola, PA: National Sexual Violence Resource Center.

Edwards, D. (2014). *Research-informed prevention strategies part 2: Disseminating bystander programs.* Atlanta, GA: Office on Violence Against Women Technical Assistance Training: Mandatory Prevention Education.

Fisher, B.S., Cullen, F.T., & Turner, M.G. (2002). Being pursued: Stalking victimization in a national study of college women. *Criminology & Public Policy, 1,* 257–308.

Fisher, B.S., Cullen, F.T., & Turner, M.G. (2000). *The sexual victimization of college women.* Washington, DC: U.S. Department of Justice, Office of Justice Programs, National Institute of Justice. Retrieved from www.ncjrs.gov/pdffiles1/nij/182369.pdf.

Fisher, B.S., Daigle, L.E., & Cullen, F.T. (2010). What distinguishes single from recurrent sexual victims? The role of lifestyle-routine activities and first-incident characteristics. *Justice Quarterly, 27,* 102–129.

Fox, K.A., Gover, A.R., & Kaukinen, C. (2009). The effects of low self-control and childhood maltreatment on stalking victimization among men and women. *American Journal of Criminal Justice, 34,* 181–197.

Garner, J.H., & Maxwell, C.D. (2008). Coordinated community responses to intimate partner violence in the 20th and 21st centuries. *Criminology & Public Policy, 7*(4), 525–535.

Higher Education Research Institute. (1996). *A social change model of leadership development guidebook.* Version III. Los Angeles, CA: Higher Education Research Institute.

Holland, B.A., & Gelmon, S.B. (1998). The state of the "engaged campus": What have we learned about building and sustaining university-community partnerships. *American Association of Higher Education Bulletin,* 3–6.

Jordan, C.E., Wilcox, P., & Pritchard, A.J. (2007). Stalking acknowledgement and reporting among college women experiencing intrusive behaviors: Implications for the emergence of a "classic stalking case." *Journal of Criminal Justice, 35,* 556–569.

Leiderman, S., Furco, A., Zapf, J., & Goss, M. (2002). *Building partnerships with college campuses: Community perspectives.* Washington, DC: U.S. Department of Education, Office of Educational Research and Improvement, Educational Resources Information Center. Retrieved from www.cic.edu/News-and-Publications/CIC-Books-and-Reports/Documents/engaging_monograph.pdf.

Mustaine, E.E., & Tewksbury R. (1999). A routine activity theory explanation of women's stalking victimizations. *Violence Against Women, 5,* 43–62.

Nobles, M.R., Fox, K.A., Piquero, N.L., & Piquero, A.R. (2009). Career dimensions of stalking victimization and perpetration. *Justice Quarterly, 26*(3), 476–503.

Rankin, S.R. (2005). Campus climates for sexual minorities. *New Directions for Student Services, 111,* 17–23.

Robinson, A.L. (2006). Reducing repeat victimization among high-risk victims of domestic violence: The benefits of a coordinated community response in Cardiff, Wales. *Violence Against Women, 12*(8), 761–788.

Rogers, E.M. (1995). Diffusion of innovations (4th ed). New York: The Free Press.

Sabina, C., & Straus, M.A. (2008). Polyvictimization by dating partners and mental health among U.S. college students. *Violence and Victims, 23*(6), 667–682.

Sandy, M., & Holland, B.A. (2006). Different worlds and common ground: Community partner perspectives on campus-community partnerships. *Michigan Journal of Community Service Learning, 13*(1), 30–43.

Scheibel, J., Bowley, E.M., & Jones, S. (2005). *The promise of partnerships: Tapping into the college as a community asset.* Providence, RI: Campus Compact.

Shepard, M.F., Falk, D.R., & Elliott, B.A. (2002). Enhancing coordinated community responses to reduce recidivism in cases of domestic violence. *Journal of Interpersonal Violence, 17*(5), 551–569.

Sinozich, S., & Langton, L. (2014). *Rape and sexual assault victimization among college-age females, 1995–2013.* Washington, DC: U.S. Department of Justice, Office of Justice Programs, Bureau of Justice Statistics. Retrieved from www.bjs.gov/content/pub/pdf/rsavcaf9513.pdf.

Smith, P.H., White, J.W., & Holland, L.J. (2003). A longitudinal perspective on dating violence among adolescent and college-age women. *American Journal of Public Health, 93*(7), 1104–1109.

The Cleary Center (2012) Overview: The Jeanne Clery Act. Retrieved from http://clerycenter.org/summary-jeanne-clery-act#Overview.

Tjaden, P., & Thoennes, N. (2000). *Full report of the prevalence, incidence, and consequences of violence against women.* Washington, DC: U.S. Department of Justice, Office of Justice Programs, National Institute of Justice. Retrieved from www.ncjrs.gov/pdffiles1/nij/183781.pdf.

Torres, J., & Schaffer, J. (2000). Benchmarks for campus/community partnerships. *Introduction to Service Learning Toolkit.* Boston, MA: Campus Compact. Retrieved from www.virginia.edu/jpc/docs/benchmarks.pdf.

United Nations Children's Fund. (2010). *Handbook for coordinating gender-based violence interventions in humanitarian settings.* Retrieved from www.unicef.org/ecuador/GBV_Handbook_Long_Version.pdf.

Vernon, A., & Ward, K. (1999). Campus and community partnerships: Assessing impacts & strengthening connections. *Michigan Journal of Community Service Learning, 6*, 30–37.

White, J.W., & Koss, M.P. (1991). Courtship violence: Incidence and prevalence in a national sample of higher education students. *Violence and Victims, 6*, 247–256.

White House Task Force to Protect Students from Sexual Assault. (2014). *Not alone.* Washington, DC. Retrieved from www.notalone.gov/assets/report.pdf.

Wilcox, P., Jordan, C.E., & Pritchard, A.J. (2007). A multidimensional examination of campus safety: Victimization, perceptions of danger, worry about crime, and precautionary behavior among college women in the post-Clery era. *Crime and Delinquency, 53*, 219–254.

AFTERWORD

The Anti-Campus Sexual Assault Activism Movement Under Title IX

Laura L. Dunn

The current movement occurring on college campuses across the country to both prevent and address sexual assault is attributable in large part to the federal civil rights law known as Title IX. As many of the chapters in this volume make mention, the Title IX guidance specific to campus sexual assault from the 2011 Dear Colleague Letter has had a profound impact on institutional efforts to not only be in compliance with the law, but also to proactively address the issue through prevention programming. As a concluding commentary to this volume, I will briefly address the history and legacy of Title IX and related federal legislation that provoked such efforts on campus. It is critical for administrators and leadership in higher education to have an accurate history of the coalition building and incredible survivor-led efforts that have drawn national interest in and concern around combatting sexual assault on campus. As those of us actively working to reduce the prevalence of campus sexual violence look to the future, the success of our collective action will demand continued strengthening of federal, state, and local laws, as well as efforts to get institutions of higher education to double-down on proactive, rather than reactive, programming and resource development. As this concluding chapter will demonstrate, student survivors have made this movement possible in large part through their sacrifice and tireless advocacy. In honor of such courage, educational institutions should continue to ensure students are the central focus in prevention and response efforts against sexual violence.

Title IX and the Office of Civil Rights

Since its passage in 1972, Title IX has prohibited discrimination on the basis of sex within educational programs or activities that receive federal funds (Maatz & Graves, 2012). The law succinctly states that "[n]o person in the United States shall, on the basis of sex, be excluded from participation in, be denied the benefit of, or be subjected to discrimination. . . ." (Title IX of the Higher Education Amendments of 1972). It has been used to prohibit institutions of higher education from denying female applicants admission into graduate and professional programs solely on the basis of their sex (*Cannon v. Univ. of Chicago*, 1979). It is also well known for equaling the playing field so that female students have equitable access to athletic opportunities and programs as compared to their male counterparts (Anderson, 2012; Heckman, 1992). Within the last two decades, Title IX has also become known for addressing sexual harassment and violence occurring within educational settings.

Following the U.S. Supreme Court's decision that employers are liable under Title VII for sexual harassment within the workplace because such harassment is a form of sex discrimination (*Meritor Savings Bank v. Vinson*, 1986), similar cases had arisen against schools under Title IX. Through these cases, the Court has established that Title IX prohibits sex discrimination in the form of sexual harassment or violence within educational settings (*Franklin v. Gwinnett Cnty. Public Sch.*, 1992; *Gebser v. Lago Vista Indep. Sch. Dist.*, 1998). Additionally, the Court has found educational institutions liable under Title IX when they act with "deliberate indifference" to the actual knowledge that sexual harassment or abuse is affecting a student's access to educational programs or activities (*Franklin v. Gwinnett Cnty. Public Sch.*, 1992; *Gebser v. Lago Vista Indep. Sch. Dist.*, 1998). This liability attaches even when the sexual harassment or violence is perpetrated by students, as schools have substantial control over educational settings to address the resulting hostile environment created by such forms of sex discrimination (*Davis v. Monroe Cnty. Bd. of Educ.*, 1999). These cases have resulted in the Court's extensive interpretation of Title IX beyond its succinct statutory framing to create significant obligations for educational institutions to address sexual harassment and violence upon receipt of actual notice. The U.S. Department of Education has assisted schools in meeting such obligations by providing extensive guidance about Title IX in the wake of these decisions by the Court.

While any federal agency that disperses federal funds to an educational institution can enforce Title IX, the U.S. Department of Education has primary enforcement under the civil rights statute (20 U.S.C. § 1682). The Department therefore has the authority to promulgate implementing regulations as part of its authority to interpret and enforce Title IX. It also releases guidance materials to further support schools in compliance efforts by signaling its investigation and administrative enforcement of Title IX through such materials (Revised Sexual Harassment Guidance, 2001). Specifically, the Department's Office for Civil Rights (OCR) has developed significant guidance over the last two decades to ensure that schools understand their obligations to address sexual violence and harassment under Title IX (Dear Colleague Letter, 2011; Dear Colleague Letter, 2013; Questions and Answers on Title IX and Sexual Violence, 2014; Revised Sexual Harassment Guidance, 2001; Sexual Harassment Guidance, 1997; Sexual

Harassment: It's Not Academic, 2008; Title IX Resource Guide, 2015). In addition to unpacking institutional obligations under relevant case law, OCR uses guidance materials to encourage educational institutions to develop and implement effective prevention and response efforts pursuant to their obligations under the law (Sexual Harassment Guidance, 1997).

In particular, OCR provides significant guidance around a school's regulatory-based obligation to ensure prompt and equitable resolutions of complaints regarding sex discrimination through the provision of a grievance procedure (34 C.F.R. § 106.8; Dear Colleague Letter, 2011; Questions and Answers on Title IX and Sexual Violence, 2014; Revised Sexual Harassment Guidance, 2001; Sexual Harassment Guidance, 1997). Its initial Title IX guidance encourages schools to take "immediate and appropriate steps to remedy the hostile environment" through such a grievance procedure as liability under Title IX only attaches when a school discriminates by "failing to remedy" the harassment of the accused perpetrator (Sexual Harassment Guidance, 1997). It also encourages schools to undertake relevant prevention efforts through the dissemination of nondiscrimination policies and the grievance procedure as well as through training staff and students alike on such policies and procedures (Sexual Harassment Guidance, 1997). Such OCR guidance materials therefore outline institutional requirements under Title IX as well as provide suggestions for schools to ensure their procedures effectively remedy the hostile environment created by sexual violence or harassment. Such policies and procedures, as well as remedies provided thereunder, are meant to ensure students' ongoing access to educational programs, opportunities, and benefits. Despite these early guidance materials provided to schools by OCR, prior to 2011 many schools failed to fully implement the requirements of Title IX when it came to the issue of sexual assault on campus.

The 2011 Dear Colleague Letter

Starting around 2009, the Center for Public Integrity took an interest in the issue of campus sexual assault (Jones, 2009; Lombardi, 2009, 2010). It then undertook the first investigative journalism series on this issue, which is entitled "Sexual Assault on Campus: A Frustrating Search for Justice" (Center for Public Integrity, 2010). Through its partnership with National Public Radio, the Center released its series in 2010 to draw national media attention to the issue of campus sexual assault. The articles featured stories of student survivors who had turned to their schools for help after rape by fellow students (Jones, 2010; Lombardi, 2010). It also highlighted the realities of repeat perpetration on campus (Jones, 2010; Peebles & Lombardi, 2010). The series used these stories of campus sexual assault to expose the lack of consequences at the campus level for reports of student-perpetrated sexual assault (Lombardi, 2010). It also raised public awareness about the role Title IX could play in requiring schools to address such complaints as civil rights violations, not merely as crimes (Jones, 2010). The series went further to critique the lax administrative enforcement of Title IX by OCR for the few students who knew enough about the civil right to file such a complaint with the U.S. Department of Education (Jones, 2010; Shapiro, 2010). As a result of the series' coverage by National Public Radio, Title IX gained awareness as a tool for survivors to use as they struggled for justice after a campus sexual assault. It also brought scrutiny on OCR, which provided an opportunity capitalized on by several national experts and advocates.

As part of the investigative series exposing the plague of campus sexual assault, Assistance Secretary for Civil Rights Russlynn Ali responded with a pledge to do more (Shapiro, 2010). After meeting with several national experts and advocates, she authored a new Title IX guidance focused specifically on the issue of campus sexual violence (Dear Colleague Letter, 2011) rather than sexual harassment more generally (Sexual Harassment Guidance, 1997; Revised Sexual Harassment Guidance, 2001). On April 4, 2011, Vice President Biden and the Secretary of Education Arne Duncan announced the release of this guidance, known commonly as the "Dear Colleague Letter," which occurred at the University of New Hampshire (Vice President Biden Announces New Administrative, 2011). This guidance marked a sea change for the administrative enforcement of Title IX as well as a new focus by the Obama administration on the issue of campus sexual assault. While it built upon OCR's previous sexual harassment guidance (Revised Sexual Harassment Guidance, 2001), it was unique in articulating that sexual violence was a form of sexual harassment schools had to address under Title IX (Dear Colleague Letter, 2011; Grasgreen, 2011). It thus provided a definition of sexual violence, as distinct from sexual harassment, which is "physical sexual acts perpetrated against a person's will or where a person is incapable of giving consent due to the victim's use of drugs or alcohol" as well as intellectual or other disability (Dear Colleague Letter, 2011). In reiterating previous guidance on how schools should promptly and equitably address sexual harassment, it highlighted some unique considerations for instances of sexual violence (Dear Colleague Letter, 2011). These distinctions have been responsible for the shift in response and prevention efforts of many institutions of higher education across the country.

One key distinction outlined by the Dear Colleague Letter is that sexual violence is sufficiently severe to immediately trigger institutional obligations under Title IX (Dear Colleague Letter, 2011; *Jennings v. Univ. of N.C.*, 2006), unlike sexual harassment that has to be severe, pervasive, and objectively offensive before such obligations attach (*Davis v. Monroe Cnty. Bd. of Educ.*, 1999; Revised Sexual Harassment Guidance, 2001). Given its severe nature, OCR reiterated that schools were prohibited from using mediation as an informal mechanism to resolve sexual violence complaints, which is otherwise permissible to resolve complaints of sexual harassment (Dear Colleague Letter, 2011; Revised Sexual Harassment Guidance, 2001; Sexual Harassment Guidance, 1997). Additionally, the Dear Colleague Letter clarified to schools that they had an independent obligation to investigate and address sexual violence as a civil rights violation under Title IX rather than merely deferring the matter to law enforcement to be addressed solely as a crime (Dear Colleague Letter, 2011). OCR explained that this independent obligation attached to schools, which are obligated to use the preponderance of the evidence standard to address the complaint as a civil rights violation rather than using elevated standards, such as the beyond a reasonable doubt standard used within the criminal system (Cantalupo, 2012; Dear Colleague Letter, 2011). The Dear Colleague Letter also reiterated that off-campus sexual violence may trigger a school's Title IX obligations when there are "continuing effects" from the assault to create a hostile environment within the educational setting (Dear Colleague Letter, 2011). These provisions within the Dear Colleague Letter caused many educational institutions to review their current practices and ultimately undertake dramatic administrative changes regarding their policies and procedures as well as staffing.

Since the Dear Colleague Letter, the U.S. Department of Education has increased its focus on addressing campus sexual assault under Title IX to lead many institutions of higher education to undertake prompt and comprehensive compliance efforts on campus (Hartocollis, 2016). Many smaller institutions of higher education have hired Title IX Coordinators for the first time while larger colleges and universities have hired entire teams to develop comprehensive TitleIX offices (Hartocollis, 2016). New staff has tended to include more legal professionals and trained investigators to ensure that prompt, thorough, and impartial investigations are occurring at the campus level in compliance with Title IX. This increased infrastructure timed to meet the increasing reports of campus sexual assault that resulted from the growing public attention to the issue (Shapiro, 2014). Beyond spurring improvements to an educational institution's response to reports of sexual violence, the Dear Colleague Letter has also led to more prevention education efforts on campus. The Dear Colleague Letter encourages prevention efforts by asking schools to improve their Title IX policies that are required by regulation to be disseminated publicly to the campus community (34 C.F.R. § 106.9). While educational institutions were not legally required to state in their Title IX policies that sexual violence or harassment were prohibited forms of sex discrimination, the Dear Colleague Letter encouraged schools to do so and provide examples to ensure policies could assist survivors in identifying the applicability of such policies to their experiences (Dear Colleague Letter, 2011). Though a seemingly small change, it had a large impact on prevention efforts. First, the dissemination of these policies provided an opportunity for Title IX Coordinators and related campus personnel to incorporate prevention education into the policy dissemination efforts. Second, the provision of examples within the policy of prohibited forms of sex discrimination created educational opportunities and dialogue around what sexual violence and harassment looks like on a college campus. Rather than the traditional image of a violent stranger attack at night in an alley, examples were added around acquaintance rape and dating violence as common forms of student-perpetrated sexual assault, which were the focus of the Dear Colleague Letter. Additionally, many Title IX Coordinators and their office staff finally had leverage to demand administrative support in performing their duties, which includes both "identifying and addressing any patterns or systemic problems that arise" regarding sexual violence and harassment on campus as well as responding to related complaints (Dear Colleague Letter, 2011). One permissible way for an institution of education to address patterns and systematic discrimination occurring on campus is through violence prevention programming. While some schools used the release of the Dear Colleague Letter as an opportunity to improve campus sexual assault response and prevention efforts, many others had to face the threat of federal investigation before taking up such reforms.

Prior to the 2011 Dear Colleague Letter, few students knew about their rights under Title IX (Jones, 2010; Shapiro, 2010). With the recent national media coverage on campus sexual assault, along with the heralded release of the Dear Colleague Letter, many more student survivors started to speak out about their experiences with campus sexual assault (Grasgreen, 2013; Grinberg, 2014; Grigoriadis, 2014; Kingkade, 2014; Ludden, 2014; Pérez-Peña, 2013; Webley, 2011). Many of these survivors had learned about their Title IX rights from the Dear Colleague Letter and thus filed their own administrative complaints with OCR against their schools (Webley, 2011). Many student survivors also went on to take leadership roles, both on campus and at the national level, to organize student movements that protest the institutional indifference to complaints of campus sexual violence (Groden, 2013; Schonfeld, 2014; Testa, 2014). This leadership spread online as student survivors created activism networks via social media where they shared their strategies around filing Title IX complaints and gaining media attention around their campus activism efforts (Pérez-Peña, 2012). Through these efforts, which were fueled by the release of the Dear Colleague Letter, student activists created a tidal wave of Title IX complaints that took over the headlines (Burleigh, 2014; Gray, 2014). Such bad publicity further incentivized colleges and universities to improve prevention and response efforts to avoid the public relations nightmare that would result if their institution faced the next public Title IX complaint.

Beyond Title IX: The Violence Against Women Act & ED ACT NOW

While the Dear Colleague Letter marked a significant moment in Title IX's history, as administrative guidance it does not enjoy the force of law (*Chevron v. Nat. Res. Def. Counsel*, 1984; Dunn, 2014). Therefore, many national experts and advocates moved to ensure that the growing momentum to hold institutions accountable for preventing and addressing campus sexual assault would be codified into federal law through the Campus Sexual Violence Elimination (SaVE) Act (H.R. 2016; S. 834). In 2013, the Campus SaVE Act passed as Section 304 of the VAWA Reauthorization to amend the Clery Act (20 U.S.C. § 1092(f)). While the Clery Act had previously focused on reporting campus crime statistics, which included sex offenses (20 U.S.C. § 1092(f)(1)(F)), Section 304 of VAWA amended the Act to also report on sexual assault, dating violence, domestic violence, and stalking (Violence Against Women Act Reauthorization of 2013). Furthermore, it codified important equitable procedural rights to ensure victims and the accused enjoyed prompt, fair, and impartial investigations and proceedings to address reports of gender violence on campus (20 U.S.C. § 1092(f)(8)(B)). This furthered the requirements established by OCR guidance and pursuant to Title IX regulation that schools must ensure prompt and equitable proceedings into complaints of sexual violence (34 C.F.R. § 106.8; Dear Colleague Letter, 2011; Questions and Answers on Title IX and Sexual Violence, 2014). Most notably, the VAWA amendments under the Campus SaVE Act went beyond the suggestions and encouragement provided by OCR for schools to undertake prevention education programs in order to make such programs a requirement for campus policies under federal law.

Pursuant to VAWA, the Clery Act now requires colleges and universities to report on their prevention education programs that are provided to all incoming students and new employees (20 U.S.C. § 1092(f)(8)(B)). Beyond risk reduction messages, such orientation programs must focus on "primary prevention and awareness efforts" (20 U.S.C. § 1092(f)(8)(B)(i)(I); 34 C.F.R. § 668.46(j)(1)(i)). VAWA requires that such efforts ensure students know the definition of "domestic violence, dating violence, sexual assault, and stalking" as well as the meaning of consent in regards to sexual activity within the local jurisdiction (20 U.S.C. § 1092(f)(8)(B)(i); 34 C.F.R. § 668.46(j)). VAWA also requires college and universities to include "options for bystander intervention" (20 U.S.C. § 1092(f)(8)(B)(i)(I)(dd); 34 C.F.R. § 668.46(j)(1)(i)(D)) to ensure that prevention is seen as a community issue rather than perpetuating it as a "women's issue" by focusing solely on risk reduction. Additional requirements for prevention education are found in the implementing regulations for VAWA, which require prevention education programs to be "culturally relevant" and "responsive to community needs" while ensuring the inclusion of "diverse communities and identities" within such programming (34 C.F.R. § 668.46(a)). These requirements ensure colleges and universities are targeting all forms of gender violence, not merely the traditional narrow focus of heterosexual normative sexual violence committed by men against women.

In addition to ensuring prevention education occurs during orientation for new students and employees, VAWA requires schools to engage in ongoing prevention campaigns (20 U.S.C. § 1092(f)(8)(B)(i)(II)). Such campaigns must either be "community-wide or audience-specific programming, initiatives, and strategies that increase audience knowledge and share information and resources to prevent violence, promote safety, and reduce perpetration" (34 C.F.R. § 668.46(j)(2)(i)). Beyond the subject matter and timing of prevention education,

VAWA has pushed institutions of higher education to be critical about the effectiveness of prevention programming. Under VAWA's implementing regulations, all prevention education programs and campaigns offered on gender violence must be "informed by research or assessed for value, effectiveness, or outcome" (34 C.F.R. § 668.46(a)). This has led to institutions of higher education critically assessing their current choices of prevention education while spurring others to continue developing and researching and determining measures for effective prevention education programming. Unlike Title IX, VAWA has set clear benchmarks for prevention education programs to improve efforts around institutional efforts to proactively respond to the issue of sexual assault on campus.

With increased federal efforts and administrative enforcement around VAWA and Title IX, student activism moved beyond campus to the White House. In July 2013, several student activists and survivors from across the country converged outside of the U.S. Department of Education as part of the "ED ACT NOW" protest, which was organized by Know Your IX (Kingkade, 2013). This protest included a petition demanding that the Department improve enforcement of Title IX, which ultimately gained over 175,000 signatures (Bolger, 2014). As a result of the protest and petition, Secretary Duncan and the leadership of OCR met with the ED ACT NOW organizers to hear their list of policy demands, which were developed in partnership with SurvJustice. After meeting with the Department, the student activists likewise met with the White House Counsel on Women and Girls as well as the Vice President's Office. The list of demands presented to these executive offices included demands that OCR's voluntary resolution agreements under Title IX ensure direct remedies for survivors, that OCR provide further guidance for schools to ensure more cultural competence around administrative response to reports of sexual violence within marginalized student populations, and included a request for increased transparency around the list of active federal investigations into mishandled campus sexual assault cases under Title IX as well as the Clery Act. Throughout the coming months, the ED ACT NOW organizers continued meeting with OCR to discuss progress on the policy demands from the protest and petition, which eventually led to a special announcement from the White House.

The White House Task Force to Protect Students from Sexual Assault

The efforts outlined above resulted in President Obama's announcement in January 2014 that the White House would form a Task Force to Protect Students Against Sexual Assault (White House, 2014a, b). Through the White House Task Force to Protect Students Against Sexual Assault, the White House Counsel on Women and Girls, the Vice President's Office, and several heads of federal agencies conducted listening sessions with survivors, student activists, advocates, and national experts from across the country that were focused on how to better address and prevent campus sexual assault (White House, 2014a, b). In April 2014, the Task Force released the results of its listening sessions through its first report entitled "Not Alone" (White House, 2014a, b).

The Not Alone report focused on supporting institutions of higher education in tackling the issue of campus sexual violence (White House, 2014a, b). It proposed the implementation of campus climate surveys, which would gauge the true prevalence of sexual violence on campus through victimization surveys while also gaining feedback on student awareness about their rights and options under Title IX as well as the effectiveness of prevention education and institutional resources on campus (Bureau of Justice Statistics, 2016; White House, 2014a, b). It also included information on best practices and cutting-edge research on prevention education programs as well as draft policies to facilitate improved institutional responses to reports of sexual violence (White House, 2014a, b). Additionally, the report pledged ongoing support and resources from the federal government to support schools and research best methods for addressing and preventing sexual violence on campus (White House, 2014a, b).

Of all the recommendations from the Not Alone report, the recommendation for campus climate surveys had the greatest immediate impact on colleges and universities. After the report, some schools conducted their own surveys (Massachusetts Institute of Technology, 2014) while others joined on with professional associations to compare their data nationwide to other institutions of higher education (Cantor, 2015), or participated in the Bureau of Justice Statistics' pilot research (Bureau of Justice Statistics, 2016). Some states, like Maryland (Richards & Palmer, 2015) and New York (Cuomo, 2015), even passed legislation to implement climate surveys immediately rather than waiting for it to become a federal mandate. Through such campus-specific research, schools were able to face the reality that sexual violence was a problem occurring on their campus to begin a dialogue about the campus climate and culture as well as gauge areas for improvement within their prevention programming and response efforts.

Beyond climate surveys, the White House Task Force encourages schools to improve their policies around campus sexual violence prevention and response. To facilitate these improvements, the White House Task Force developed a new government website, NotAlone.gov, which contained a list of national organizations and resources available to support victims of sexual assaults, drafts of sample policies to support improved institutional responses to campus sexual assault, research and best practices regarding prevention education programs, OCR's guidance materials around Title IX, as well as previous findings and enforcement actions taken by the federal government against noncompliant schools. This website became a critical source of information for smaller colleges and universities with limited resources to support improvement to their policies in response to the Dear Colleague Letter and VAWA. Rather than requiring such schools to obtain costly consultants and undertake intensive efforts to reform their policies, NotAlone.gov provided a one-stop-shop of all the materials necessary for schools to ensure their compliance with Title IX as well as improve on their prevention education programs mandated by VAWA. Included in the policy materials were definitions of consent, which subsequently inspired state legislation in California (Chappell, 2014) and New York (Craig & McKinley, 2015) to mandate uniform statewide policies regarding affirmative consent to help guide institutional prevention and response efforts to campus sexual assault.

In addition to supporting educational institutions the White House Task Force also granted several policy demands from the ED ACT NOW protest. For example, the Task Force worked with OCR to ensure the release the 2014 Title IX Guidance, which summarized previous guidance materials in question and answer form while also providing further information about institutional responses to sexual violence within marginalized student groups (Questions and Answers on Title IX and Sexual Violence, 2014). The Task Force also required OCR to provide a public list of college and universities currently facing federal investigation for mishandling campus sexual assault under Title IX that could be requested by the public (U.S. Department of Education, 2014). To date, this list shows close to 200 institutions of higher education are under federal investigation (Hartocollis, 2016; Kingkade, 2016; Stuckey, 2016). While countless other colleges and universities face federal investigation under the Clery Act for violations of VAWA, the growing federal scrutiny has encouraged educational institutions across the country to rapidly improve their response to campus sexual violence to avoid being listed publicly.

Conclusion

While there are several driving forces behind higher education's increasing commitment to addressing campus sexual assault, the core of the movement has been Title IX. Through the Dear Colleague Letter, OCR has made the civil rights provided by Title IX accessible to students who face sexual violence and harassment on campus. It is through the courage of these student survivors both in speaking out publicly to report sexual violence and in seeking federal enforcement of their rights under Title IX that there has been an increase in political will to address campus sexual violence. As the list of colleges and universities under federal investigation for Title IX violations continues to grow, there is a need for ongoing federal and state level legislation to continue demanding and supporting schools to do more to prevent and address sexual violence. As the authors in this volume have demonstrated, there is a strong movement of thoughtful, innovative, and active administrators utilizing the mandates of Title IX to develop new programmatic interventions on their campuses. The approaches to sexual violence prevention described in this volume can serve as models for colleges and universities as they seek to demonstrate their commitment to ending sexual violence on their campuses. Through ongoing research and program development within institutions of higher education, our nation will be able to meaningfully decrease the prevalence of sexual violence and create safer educational settings where all students can learn free from sexual violence and harassment.

References

Anderson, P. (2012). Title IX at forty: An introduction and historical review of forty legal developments that shaped gender equity law. 22 Marq. Sports L. Rev. 325.

Bolger, D. (2014, May 3). White house uses college-shaming to fight campus sexual violence. *Al Jazeera America*. Retrieved from http://america.aljazeera.com/opinions/2014/5/sexual-assault-collegecampusrapedepartmentofeducationtitleix.html.

Bureau of Justice Statistics (BJS). (2016). Campus climate survey validation study final technical report. Retrieved from www.bjs.gov/content/pub/pdf/ccsvsftr.pdf.

Burleigh, N. (2014, June 19). Confronting campus rape: A growing wave of grassroots activists is forcing universities to take a stronger stand against sexual abuse—and now the Obama administration is joining the fight. *Rolling Stone Magazine*. Retrieved from www.rollingstone.com/politics/news/confronting-campus-rape-20140604.

Campus Sexual Violence Elimination (SaVE) Act (H.R. 2016; S. 834).

Cannon v. University of Chicago, 441 U.S. 677 (1979).

Cantalupo, N. (2012). "Decriminalizing" campus institutional responses to peer sexual violence. *Journal of College and University Law, 38*(3), 483–525.

Cantor, D., Fisher, B., Chibnall, S., Townsend, R., Lee, H., Bruce, C., & Thomas, G. (2015). *Report on AAU campus climate survey on sexual assault and sexual misconduct*. Retrieved from www.aau.edu/uploadedFiles/AAU_Publications/AAU_Reports/Sexual_Assault_Campus_Survey/AAU_Campus_Climate_Survey_12_14_15.pdf.

Center for Public Integrity (CPI). (2010). Sexual assault on campus: A frustrating search for justice.

Chappell, B. (2014, September 29). California enacts "Yes Means Yes" law, defining sexual consent. *National Public Radio*. Retrieved from www.npr.org/sections/thetwo-way/2014/09/29/352482932/california-enacts-yes-means-yes-law-defining-sexual-consent.

Chevron v. Nat. Res. Def. Counsel, 467 U.S. 837 (1984).

Craig, S., & McKinley, J. (2015, June 16). New York's lawmakers agree on campus sexual assault law. *New York Times*. Retrieved from www.nytimes.com/2015/06/17/nyregion/new-yorks-lawmakers-agree-on-campus-sexual-assault-laws.html.

Cuomo, A. (2015, May 20). Andrew Cuomo on campus sexual assault: "Enough is enough." *News Day*. Retrieved from www.newsday.com/opinion/oped/enough-is-enough-on-campus-sex-assaults-andrew-cuomo-1.10453713.

Davis v. Monroe County Board of Education, 529 U.S. 629 (1999).

Dunn, L. (2014). Addressing sexual violence in higher education: Ensuring compliance with Clery Act, Title IX and VAWA. *15 Georgetown Journal of Gender and the Law 563*.

Franklin v. Gwinnett County Public Schools, 503 U.S. 60 (1992).

Gebser v. Lago Vista Independent School District, 524 U.S. 274 (1998).

Grasgreen, A. (2011, April 4). Call to action on sexual harassment. *Inside Higher Ed.* Retrieved from www.insidehighered.com/news/2011/04/04/education_department_civil_rights_office_clarifies_colleges_sexual_harassment_obligations_title_ix.

Grasgreen, A. (2013, June 11). Student activists spur sexual assault complaints, but some say education department is overstepping its bounds. *Inside Higher Ed.* Retrieved from www.insidehighered.com/news/2013/06/11/student-activists-spur-sexual-assault-complaints-some-say-education-department.

Gray, E. (2014) Rape: The sexual assault crisis on American campuses. *TIME Magazine.* Retrieved from http://time.com/100542/the-sexual-assault-crisis-on-american-campuses/.

Grigoriadis, V. (2014, September 21). Meet the college women who are starting a revolution against campus sexual assault. *New York Magazine.* Retrieved from http://nymag.com/thecut/2014/09/emma-sulkowicz-campus-sexual-assault-activism.html.

Grinberg, E. (2014, February 12). Ending rape on campus: Activism takes several forms. *CNN.* Retrieved from www.cnn.com/2014/02/09/living/campus-sexual-violence-students-schools/.

Groden, C. (2013, August 8). Campus rape victims find a voice. *TIME Magazine.* Retrieved from http://nation.time.com/2013/08/08/campus-rape-victims-find-a-voice/.

Hartocollis, A. (2016, March 29). Colleges spending millions to deal with sexual misconduct complaints. *New York Times.* Retrieved from www.nytimes.com/2016/03/30/us/colleges-beef-up-bureaucracies-to-deal-with-sexual-misconduct.html.

Heckman, D. (1992). Women & athletics: A twenty year retrospective on Title IX. *9 University of Miami Entertainment & Sports Law Review 1.*

Jeanne Clery Disclosure of Campus Security Policy and Campus Crime Statistics Act of 1990, Pub. L. 101–542, 104 Stat. 2381, codified at 20 U.S.C. § 1092(f)), implementing regulations at 34 C.F.R. § 668.46.

Jennings v. Univ. of N.C., 444 F.3d 255, 268, 274 n.12 (4th Cir. 2006).

Jones, K. (2009, December 2). Barriers Curb Reporting of Campus Sexual Assault. *Center for Public Integrity.* Retrieved from www.publicintegrity.org/2009/12/02/9046/barriers-curb-reporting-campus-sexual-assault.

Jones, K. (2010, February 24). An uncommon outcome at Holy Cross. *Center for Public Integrity.* Retrieved from www.publicintegrity.org/2010/02/24/4373/uncommon-outcome-holy-cross-0.

Jones, K. (2010, February 25). Lax enforcement of Title IX in campus sexual assault cases. *Center for Public Integrity.* Retrieved from www.publicintegrity.org/2010/02/25/4374/lax-enforcement-title-ix-campus-sexual-assault-cases-0.

Kingkade, T. (2013, January 23). Group pushes Department of Education to get tougher on colleges mishandling sexual misconduct. *Huffington Post.* Retrieved from www.huffingtonpost.com/2013/07/02/colleges-sexual-misconduct-department-of-education_n_3531257.html.

Kingkade, T. (2014, February 26). UC-Berkeley faces new complaint it failed sexual assault survivors. *Huffington Post.* Retrieved from www.huffingtonpost.com/2014/02/26/uc-berkeley-rape-students-complaint_n_4855816.html.

Kingkade, T. (2016, January 5). Federal campus rape investigations near 200, and finally getting more funding. *Huffington Post.* Retrieved from www.huffingtonpost.com/entry/federal-funding-campus-rape-investigations_us_568af080e4b014efe0db5f76.

Lombardi, K. (2009, December 1). Sexual assault on campus shrouded in secrecy. *Center for Public Integrity.* Retrieved from www.publicintegrity.org/2009/12/01/9047/sexual-assault-campus-shrouded-secrecy.

Lombardi, K., & Jones, K. (2009, December 3). Campus sexual assault statistics don't add up. *Center for Public Integrity.* Retrieved from www.publicintegrity.org/2009/12/02/9045/campus-sexual-assault-statistics-don-t-add.

Lombardi, K. (2010, February 24). A lack of consequences for sexual assault. *Center for Public Integrity.* Retrieved from www.publicintegrity.org/2010/02/24/4360/lack-consequences-sexual-assault.

Ludden, J. (2014, August 26). Student activists keep pressure on campus sexual assault. *National Public Radio.* Retrieved from www.npr.org/2014/08/26/343352075/student-activists-keep-sexual-assault-issues-in-the-spotlight.

Massachusetts Institute of Technology (MIT). (2014). Survey results: 2014 community attitudes on sexual assault.

Meritor Savings Bank v. Vinson, 477 U.S. 57 (1986).

Maatz, L., & Graves, F. (2012). Title IX at 40: Working to ensure gender equity in education. *National Coalition for Women and Girls in Education (NCWGE).*

Peebles, J., & Lombardi, K. (2010, February 26). "Undetected rapists" on campus: A troubling plague of repeat offenders. *Center for Public Integrity.* Retrieved from www.publicintegrity.org/2010/02/26/4404/undetected-rapists-campus-troubling-plague-repeat-offenders.

Pérez-Peña, R. (2013, March 19). College groups connect to fight sexual assault. *New York Times.* Retrieved from www.nytimes.com/2013/03/20/education/activists-at-colleges-network-to-fight-sexual-assault.html.

Richards, T., & Palmer, J. (2015, June 29). New sexual assault reporting law should improve prevention. *Baltimore Sun.* Retrieved from www.baltimoresun.com/news/opinion/oped/bs-ed-assault-reporting-20150628-story.html.

Schonfeld, Z. (2014, April 10). Columbia accused of silencing sexual assault protest as prospective students watch. *Newsweek.* Retrieved from www.newsweek.com/columbia-accused-silencing-sexual-assault-protest-prospective-students-watch-245800.

Shapiro, J. (2010, February 24). Campus rape victims: A struggle for justice. *National Public Radio.* Retrieved from www.npr.org/templates/story/story.php?storyId=124001493.

Shapiro, J. (2014, April 30). Campus rape reports are up, and assaults aren't the only reason. *National Public Radio.* Retrieved from www.npr.org/2014/04/30/308276181/campus-rape-reports-are-up-and-there-might-be-some-good-in-that.

Stuckey, A. (May 4, 2016). Former U. student files federal complaint, says school investigation into her sexual assault was unduly long. Retrieved from www.sltrib.com/home/3850379-155/new-graduate-says-university-of-utah.

Testa, J. (2014, March 26). Inside the sexual assault war at Occidental College. *BuzzFeed.* Retrieved from www.buzzfeed.com/jtes/inside-the-sexual-assault-civil-war-at-occidental-college.

Title IX of the Higher Education Amendments of 1972, Pub. L. 92–318, 86 Stat. 373, codified at 20 U.S.C. § 1682 *et seq.,* implementing regulations at 34 C.F.R. Pt. 106.

U.S. Department of Education, OCR, Sexual Harassment Guidance: Harassment of Students by School Employees, other Students, or Third Parties (1997).

U.S. Department of Education, OCR, Revised Sexual Harassment Guidance: Harassment of Students by School Employees, other Students, or Third Parties (2001).

U.S. Department of Education, OCR, Sexual Harassment: It's Not Academic (2008).

U.S. Department of Education, Vice President Biden Announces New Administrative Effort to Help Nation's Schools Address Sexual Violence [Press Release] (2011). Retrieved from www.whitehouse.gov/the-press-office/2011/04/04/vice-president-biden-announces-new-administration-effort-help-nation-s-s.

U.S. Department of Education, OCR, Dear Colleague Letter (2011).

U.S. Department of Education, OCR, Dear Colleague Letter (2013).

U.S. Department of Education, OCR, Questions and Answers on Title IX and Sexual Violence (2014).

U.S. Department of Education, U.S. Department of Education Announces Final Rule to Help Colleges Keep Campuses Safe [Press Release] (2014). Retrieved from www.ed.gov/news/press-releases/us-department-education-announces-final-rule-help-colleges-keep-campuses-safe.

U.S. Department of Education, OCR, Title IX Resource Guide (2015).

Violence Against Women Act Reauthorization of 2013, Pub. L. 113–4, 127 Stat. 54, codified at 20 U.S.C. § 1092(f).

Webley, K. (2011, April 18). It's not just Yale: Are colleges doing enough to combat sexual violence? *TIME Magazine*. Retrieved from http://content.time.com/time/nation/article/0,8599,2065849,00.html.

White House, Not Alone: The First Report of the White House Task Force to Protect Students Against Sexual Assault (April 2014a).

White House, Office of the Press Secretary, Establishing a White House Task Force to Protect Students Against Sexual Assault [Press Release] (2014b). Retrieved from www.whitehouse.gov/the-press-office/2014/01/22/memorandum-establishing-white-house-task-force-protect-students-sexual-a.

CONTRIBUTORS

Adriane Bang, LMSW, serves as a Licensed Master Social Worker and the Director of the Boise State University Gender Equity Center. In this role, she supports a team of passionate students and professional staff in offering educational outreach, confidential support services, and a safe space for campus members to gather. As a team, the staff of the Gender Equity Center partner with student organizations, departments, and community organizations to offer original programs that examine intersectionality and highlight LGBT experiences, body image, masculinity, healthy relationships, consent, ally development, bystander intervention, women in STEM, pay equity, etc. In addition to facilitating educational outreach and advocating for increasingly inclusive campus programs and policies, Adriane offers confidential crisis support services to all members of the campus community. She most commonly serves students who are victims of gender-based violence and students who identify as Trans★. Adriane earned both her bachelor and master's degrees in social work from Boise State. She has been with the Gender Equity Center since 2007, and has a strong interest in collaborating with others to form a more just and equitable world for all people.

Carrie L. Cook, PhD, is an Associate Professor in the Department of Government and Sociology at Georgia College. Dr. Cook earned her PhD in Criminology, Law and Society from the University of Florida. Her research interests include victimization, fear of crime, corrections, and program evaluation. Her work has appeared in *Journal of Criminal Justice*, *Journal of Interpersonal Violence*, *Crime & Delinquency*, and *Violence and Victims*.

Jill Dunlap is the Director for Equity, Inclusion and Violence Prevention at NASPA-Student Affairs Administrators in Higher Education. Prior to joining

NASPA, Jill was Director of the University of California, Santa Barbara Campus Advocacy, Resources & Education (CARE) Program for 4 years. Jill has also served as the Director of the Women's Center at Northern Illinois University for 5 years, and the Assistant Director of the Women's Resource Center at the University of Missouri-Kansas City for 5 years. In 2014, Jill served as the nonfederal negotiator representing 4-year, public institutions on the Violence Against Women Act negotiated rulemaking committee.

Laura L. Dunn, Esq., is the Founder and Executive Director of SurvJustice, which is a national not-for-profit organization that increases the prospect of justice for survivors by providing effective legal assistance, institutional trainings, and change-maker support. In 2007, Dunn graduated from the University of Wisconsin-Madison with a BA in Psychology & Pre-Law and a Certificate in Criminal Justice. In 2014, Dunn received a JD from the University of Maryland Carey School of Law, graduating Order of the Barristers and receiving the William P. Cunningham Award for her national advocacy on campus sexual assault, which included lobbying to pass the 2013 Violence Against Women Act (VAWA) Reauthorization, advising the White House Task Force to Protect Students Against Sexual Assault, and serving as a primary negotiator on the U.S. Department of Education's VAWA Rulemaking Committee. Dunn is also a published legal scholar in the *Georgetown Journal of Gender & Law*, an adjunct at the University of Maryland Carey School of Law teaching the course Sexual Violence & Harassment in Education, and a 2015 Global Fellow through Echoing Green for her work with SurvJustice.

Katie Eichele is the Director of The Aurora Center for Advocacy & Education at the University of Minnesota, Twin Cities. She served as the Coordinator of Judicial Affairs in campus residential life before providing leadership at The Aurora Center, around issues of sexual assault, relationship violence, and stalking. Her background and professional experience stem from social justice, university conduct, student development, and crisis management. Eichele is Vice-Chair of the Board of Director for the Minnesota Coalition Against Sexual Assault. She was a campus sexual assault representative in Washington D.C. to U.S. Senate round table discussions, and she has coauthored chapters through Routledge Publishing in *The Crisis of Campus Sexual Violence*.

Stephanie Erdice is the Director of the Women's Center at Shippensburg University. She works on major programs like Take Back the Night and the Ship Says No More Campaign, as well as advising several feminist organizations and working to promote and develop women's leadership on campus. She also works to advocate for students that have been victims of harassment and sexual misconduct. Before joining, she graduated with a BA in Political Science and Broadcasting from Baldwin-Wallace College, in Berea, OH, and earned her MS in Business Ethics and Leadership from Duquesne University.

Mary Geller is in her 16th year as Vice President for Student Development at the College of Saint Benedict. She serves as a Title IX deputy and the appeals officer for sexual misconduct cases on her campus. She co-chairs the Title IX team along with her counterpart at SJU.

Melissa Gerrior, MEd, serves as the Project BRAVE Program Assistant in the Georgia College Women's Center in Milledgeville, GA. Project BRAVE (Bobcats Rising Against Violence Everywhere) is GC's comprehensive power-based interpersonal violence prevention, education, and advocacy initiative. Prior to her current position, Melissa worked as a graduate assistant at the Georgia Tech Women's Resource Center while obtaining her MEd in College Student Affairs Administration from the University of Georgia.

Jennifer L. Graham, MPA, is the Coordinator of the Women's Center and Program Director of Project BRAVE at Georgia College & State University. Ms. Graham earned her Master's in Public Administration at Georgia College & State University and is a doctoral student in Student Affairs Leadership at the University of Georgia. She served as the Primary Investigator on a number of grants focused on power-based interpersonal violence prevention, including the U.S. Department of Justice Office on Violence Against Women's Campus Grant Program, the American Association of University Women's Community Action Grant and the Georgia Department of Public Health's One in Four and Beyond Grant.

Rachel Alicia Griffin, PhD, is a newly appointed Assistant Professor of Race and Communication in the Department of Communication at the University of Utah. Previously tenured at Southern Illinois University (SIU), as a critical intercultural scholar, her research interests span Black feminist thought, critical race theory, popular culture, sport, education, and sexual violence. Currently serving as the Book and Media Review Editor for *Women's Studies in Communication*, Dr. Griffin has also published in several journals including *Women's Studies in Communication*, *Critical Studies in Media Communication*, the *International Journal of Qualitative Studies in Education*, *The Howard Journal of Communications*, the *Journal of International and Intercultural Communication*, and *Departures in Critical Qualitative Research*. She has delivered well over 100 antisexual violence and Inclusive Excellence presentations on campuses and at conferences nationally and internationally—and especially prizes having spoken for U.S. state coalitions against sexual violence in North Carolina, Oregon, Texas, Maryland, California, Illinois, and Washington.

Cecil Howard is the Executive Director of Social Equity and Title IX Coordinator at Shippensburg University in Shippensburg. He is a graduate of Florida State University and Thurgood Marshall School of Law at Texas Southern University. He is a licensed attorney, and has been a member of the Florida Bar since 1985. Prior to going to Shippensburg, Cecil served as the Director of Equal Opportunity and Chief Diversity Officer for the City of Gainesville, Florida. Prior to Gainesville, Cecil was Chief Legal Counsel at the Florida Commission on Human Relations (FCHR). The FCHR is Florida's EEOC-equivalent agency that investigates allegations of discrimination in employment. Cecil is a certified mediator, EEO investigator, and Diversity Trainer. He is also a frequent conference speaker and workshop leader on all aspects of employment discrimination, diversity, and inclusion.

Susan V. Iverson is Professor of Higher Education Leadership at Manhattanville College. Iverson's research interests focus on equity and diversity, status of women in higher education, feminist pedagogy, and the role of policy (e.g., sexual violence) in shaping perceptions and culture. She has two co-edited volumes: *Feminist community engagement: Achieving praxis* (Palgrave, 2014) and *Reconstructing policy analysis in higher education: Feminist poststructural perspectives* (Routledge, 2010). Iverson earned her doctorate in higher educational leadership, with a concentration in women's studies, from the University of Maine.

Kristina M. Kamis is a first-year graduate student pursing her MEd in Higher Education Administration and Student Personnel at Kent State University. She graduated from Kent State University with a BA in Psychology and a minor in Communication Studies. She recently completed her Senior Honors Thesis entitled "Powerful or Playful? An Investigation of the Effectiveness of Walk a Mile in Her Shoes Events."

Annie Kerrick, JD, is the Director of Title IX/ADA/504 Compliance at Boise State University. Kerrick coordinates university compliance with state and federal laws and regulations regarding gender and disability-based discrimination. She facilitates student, faculty, and staff training to advance Boise State's commitment to provide an environment free from unlawful discrimination and harassment. Prior to beginning at Boise State in 2013, Kerrick was a staff attorney at the Idaho Coalition Against Sexual & Domestic Violence. There, she designed and implemented interpersonal violence prevention activities and strategies for middle and high school students; provided training and guidance for Idaho schools on the implementation of Title IX; worked closely with the Idaho Department of Education to present and promulgate an Idaho Board of Education rule change requiring all public schools in Idaho to have a policy on adolescent relationship abuse and sexual assault prevention, intervention, and response; and testified in front of the U.S. Attorney General's Defending Childhood Task Force on the importance of prevention and intervention of teen dating violence and sexual assault. Kerrick is a contributing editor for *Title IX Today*, and an editorial board member for *The Journal of Campus Title IX Compliance and Best Practices*. Kerrick is a Ph.D. student studying Public Policy and Administration with a focus on reducing gender-based violence on college campuses.

Lori Klapperich, MS, is the Assistant Director of Health Promotion at the College of St. Benedict & St. John's University. She has a BA in Business Administration from Augsburg College. She received her Master's degree in Physical Education specializing in Exercise Physiology and Health Promotion from Montana State University in Bozeman. Lori is in charge of the men's & women's health promotion plans, including the student surveys in alcohol and drug use, general health, as well as the development of the sexual assault campus climate survey. She developed, piloted, and has instituted the CSB/SJU bystander intervention program. She is also working with a faculty/staff group to look at campus-wide sexual assault initiatives and is currently implementing Title IX related resources developed for faculty/staff.

Lauren "LB" Klein is a doctoral student in the University of North Carolina at Chapel Hill School of Social Work. LB also serves as a lead trainer and curriculum development specialist for Prevention Innovations Research Center at the University of New Hampshire. She has served as a consultant for organizations and coalitions across the United States and Canada on gender-based violence prevention and advocacy with a particular focus on mobilizing college and university communities. She previously led Emory University's Respect Program and founded the volunteer advocate program within St. Louis County's specialized domestic violence court. LB received a Master's degree in public administration from the Program on Gender-Based Violence at the University of Colorado Denver as well as a Master's degree in clinical social work and a Bachelor's degree in history from Washington University in St. Louis. She also holds a certificate in lesbian, gay, bisexual, and transgender health from Drexel University's School of Public Health. She is a founder and leadership council member of the Campus Advocates & Prevention Professionals Association (CAPPA).

Chris Loschiavo is Associate Dean of Students and Director of Student Conduct and Conflict Resolution at the University of Florida. He is responsible for oversight of the campus response to student behavioral and honor code-related issues from cheating and plagiarism, alcohol and other drug issues and physical, violence, dating violence, and sexual misconduct. He is also Deputy Title IX Coordinator for Students and also serves on the institution's Behavioral Consultation Team (threat assessment team). Chris also teaches a conduct committee training class each spring semester. Chris currently serves as the Chair of the ASCA Gehring Academy and is a past president of the Association for Student Conduct Administration (ASCA), the premier authority for student conduct and conflict resolution administration in higher education, which has over 2800 members at over 900 institutions. Chris has also served as a faculty member at the ASCA Gehring Academy, teaching new conduct professionals about conduct and conflict resolution work since 2011.

Beverly A. McPhail has her PhD in Social Work and a Portfolio in Women Studies from the University of Texas at Austin. Her scholarship focuses on violence against women such as sexual assault, intimate partner violence, gender-biased hate crimes, and feminist policy analysis. She is coauthor of a textbook on women, *Confronting Sexism and Violence Against Women* (1998, Longman). She teaches courses at the *University of Houston Graduate School of Social Work* in women's issues and feminist practice. She recently retired as the director of the Women's Resource Center at the University of Houston after serving in that position for 8 years where she developed and presented sexual assault prevention programs.

Roland W. Mitchell is Jo Ellen Levy Yates Endowed Professor and Interim Associate Dean of Research Engagement and Graduate Studies in the College of Human Sciences and Education at Louisiana State University. He has a BA in History from Fisk University, an MEd in Higher Education from Vanderbilt University, and a PhD in Educational Research from the University of Alabama. He teaches courses that focus on the history of higher education and college teaching, and his articles have appeared in leading education journals such as *Urban Education*, *International Journal of Qualitative Studies in Education*, and *The Review of Education Pedagogy and Cultural Studies*. His current research interests include theorizing the impact of historical and communal knowledge on pedagogy.

Andrew "Drew" Rizzo is a doctoral student in the University of New Hampshire's Social Psychology program. Drew grew up in Wilmington, DE, and earned degrees from the University of Pennsylvania and Oklahoma State University in psychology and higher education. He previously led Emory University's Respect Program, worked with the Prevention Innovations Research Center at UNH, and has worked at institutions of higher education as a researcher and educator in public health, psychology, education, and student affairs. He believes that educational systems can be a powerful engine for social change. His scholarship focuses on exploring interdisciplinary pedagogies to more effectively address root causes of oppression, violence, and other social issues. He is a founder and current member of the leadership council for the Campus Advocates & Prevention Professionals Association (CAPPA).

Matthew R. Shupp is an assistant professor in the Department of Counseling and College Student Personnel at Shippensburg University, and coordinates the College Counseling and College Student Personnel specializations. He joined the faculty after serving as a student affairs administrator for 12 years in a variety of institutional settings. He is a graduate of Widener University's EdD program in Higher Education—Administrative Leadership. Dr. Shupp is both a National Certified Counselor (NCC) through the National Board for Certified Counselors (NBCC), as well as a Distance Credentialed Counselor (DCC). He is past president of the Pennsylvania College Personnel Association (PCPA) and currently serves as co-chair for the Senior Student Affairs Officers Community of Practice. Dr. Shupp has spoken at international and national higher education and student leadership conferences. His research focuses on staff supervision, student leadership, multicultural competence, and inclusive supervisory practices.

Traci Thomas-Card is the Prevention Program Coordinator for The Aurora Center for Advocacy & Education and Boynton Health Service at the University of Minnesota, Twin Cities. She began her work in sexual violence prevention in 2004, and is responsible for education and outreach to the campus community on bystander intervention, consent, and general issues surrounding sexual harassment, sexual assault, relationship violence, and stalking prevention. Traci is certified as a Title IX Investigator and also an instructor in the Leadership Minor Program. She is currently pursuing her EdD in Higher Education through the department of Organizational Leadership, Policy, and Development at the University of Minnesota. Her current research interests include the LGBTQIA+ college student population, intersectionality, student development, and violence prevention.

Sara Carrigan Wooten is a doctoral candidate in Educational Leadership and Research at Louisiana State University. She completed her BA in Women's Studies at Purdue University, received an MA in Sociology & Women's and Gender Studies from Brandeis University, and received an additional MA in Educational Studies from Tufts University. Her research interests include heterosexism and heteronormativity in sexual violence prevention and response resources, critical discourse analysis, and higher education policy development.

Christian K. Wuthrich, PhD, serves as the Dean of Students at Boise State University where he supervises multiple departments dedicated to student success, advocacy, and retention. As a long serving higher education administrator and faculty member, his career spans 3 decades serving multiple campuses and thousands of students. As a practitioner scholar, his interests are faculty work life, underrepresented students, and social justice issues. His passion for higher education effectiveness and student-centered engagement has called him to develop programs related to veteran's success, service learning, academic integrity, and student leadership. As an active professional and volunteer, he has served as an editorial board member and reviewer for journals and monographs, presented research findings at scholarly meetings, and been a director for several nonprofit organizations.

INDEX

CPSIA information can be obtained
at www.ICGtesting.com
Printed in the USA
LVHW04s1813070518
576287LV00012B/1106/P